Armadale in Minutes

A Chronological History
by Robert Kerr

Edited by
Jim McGregor

Published by the
History of Armadale Association
2008

Printed by
The Print Consultancy

ISBN 978-0-9514941-2-7

The Author

Robert Kerr, was born to James and Mary Kerr in Armadale, West Lothian on September 7th 1927. He was educated at Armadale Primary School, completing his education at the old Bathgate Academy. He also attended the Glasgow School of Art and Heriot Watt College, Edinburgh, before starting work in the building industry as an apprentice architect with Thomas Roberts, Architects, of Bathgate. His career took him through many aspects of the building industry and he was employed with West Lothian Council as draughtsman / surveyor prior to his retirement in 1991. He also served with the Royal Engineers during his spell of National Service.

He and his wife Jessie Brown, whom he married in 1953, first set up house at Avoncrook, Westfield, before moving to Torphichen where they reared their family of two sons and two daughters. Recently, a debilitating illness necessitated that he and Jessie move to more suitable accommodation in Bathgate.

Robert is a man of many interests: he recalls his happy days camping with the Scouts, playing in the Armadale and Whitrigg Pipe Bands and the excitement of wartime activities during his teenage years. He was also a keen sportsman and trained as a football referee. An active politician, Scotland's heritage and culture always came high on his priority list and the enormous amount of research that he undertook into its history, geography and languages etc. confirms that priority.

Armadale in Minutes

Foreword

Writing an introduction to a book can quite often be the part which potential readers will look at first before buying or borrowing.

Being asked to write the foreword to this book is an honour since I have known Robert Kerr for over 30 years and shared his interest in local and Scottish history. Many a time he would be able to come out with some detailed information on a topic which would make you think "Where did he source that kind of information?".

This book is a reflection on the detailed research which Robert did in all things and it gives an insight into the many mundane, funny, historical and hilarious events that took place in Armadale's past.

What evidence there was of early settlement in the area, where was the first school in the burgh and how did Armadale get its name are many of the fascinating questions answered in this book.

The time taken to go through the old Armadale Council minutes must have been immense but I'm sure that readers will find them quite entertaining at times with familiar names from the past appearing in the pages.

Robert's research was a labour of love and I would like to think that his efforts will be appreciated by those of you who read this book.

The History of Armadale Association felt that Robert's work should be preserved for posterity and be the 21st century's version of "Armadale Past and Present".

Ron Dingwall
Chairman
History of Armadale Association

History of Armadale (West Lothian)

Prehistoric

The earliest evidence of human habitation in the Armadale area appears to be the 5-inch high food vessel that was found in 1905 at Cowdenhead Farm. (Coldounheides of 1614) The vessel, which was in a short stone kist (i.e. coffin) with un-burnt remains, was given to a museum. The people who buried the vessel and the kist probably lived B.C. in the Roman Era. It is recorded that Roman coins were found at Cowhill near Tippethill.

At Tantallon Hill, about two miles north of Armadale, stood an ancient building which was identified by James Young, discoverer of chloroform, as a Pictish broch. Stone kists were also found buried in the sand of Tantallon Hill.

Local Place Names

Two local names seem to remind us that Cymric / Welsh was a language spoken long ago in the Armadale area. These are Ogilface (which gave its name to a Barony, a castle and a Regality) and Tarbantree where tarban seems Gaelic and tree from the Welsh word tref. Ogilface (first recorded in 1165) is said to be Cymric / Welsh for high field or plateau, while Tarbantree (first recorded 1558) could be interpreted as 'Settlement by the White Hill'.

Circa 1018 A.D., when Lothian and Strathclyde joined with Alba to form Scotland, the Gaelic language seems to have spread into Lothian, thus many of the older local place names that are Gaelic in origin, probably date from the 11th or 12th centuries.

Here are some of these places, with date first recorded, some early spellings and possible meanings - note that the name sometimes describes the area:

1335: Barbauchlaw	Balbaughlagh, the settlement of the crozier.
1386: Muckraw	Farm of the pigs (Pig Farm).
1426: Craigengall	Craiginga, rock of the stranger.

1426: Killycanty — Kaillyfranky near Birkenshaw Mill, later Muirhall (near Woodbank).
1607: Craigmarie — Kraigmary, Mary's Rock, rock of slaughter.
1667: Drumbowie — Yellow ridge.
1684: Tannoch — Green or fertile field near Craig Hills.
1820: Cappers — High place (originally near Tippethill).

Other old place names, mainly of Anglo Saxon or Middle English:

1386: Andros Yeard, Andrews Garden renamed Gowanbank about 1840. It was built by Walter Gowans, mason / engineer / builder; his son was Sir James Gowans, architect.
1409: Brighous, Bridgehouse in an area known as 'The Briggist'.
1480: Hillhous, Hillhouse near a brae known as 'The Hillus Brae'.
1538: Birkenshaw, Birchwood.
1538: Netherhillhouse, nether means lower as in Netherlands.
1691: Wateacre, wet acre to the west of Craigrigg Cottages.
1773: Hagieslap, a slap is a cutting or ravine through high ground.
1773: Gowkstone, cuckoo's stone - Gowkstone was where the Atlas Foundry stood.
1773: Colinshiel, Colin's cottage - Colinshiel was a mining community in 1841.
1773: Knowes, Hillocks near Springfield.
1818: Newbigging, bigging = building.
1818: Snab, a short steep incline.
1820: Todholes, a tod was a fox.

Other interesting old place-names from Armadale area are:

1538: Overhillhouse.
1614: Whitockbrae (Quhythokebray).
1630: Hardhill (Harrhill).
1649: Middlerig.
1665: Harestanes (from hare= a boundary stone).
1673: Blackdub.
1773: Muirhall, Stanerig, Northrigg, Snipedub.
1820: Woodhead, Springfield, Cocksmuir.
1891: Woodbank.

1590's: Local places surveyed by Timothy Pont - Kaillyfranky (now Woodbank), Balbachlaw, Kraigmary, Woodend and Harrhill.
1603: Bridgecastle was the seat of Livingstone, Earls of Linlithgow and Callendar.

1691: Map shows Broxburn to Woodend via Bangour / Drumcross, and Colinsheil as "The Middle Way to Glasgow".

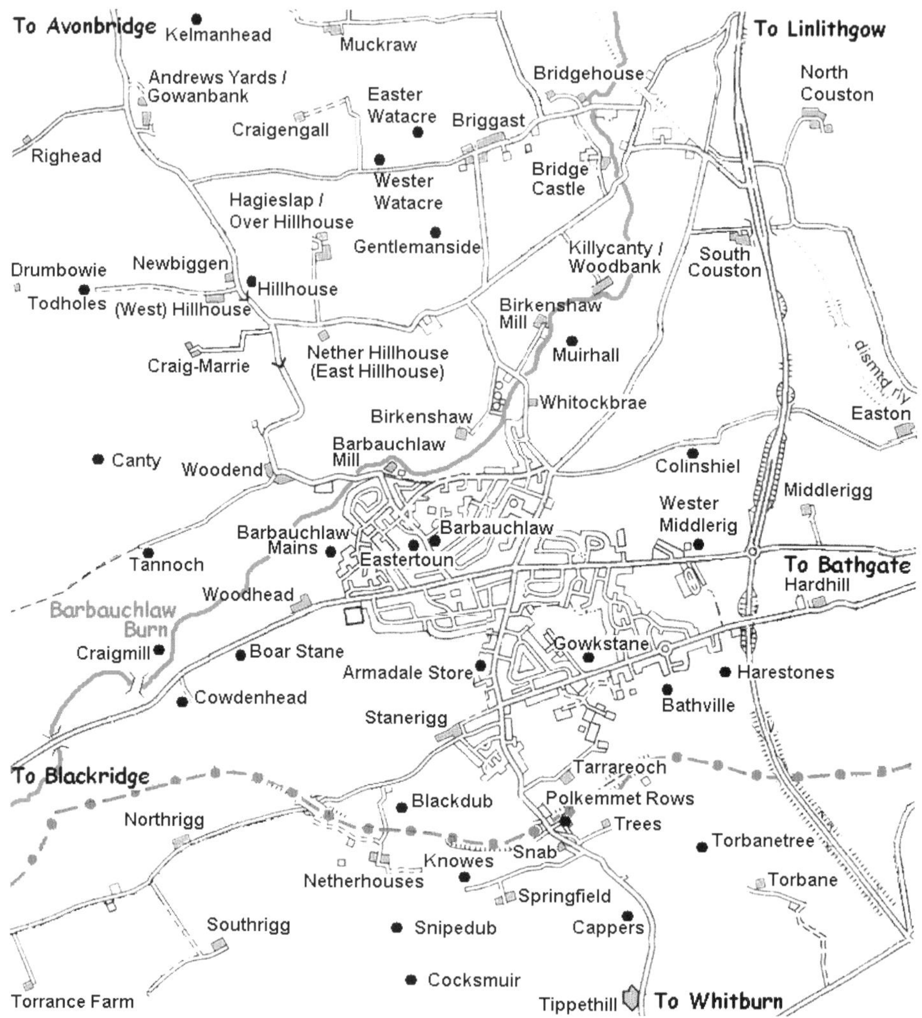

Some of the earliest estates in the Armadale area:

Bridgehouse (Brighous or the Briggast) the original house was demolished in 1629, a stone lintel with a 17th century date can be seen at West Lodge, Bridgecastle, Couston, Barbauchlaw, Hardhill and Bathville are old estates.

Polkemmet Estate seems to have shared a boundary with Barbauchlaw.

Capper's Rows at Armadale Station appears to have earlier been Polkemmet Rows.
To the north of the Barbauchlaw Burn was the big estate and one time Barony of Ogilface.
For a time the lands of Hardhill were part of Hopetoun Estate.

Earliest places of the Armadale area from old maps:
1630 map: shows Kaillyfranky and Harrhill.
1650 map: (from survey of c.1590) shows Kraigmary, West Balbachla and Woodend.
1654 map: (from 1590 survey) shows West Torbain.
1681 map shows Nedderhillhouse, Wateacre, Brighous Castle.
1691 map shows Canty, Barntoun, Hairstons, Tarbantree, Tarban, Tarryryoh, Midlerig, Craiginga and Andrewsyeards.
1744 map shows Muckra and Whitebrea.

Barbauchlaw

Most of present day Armadale stands on land that was once part of the lands or estate of Barbauchlaw. The original Barbauchlaw Estate seems to have stretched from Colinburn, at the Marches, to Cowdenhead and lay to the south of Barbauchlaw Burn (though several centuries later part of Barbauchlaw Estate lay to the north of Barbauchlaw Burn within the Barony of Ogilface and Parish of Torphichen).

Between 1156 and 1158, King Malcolm IV granted by Charter to the Monks and Abbacy of Holyrood, the Church and Lands of Batket (Bathgate). As the original land of Barbauchlaw was entirely within the Parish of Bathgate, it is possible that the Monks of Holyrood owned Barbauchlaw from as early as the 12th century.

As there was a Barony of Ogilface (owned by De Bosco) to the north of the Barbauchlaw Burn from 1165 until the 14th century, it is possible that there was a Barony of Bathgate during a similar period and that the lands of Barbauchlaw were in that Barony. (If there was a Barony of Bathgate between c.1165 till c.1315, it might have been a Secular Barony, belonging to Holyrood Abbey).

It is conceivable that as early as the 12th or 13th century, the Monks of Holyrood owned and operated a mill at Barbauchlaw. During the pre-Reformation period, Holyrood monks might also have built and used the old square stone building near Woodend, which the mapmakers of the 1890's Ordnance Survey map may have wrongly called 'Site of Ogilface Castle'.

In 1315, when the castle and lands (or Barony) of Bathgate was given by Robert the Bruce as a wedding dowry, when his daughter Marjorie married Walter Fitzallan, High Steward of Scotland, the lands of Barbauchlaw might have been included in the dowry. On the death of Walter the Steward on 9th April 1327, at Bathgate Castle, his lands of Bathgate possibly became Crown property.

It is not known for sure who owned the lands of Barbauchlaw before it was first recorded in 1335. Four possible owners were the monks of Holyrood, who are likely to have travelled from Holyrood to Monklands via Barbauchlaw from about 1162, or De Bosco of Ogilface, or Walter Stewart or the Crown.

'Balbaghlach' was first recorded in 1335-36 and 'Balbachlathe' in 1336-37. Both of these names could be Gaelic for settlement or place of the crozier, i.e. belonging to an Abbey.

In 1327, Bathgate's Kirkton Kirk, and possibly the lands of the Parish or Barony of Bathgate, was transferred from Holyrood Abbey to Newbattle Abbey. The kirk at Kirkton seems to have been the original pre-Reformation Bathgate Parish Kirk. The lands of Barbauchlaw might have been included in the transfer, so the lands of Barbauchlaw could have belonged to Newbattle Abbey until the Reformation in 1560.

It is recorded that, in 1333, the monks of Newbattle were allowed to pass through the Barony of Bathgate on the way to Monklands. It is possible that the monks of Newbattle had established a meal, barley or flourmill at Barbauchlaw Mill about, or before, 1335. Barbauchlaw Mill is now a flourishing market garden / nursery and several old stone farm buildings survive. Thomas Harvie once lived at Barbauchlaw Mill.

The monks of Newbattle and Holyrood probably played a part in the construction of the old Drove Coach, or Turnpike road between Edinburgh and Monklands and in the erection of the old drystane dykes.

The land north of the Barbauchlaw Burn was part of the ancient Barony of Ogilface. From 1165 until the 14th century, the De Bosco family owned the Barony. The Barony seat was Ogilface Castle which was situated either in the Craig Hills at Blackridge or at Woodend.

The Canons of Holyrood Abbey were granted a regal jurisdiction over the Barony between 1390 and 1406. Nicholas de Bothville worked on Linlithgow Castle around 1300.

1506: Balbachio recorded.
1558: Barbachlach and Barbaychlaych.
1562: Barbauchlecht and Barbauchlaw.
1538: Part of the Barony of Ogilface was given or sold to Rab Gibb of Carriber. The lands stretched from Barbauchlaw Burn to the River Avon and included Birkenshaw. (The lands involved in the transaction seem to have belonged to the Abbacy of Holyrood).
1555: There was a Sasine in favour of the son and heir of Robert Wetherspoune of Brighous. Alex Cochran was a witness.
1566: It was recorded that Adam Cuthbart, who formerly resided in Bawbauchloch, borrowed £10.5/4. He was possibly the first post-Reformation owner or lessee of the lands of Barbauchlaw.
1577-8: Barbachlay recorded.
1579: Barbachlaw recorded.
1584: Barbauchlaw became the property of James Cochrane of the family of Cochrane of Dundonald in Ayrshire and Renfrewshire.
1584-1789: During the Cochrane ownership of Barbauchlaw, several Cochranes held key judicial and administrative positions in Linlithgowshire.
1587: James Cochrane of Barbauchlaw failed to respond to the call to military conscription and was found guilty of treason.
1588: James Cochrane of Barbauchlaw recorded.
1590: West Balbachla was on the old Coach or Drove Road.
1614: Easter Barbachlaw was recorded.
1622: A James Cochrane was appointed Sheriff of Linlithgowshire.
1642: James Cochrane of Barbachla was recorded.

1651: A stone at Barbauchlaw Mill records this date. Another stone has the letters P.B. possibly standing for Phineas Bennie or Binnie, who was probably the resident miller.

1654: On a map, there was an East and a West Balbachla.

1662: James Cochrane was Sheriff of Linlithgowshire.

1662: A Cochrane signed a kirk document.

1673: James Davie, Covenanter, was shot by Dragoons at Blackdub. He was buried in Bathgate's Kirkton Graveyard. Blackdub seems to have been renamed Netherhouses in 19th century.

1679: Alex Cochrane was Chief Heritor of the Parish of Bathgate; Barbauchlaw was at that time within the civil and religious Parish of Bathgate. Alexander Cochrane was a Commissioner of Justiciary who tried six Bo'ness people, and found them guilty of practising witchcraft (they were burned at the stake).

1683: Alexander Cochrane was restored to the office of Sheriff of Bathgate.

1691: It would seem that part of the lands of Barbauchlaw was in Torphichen Parish and part in Bathgate Parish. According to the Hearth Tax Records of 1691, Barbachlaw's land's mansion house and office house had 14 hearths. Barbachlaw's tenants in Torphichen Parish were Marshell in Back of the Moss, Walker in Craigend, Nimmo in Cante, Walker in Gartmore, Fleyming in Woodquarter, Brook (or Brock?) in Tannochhead.

1703-1710: A Cochrane of Barbauchlaw was Sheriff of Bathgate.

c.1720: A Cochrane was Sheriff of Bathgate as well as of Linlithgow. The seat of Cochrane's Barbauchlaw Estate was a house called 'The Place'. It was situated to the north of the old manse at the Beeches. Barntoun, later renamed Eastertoun, was possibly the original Barbauchlaw Home Farm. Barbauchlaw Farm was demolished c.1952 and Barbauchlaw Mains c.1992, both to make way for housing.

1734: The last Royal Charter granting Barbauchlaw Estate to a member of the Cochrane family granted it to Harry Cochrane.

1737: On a map of that date, there was Barnbachla and Barntoun.

1747: Margaret Cochrane of Barbauchlaw (daughter of the late Alex Cochrane and sister of Alex Cochrane) married Alex Hamilton of Pumpherston.

1760: The first two feus sold by the estate were close to Eastertoun, one was sold in 1760 to William Gardner, shoemaker, and the second sold to John Brock, butcher, in 1773.

1789: Helen Bell, daughter of Robert Bell, died in Barbauchlaw Mill.

1789: The last of the Cochranes of Barbauchlaw seems to have died, without heir, he was Harry Cochrane.

1790-1800: The old farmhouse at Barbauchlaw Mill was built, making it possibly the oldest inhabited house in Armadale.

1790: Barbauchlaw Estate was auctioned by the Crown and was bought by Sir William Honeyman.

1795: The first feuar to buy a feu from the new owner of Barbauchlaw Estate was John Russell, joiner / wright. It was west of the Cross and was later the site of the old Police Station.

1797: George Swan built an inn near the Cross, where the Regal Bar stands now, naming it Armadale Inn. This was an important year in Armadale's history for Sir William Honeyman, owner of Barbauchlaw Estate, became Lord Armadale.

Lord Armadale (Sir William Honeyman) after whom Armadale is named - from Kay's Edinburgh Portraits 1790's

Sir William Honeyman was the eldest son of Patrick Honyman of Graemsay in Orkney. He was born in 1756 and was fourth in descent from Andrew Honyman, Bishop of Orkney. In 1777 he was admitted to the Bar and became Sheriff Depute for Lanarkshire in 1786. In 1797 he was promoted to the Bench and assumed the title of Lord Armadale from landed property that he inherited from his mother Margaret McKay, daughter and heiress of McKay of Strathy. In 1799 he became a Lord of Justiciary and a Baronet in 1804. In 1811 he retired to Smyllum Park, Lanark, and died in 1825.

Sir William Honeyman of Graemsay, Lord Armadale, 4th from the bottom on the left at the last sitting of the Old Court of Session, 11/07/1808, caricature by John Kay

Owners of Barbauchlaw Estate after Lord Armadale, were Andrew Thomson (1813-1818), James Dennistoun (1818-1835), Alex Dennistoun (1835-1861), Alex Turner (c.1861–c.1871), John Moffat (c.1871–c.1881), George Readman (c.1881-1893) and George Readman (c.1893–1906+).

1836: The population of Barbauchlaw Estate was 217.

Farmer Brock of Barbauchlaw Mill was a well-known poet in the 19th century. Jessie Harvie, daughter of Thomas Harvie of the same place, was the Jessie of teacher William Cameron's song 'Jessie o the Mill'. He changed the words to 'Jessie o the Dell'. It was set to music and published by Thomas Brown, music seller, Glasgow, in 1835.

Jessie o the Dell, Victorian illustration

Bathville

The Estate of Harestanes was part of Hopetoun Estate for a number of years before, and until, 1797. In that year, it was sold to William Davidson who, right away, changed its name to Bathville Estate. He probably built Bathville House soon after becoming the laird and he lived at Bathville House till about 1820.

Between 1975 and 1996, two local authority electoral wards were named after two old local estates, they were Bathville and Barbauchlaw.

The Shepherd's Stanes

The Shepherd's Stones (or Stanes) - a big stone (it may possibly be a block of concrete) sits inside a field close to the Northrigg Road a few hundred yards from Stanerig Filters. A group of three stones nearby was probably a similar stone before being broken.

The Shepherd's Stanes

A local legend has it that two shepherds had a disagreement - but this story seems to be without foundation. As the stones lie not far from Harestanes Road, it would appear that the Councillor or official who named the street, held the view that the stones were 'Hare' or Boundary stones. A standing stone on Trees Farm was described as a Hare or Boundary stone.

The suggestion that the stones were relics of the local coalmining industry can be ruled out as the stones have been lying where they are now since before the coal mining industry began in the Armadale area. (A map dated 1773 shows the stones marked "Standing Stone")

The following explanation seems the most likely - the whole stone has a hole in it about one foot square and the broken stone also had a hole in it. Similar pairs of stones in Edinburgh were the bases of a gibbet (a gallows or scaffold) for hanging criminals. It is possible that the Government or King (whose Dragoons waged a military campaign against the Scottish Covenanters) arranged for gibbets to be erected in Covenanting areas after 1670.

A local Covenanter, James Davie, was shot by a Dragoon while attending a Conventicle at Blackdub (Blackdub Farm stood about 700 yards south-west of the stones), so it is feasible that the stones were carted by the military to their position soon after Davie was shot in 1673 and were pointed out to the Armstrong Brothers in 1773 when preparing their map. (Note that in 1670 preaching at Conventicles became a capital offence).

18th Century

1710: Young was the occupant of Killiecanty. Killiecanty was Kaillyfranky at a survey of c.1590 and Killiecanty was apparently renamed Woodbank some time later or was close to Woodbank.

Before Woodbank Cemetery came into use, Armadalians were buried in Bathgate, Whitburn and Torphichen Graveyards.

These Armadalians were buried in Kirkton Graveyard, Bathgate: Robert Geddes of Torbanehill (died 1722), John Gentleman of Craigmarie (1826), William Brock of Barbauchlaw Mains (1855) and John Wilson of Whitockbrae (1865). Alex Dennistoun was buried in the Barbauchlaw Burial Ground at Kirkton.

Whitburn Graveyard: David Millar of Torbanehill was buried in 1849.

At Torphichen Graveyard, the following Armadalians lie buried:
Henry Brock of Eastertoun of Boarbachly (died 1769), John Brock of Netherhillhouse (1803), John Russell of Androsyard (1814), James Sinclair of Woodend (1815), John More of Overhillhouse (1853), James Waugh of Birkenshaw (1857), Walter Gowans of Gowanbank (1858) and William S. Addie of Trees (1865).

1744: Whitebrea recorded, also Hairstone.

1773: Places on a map of that year - the old Woodend drove road was called Glasgow Road. Also mentioned are: Drumbowie, Hagieslap, Cantiecraigs, Ogelface, Tannoch, Cowdenhead, Gowkstone (at Atlas Foundry), Oakbank, Colinshiel, Muirhall, Northrigg, Blackdub, Knows, Snipedub, Brighous, Brighouse Castle, Craiginga, Kilycanty, Cowstoun, Birkenshaw, Woodend, Barnbachla, Barntoun, Whitokbrea, Midlerig, Hardhill, Tarryryoh, Tarbane, Tarbanhall, Tarbanhill, Killicanty, Netherhillhouse, Cantie, Barbauchlaw and Mill, Muirhall, Stanerig, Hartstones, Westfield, Cocksmuir, Springfield and Hetterbane.

1791: "By an Act of Parliament, the road from Glasgow to Airdrie to be extended to Edinburgh by Bathgate and, when executed, will be the most accessible way between these cities, not only as being shortest, but most level and free from pull."

1795: By October, the new road between Newbridge and Airdrie was opened. It was part of the Edinburgh to Glasgow turnpike road. This new road, which was called 'The Great Road', replaced the old Drove, Coach or Turnpike Road that went via Bangour, Drumcross, Easton, Colinshiel and Woodend, the old road being rendered obsolete.

At certain road junctions along the Great Road were toll collecting points, called Toll Barrs or Toll Points. Three local Toll Barrs were at Guildiehaugh, Armadale Cross and Entryfoot. For a number of years after the Toll Barr was established at Armadale Cross, it was probably called Barbauchlaw Toll Barr after the estate in which it was situated. The toll-keeper's house stood at the north-east corner of Armadale Cross.

1797: On 17th May, a meeting of the Cleuch Turnpike Road Trustees authorised a Side Barr (i.e. a Toll Bar) to be erected at Woodside on the Cleuch Road. (Cleuch Road stretched from Bo'ness to Wilsontoun via Torphichen, Bathgate and Whitburn or East Whitburn). This was to collect toll dues from users of the recently built road between Woodside and Armadale via Balmuir. The first Woodside toll-keeper was John Marshall. Armadale Toll Bars was mentioned in the Cleuch Trustees minutes of that year.

19th Century

1808: Mr. Reid of Bathgate bought Armadale Inn, John Harvie, stonemason, became tenant. James Steel, shoemaker, of Woodhead died.

1809: Three local people died. They were Janet Gentleman of Craigmarie, John Brown of Barbauchlaw and Henry Gardner, tailor, of Barbauchlaw.

1810: John Wardrop was a farmer at Barbauchlaw. Elizabeth Waugh of Barbauchlaw died. Thomas Rankin, blacksmith, established his smiddy next to Russell's joiner's shop in West Main Street. James Gardner was a tailor in Eastertoun. One John Wardrop farmed Barbauchlaw, while another farmed Torbanehill.

1810-11: Armadale's first Pale House was built at the Cross to house a horse drawn funeral carriage. Thomas Brock supplied thatch and stones for its construction whilst Alex Brown, carter, John Gilchrist and William Arthur, stonemasons and thatchers, and Alex Russell, supplier of stones, all helped to build the Pale. A hearse was the chief asset of Armadale Friendly Society.

1812: William White and John Clarkson were both cautioners of a Friendly Society.

1817: Farmer Brock of Barbauchlaw Mains wrote a fine poem on the severe frost of that year which ruined the hairst. (harvest)

1818: A map of that year shows Newbigging, Drove Loan, Lintmill, coal pit, Barbauchlaw Place, Heatherfield, Little Harthill, Bathville and Snab and an inn at the Cross. Willie Rodger was a carter of salt, etc.

1819: General William Maxwell of Bellamonte, Superior of Harestanes / Bathville, confirmed William Davidson in the lands of Harestanes by a Charter of Confirmation.

1820: A map of that year showed a pigeon cote (dove-cot or doocot) to the south-west of Barbauchlaw Mill. The Toll Point at the Cross was still recorded as Barbauchlaw Toll, not Armadale Toll. Todholes was near Drumbowie, Newbigging was near Hillhouse, Drove Loan was near Woodbank Cemetery. Birkenshaw Mill was a lint mill (it processed locally grown flax). Several coal pits were on the map. Also on the map were Armadale (by 1820 the name of the village that had grown around the crossroads), Springfield, Cappers near Tippethill, Trees, Cocksmuir, Birkenhead, Barbauchlaw Place, Inn, Little Hardhill, Bathville, Blackdub, Westminster, Strand, Bargaber, Liltie Cockie, Gutter Renton, Drove Loan, Heatherfield, Muirhall, Crifts Castle near Heights, Cockup Toll, Banksgutters, Badgels, Wheatacre, Cromty Faulds, Gentlemanside, Andrews Yards and Kelmanhead.

1825: William Shaw was the Laird of Trees Farm.

1827: Rev. John Brock was a licentiate of the Church of Scotland.

1831: 12th March was the date of a daring well-planned highway robbery that involved a stagecoach between Forestfield and Bathgate when nearly £6,000 was stolen. George Gilchrist, who was a regular horse racer at Blackburn Fair, was found guilty and hung. He owned the Prince Royal stagecoach and was part owner of other coaches. He also owned nearly 50 horses. Of the four men who joined the coach at Shettleston, one was dressed as a woman.

1838: Mr. Waugh farmed Birkenshaw and Mr. Bell Whitockbrae.

Whitockbrae at the end of the 19th Century

Schooling

1819: A thatched cottage that stood about 100 yards west of the Cross became Armadale's first school. It seems to have been a Subscription School paid for by a levy on wage earners in Armadale. Armadale's first schoolteacher seems to have been William Cameron, who taught in Armadale from 1819 till 1833. He is best remembered as a poet / songwriter. He wrote 'Morag's Fairy Glen', also 'Jessie o the Dell' (where Jessie was Jessie Harvie of Barbauchlaw Mill). For ten years he lived at Whitockbrae where there was a wishing well and a trysting tree.

1833-1857: William Wilson was Armadale's second teacher and may have taught at both of Armadale's Subscription Schools.

1837: Forty Armadale parents appealed to Bathgate Academy Trustees for assistance because of the distance the children travelled from Armadale to Bathgate Academy, which had opened in 1833.

1838: A six-man committee was formed to plan Armadale's first purpose built school. The school that was built in 1838 in North Street, south of Castle Poorie, which seems to have been Armadale's second school, was also a Subscription School. It seems to have been in use from 1838-1856.

1840: A Mission Sunday School was established in Armadale. It was also described as a Mission Sabbath School.

1847: Messrs. Brock, Bell, Pollock, Harvie and Wilson and others represented Armadale School Committee.

1849: Rev. Byers was given £5 a year from the Calder Bequest to go towards educating the poor children at Armadale.

1855: The Rector of Bathgate Academy refused to accept any more children from Armadale.

1856: Mr. Hare opened a private school in MacDonald's Hall, West Main Street; John Gillespie succeeded Mr. Hare.

1858: A sixteen-man committee of management for a new Subscription School in Armadale was formed. Donations came in for the new school - £30 from Russell, £30 from Monklands Iron and Steel Co., £20 from Shotts Iron Co., £15 from J. Watson, £10 from the Earl of Rosebery and £10 from William Baillie. Armadale shop-owners donated from 5/- to £5, a Soiree / Ball raised £10 ¼ and many Armadalian miners and working people gave 6d or 1/-. David Drysdale taught in Mary Campbell's Hall in South Street. Allan Craig taught at Edward's Hall next to Armadale Inn. Cornelius Cowan taught at Bathville Row School. Elizabeth and Allan Gray taught at Mount Pleasant Row School.

1859: Armadale Subscription School was built in South Street. The North Street School sold for £50. The money was used to build a new Subscription School.

In the 1860's, Monklands Co. and Watson & Son (at Bathville), both coal-masters, built works' schools for the children of their workers.

Between 1880 and 1929, three of Armadale's public schools' buildings were built with stone from the quarry in Barbauchlaw Glen.

Armadale Public School

Mining

It is recorded that ironstone mined on Couston Estate was used to make cannons that were used at the Battle of Waterloo in 1815.

It appears that the pit that provided the ironstone was Colinshiel Pit, which was situated about one mile north of Armadale Cross. In 1819, three local men (John Harvie, John Wilson and William Roberts) formed a coal company to mine coal near Woodhead. The coal was called Boarbauchlaw coal and they took out a 10-year lease.

1819: Miners included Messrs. Henderson, Twaddle, Neil and Betty Stevenson.

1820: Miners included Easton, Watson, Baxter, Colin, Brown, Lumsdale, Hamilton, Rea and Thom.

1830: Miners included Twaddle, Baxter, Simpson, Lumsdane, McPhail, Russell, Sneddon and Pollock.

1834: Thomas Harvie fell heir to a colliery and inn from his mother's side of the family.

1835: Mr. Smillie was a miner.

1840: Armadale had about 40 miners. They probably, by then, lived mainly in miners' rows called after the name of the farm or estate whose land they were built on, e.g. Barbauchlaw Row, Colinshiel Row and Polkemmet Row. Armadale miners of 1840: Williamson, Wilson and Twaddle.

1843: Barbauchlaw Colliery was leased to Margaret Harvie innkeeper. She rented from Alex. Dennistoun, owner of Barbauchlaw Estate.

1850's: Monklands Iron and Steel Co. owned Buttries Pit on Barbauchlaw land. Boiler covers at Barbauchlaw Colliery were made of wood and heaved up with each stroke of the piston.

1850: Cannel (candle) or parrot coal was used in the manufacture of illuminating gas and was a source of oil. James 'Paraffin' Young founded the world's first oil works at Whiteside using cannel coal. The richest and best cannel coal was Torbanite or Boghead gas coal of Armadale district.

Buttries Pit Miners from 1912 – note the oil lamps in the bunnets

1855: From the Ordnance Survey map: Near Mossend / North Street (in the area of the recreation park) stood Armadale Pit N$^{o.}$3 (coal and ironstone) with two shafts and tram road. ½ mile north of Mossend, near recent (1985-90) opencast, were Colinshiel Pits N$^{os.}$1, 2 and 4 (coal and ironstone) also Pit N$^{o.}$3, brickworks and tram-road, a smithy, store and houses. At Mount Pleasant was Barbauchlaw Pit N$^{o.}$2 (coal and ironstone) with shaft and tram road. East of Bathville Cross was Hardhill Pit N$^{o.}$1 (coal and ironstone) on the north side of the road, near Wester Hardhill farm, and an old quarry. East of Bathville Cross, on the south side of the road, stood Bathville Coal Pit with weighing machine, engine house / smithy, refuse bing and two old quarries. At Woodend, there were two coal and ironstone pits (east and south of Woodend Farm), a smithy and a store.

1855: Barbauchlaw Pit No.2 had been established at Mount Pleasant. Barbauchlaw Miners' Rows had been built at Woodhead - the 'White Hooses'. There was a reference to Gowkstane Minerals (Gowkstane Farm was near the Atlas / Mayfield). There was also a reference to Trees Minerals.

Coal and ironstone mining brought prosperity to Armadale between about 1815 and 1860, but it also brought problems. One of these was the exploitation of boys and girls down the pits. A survey done about 1843 tells us that five boys, all under 13, worked down below at Barbauchlaw Pit. One of them was Peter Williamson who was 12 years old. He had been down below since he was 10; he worked 12 to 14 hours per day in seams and main roads that were 40 inches high. After work, he found time and energy to attend Mr. Wilson's night-school at Armadale. The number of children under 13 who were employed in other local pits was – Walker's Hardhill Pit employing 3, Johnston's Ballencrieff Pit, 1, and Moore's Pit at Colinshiel, 3. Sir P. Honeyman employed no children under 13 at Bargaebar Pit.

c.1850-60: Companies involved in mineral extraction in Armadale district and houses built in Armadale in same period –

Company	**Lease**	**Houses built**
Russell & Son (coal had high oil content)	Boghead, Hopetoun, Torbane, Torbanehill	Russell's Row, south side East Main Street. Russell's Square, south side West Main Street. Hardhill Row, opposite No.1 Pit. Bathville Row (demolished before 1906)
Watson, Glasgow	Bathville Estate	Bathville Row south side Upper Bathville
Monklands Iron and Steel Co. (Buttries)	Barbauchlaw Estate	Buttries Rows, both sides of North Street. Also Mount Pleasant, north side, 'Quality' or 'Dandy' Row, west side of South Street. Northrigg
Shotts Iron Co.	Polkemmet Estate	Cappers, South of Armadale Rail Station (formerly Polkemmet Rows)
Coltness Iron Co.	Woodend	Woodend

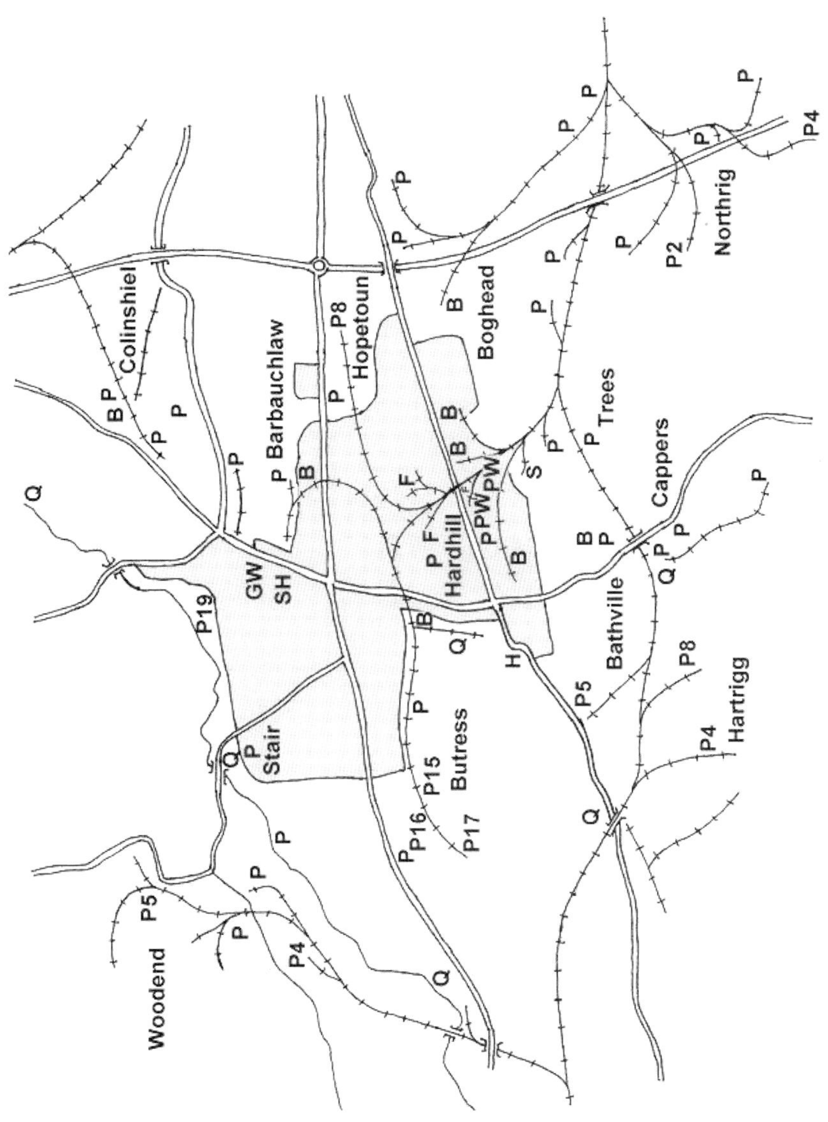

Industry in Armadale

P	Coal Pit with name & number		
B	Brick Work	**PW**	Pipe Work
F	Foundry	**S**	Steel Work
H	Hosiery	**GW**	Gas Works
Q	Quarry	**SH**	Slaughterhouse

Locally-made bricks

Mark	Maker	Production Period
ATLAS	Atlas Firebrick Works	1882-1973
ATLAS G.B.	Atlas Firebrick Works	1882-1973
ATLAS STIRLING	Atlas Firebrick Works	1882-1973
CRATER G.B.	Atlas/Etna Works	1880 or 1890-1970s
ETNA	Etna Brickworks	ca. 1890-1947
ETNA G.B.	Etna Brickworks	ca. 1890-1960
BAR-LAW	Barbachlaw Brickworks	1897-1947
MUIR	Barbauchlaw Brickworks	1897-1947
MUIR ARMADALE	Barbauchlaw Brickworks	1897-1947
BOGHEAD	Boghead Fireclay Works	ca. 1889-1930
BOGHEAD Glasgow	Boghead Fireclay Works	1889-1922
CRAIGRIGG	Craigrigg Works Westfield	ca. 1938-1950s

Brickworks and United Fireclay Pipeworks at Bathville showing chimneys and stacked-up pipes

1840's

1840: Mrs. Harvie gave up Armadale Inn and became tenant of Barbauchlaw Mill Farm. Stonemason Walter Gowans built Gowanbank House.

1841: Brock farmed Barbauchlaw Mains Farm while Orr farmed Barbauchlaw Mill.

The village of Armadale had grown very slowly from its beginnings, about 1797, until the first, all Scotland, Census of 1841. By 1841, there were only about 30 families in the village close to Armadale Cross or Toll Bar as it was then called. It had a total population of about 125.

A further ten or so miners and their families lived at Colinshiel Colliery village, about one mile north of Armadale Cross. About 50 people, all told, lived at Colinshiel village. Approximately a further 150-200 people lived in 50 or so farms and cottages within about 1½ miles of Armadale Cross.

Surnames of the families who lived in Armadale village in 1841 - Ranken, Sim, Marshall, Shanks, Smith, Neil, Docharty, Laird, Duncan, McNicol, Gray, Harvie, Thomson, Patterson, Forsyth, Campbell, McNeil, Tennant, Wilson, Finnlay, Logan, Sinclair, Dow, Neilson, Allan, Shields, Williamson, Carlaw, Pollock and Lawson.

These families lived at Colinshiel in 1841 - Duncan, Harris, Easton, Alexander, Brown, Baxter, Walker and Smellie. At least fourteen of the villagers were coal miners including two boys aged 10. About six miners wives were 'drawers', as was one girl aged 10.

Of the 350-400 people who lived within 1½ miles of Armadale Cross, around 150 were in employment split almost equally between three groups - Farming and agriculture, Coal and ironstone mining and Other trades.

The first category included farmers, agricultural labourers, farm servants, dairy-maid, and even one cow-keeper.

The second category included coal-masters, drawers, coal-miners, engine-keepers and at least one ironstone miner.

The third category comprised all trades and employment not belonging to the other two categories. This list included at least one of the following trades - blacksmith, shoemaker, roadman, tailor, miller, cotton handloom weaver, innkeeper, seamstress, tambourer, merchant, carpenter, hatter, and Toll Collector.

Among Armadale's farmers in 1841 were Bryce of Torbanhill, Bell of Terrereoch, Inglis of Standhill, Sinclair of Cowdenhead, Purves of Netherhouse, Arbuckle of Muirhall, Murray of Springfield, Peat of Staneridge, Bell of Whitockbrae, Orr of Boarbachlaw Mill, Brock of Boarbachlaw Mains, Waugh of Hetherfield, Pollock of Colinshiel, More of Overhillhouse, Brock of Netherhillhouse, Waugh (flax miller) of Birkenshaw Mill, Waugh of Birkenshaw, Sawyers of Newhouse, Waddell of Hillhouse, Gentleman of Craigmyre, Waddell of Woodend and Liddell of Craigmill.

The earliest coalminers in and around Armadale included miners with the following surnames - Marshall, Shanks, Niel, Laird, Duncan, McNicol, McNiel, Nielson, McPhail, Wilson, Harris, Easton, Alexander, Brown, Baxter, Walker, Smellie and Williamson.

The following were Armadale people whose employment was not farming or mining - Thomas Ranken, smith, Robert Sim, shoemaker, John Thomson, roadman, James Forsyth, tailor, Thomas Forsyth, blacksmith, John Smith, blacksmith, James Tennant, miller, George Finnlay, cotton handloom weaver, Margaret Harvie, innkeeper, Janet Russell, seamstress, Alex Marshall, cotton weaver, Helen Gardner, seamstress, A. Niel, tambourer, Thomas Strathern, shoemaker, John Gilmar, cotton weaver, Elizabeth Newton, merchant, David Thomson, roadman, Alex Douglas, carpenter, Louis Daves, hatter and John Lawson, Toll Collector.

Other points of interest on the Armadale of 1841, the Rentons lived at Bathville, the road from Armadale Cross to Whitburn was called Drove Road, Helen Russell appears to have put floral patterns on muslin (her livelihood), Sir R.B. Honeyman lived at Torbanehill, a row of Armadale's houses was called Collier Row, there was a brickwork at Nethermuir and a Tollhouse stood at Armadale Cross.

1846: Alex Wark attended the Parochial Board of Bathgate Parish as proxy per mandate for James McHardy of Bathville; T.D. Weir of Boghead was proxy for Alex Dennistoun of Barbauchlaw and William Brock for Margaret Gardner.

c.1847-48: William Brock, farmer, Barbauchlaw, was to arbitrate re an appeal. Geo Sinclair of Cowdenhead appealed against assessment on the grounds that his mother was infirm, his sister blind and his son was of unsound mind.

1848: Sir James Gowans, architect, enlarged Gowanbank House. Gowanbank was the new name for Andrewsyard, Andros Yeard in 1386.

Gowanbank *(DMT Davidson Associates)*

1850's

A map of 1850 shows some of the farms, places, etc. in and near Armadale - Barbauchlaw, Toll Inn Armadale, Little Hardhill Coal Pit, Colinshiel, Whitockbrae, Birkenshaw, Pigeon Cote, Barbauchlaw Place, Woodend, Stanerig, Westfield, Bathville, Taryreoch, Blackdub, Knows and Snab.

Between the 1841 and 1851 census years, Armadale and district population grew only marginally. By 1851 a number of changes had taken place, new surnames appeared in the area and there were also new trades and occupations. Since the 1851 Census, for the first time, stated the place of birth, we learn that the early inhabitants of Armadale had been born in many of Scotland's shires and parishes and some had arrived from England and Ireland.

Here are some of the names of recent incomers to Armadale, some new occupations and other observations –
Ruthven now farmed Stanerig. Netherhouses had gone, temporarily, back to its previous name 'Blackdub' - another branch of the Purves family now occupied Blackdub. Mrs. Thomson of Woodhead was a seamstress. James Wilson of Woodhead was a coal grieve. At Barbauchlaw lived a retired weaver, Blair, a handloom weaver, Gardner, a tailor, and a dressmaker. McDonald of Muirhall was a cattle dealer.

At Colinshiel Colliery village several new families had arrived, John Russell was an overseer, John Binning was an engine-keeper, a lodger with the Binnings was a cotton weaver and William Duncan was an iron miner. The Cherry, Crockston and Flucker families had all moved into Colinshiel. Salmond of Snab was a cattle dealer and Joseph Reid of Snab was a cattle drover, possibly lodging at Snab on the night of the census. At Overhillhouse lived a gamekeeper. Gillespie of Torbanehill estate owned a coal mine and employed house servants.

Thomas Ferrier, traveller, lived at Torbanehill Mains; a lodger at Torbane was a brick-maker; several coal miners and their families lived at Heatherbane. They were the Browns, Togarts and Richardsons. William Shaw of Trees was a landed proprietor, so was

Wardrop of Bridgehouse. Walter Gowans of Gowanbank was a builder and railway contractor employing 300 men. They were mainly engaged in laying the Blackston to Boghead Branch of the Monkland Railway (i.e. Bathgate to Avonbridge). Mary Steel was a tambourer and Thomas Simpson was a wright.

Bridgecastle Avenue

Thomas Harvie of Bridgecastle was a railway agent. Three wrights (wheelwrights / joiners probably) lived at Bridgecastle cottage. Bridgehouse Colliery employed a blacksmith. James Marshall of Birkenshaw Mill was a flax dresser, while Edward Marshall of the same place was a tile burner.

Waddell farmed 600 acres at Woodend and, at Tannoch, Robert McGregor, who was born at Balquhidder, was a gamekeeper. At Newbigging, Lang was a farmer, grocer and victual dealer whilst John Gentleman of Craigmarie was a farmer and landed proprietor.

Armadale village had a large number of coal miners, as well as a tailor, shoemakers, a carrier, two paupers, a grocer, a grocer / meal-dealer, an engine-keeper, a watch-maker, a toll-keeper, a stocking weaver and an embroiderer. Alex Wark, farmer, Bathville, employed three servants and an errand girl, while John Miller of Hardhill employed six servants. In 1851, about 140 people lived in the village and about 200 lived within 1½ miles of the village.

Of the several hundred people who lived in and near Armadale, around 20 were born in Ireland, another 50 born in and around Armadale, but the bulk of the adults were born in other parts of Central Scotland, mainly in towns, villages, parishes and shires within about 25 miles of Armadale - from Fintry, Glasgow, Tranent, Bo'ness, Falkirk, Dunoon, Carnwath, West Calder, Fife, Lanarkshire, Ayrshire, Stirlingshire, Slamannan, Edinburgh, Airdrie, Shotts, Whitburn, Paisley and Haddingtonshire.

A few came from other parts of Scotland such as Moray, Dunoon and Crathie in Aberdeenshire. One was born in England.

1850

About 1850, reference was made to the Laird of Boghead and Torbanehill. Hardhill Farm and lands were part of Hopetoun Estate.

In the 1850's, attempts were made to form a Brass Band in Armadale. James and Robert Thomson appealed against assessment (to Bathgate Parish Parochial Board) on grounds that the railway was going through appellant's land.

James McHardy, who died c.1850, owned Bathville.

1851

By 1851, a family of seven named Harkins, all born in Ireland, had settled at Barbauchlaw. The Cappers was mentioned in 1851.

1853

William Gillespie was in Torbanehill. His wife, a Honeyman, inherited the estate.

1854

Buttries Co. built a store and office on South Street at the entrance to Wood Park. R. Millar was proxy for John Russell of Southrigg, i.e. on the Parochial Board. John Gray of Armadale was recorded in the minutes of Bathgate Parochial Board. The Ordnance Survey map of 1854-55 shows an old coal shaft approximately opposite the Corrie public house and there was a school near the Star Inn. There was a weighing machine near the inn, a T.P. (Toll Point) was at the Cross and also a smithy. The map showed no street names in Armadale.

1855

The Burial Grounds (Scotland) Act of 1855 showed there was a need for a burial ground to be provided for the Parish of Bathgate. Armadale deaths that year - Helen Ramsay or Sinclair, of Armadale; Agnes Hunter of Bathville; Christine Easton or Murphy, Jeffrey's Row, Armadale; the husband of Margaret Davis or Jackson died of smallpox; Geo. Snedden, miner, Armadale, was killed at Hardhill Pit; William McDowall, a boy, drawer in pit, lodges with Milligan in Armadale, had smallpox; Peter Quin, an Irish labourer, was found dead; William Pollock, labourer, was killed near Bathville; Elizabeth Davis or Ramage, who lived at Woodhead to the west of Armadale; James Easton, miner, Armadale; William Lees, miner, Armadale; James Bryce, miner, Hatterbane; Archibald Hunter, miner, Armadale; Laurence McGarrie died at Bathville.

D. Lees, miner, Beeches; William Shaw, miner, Muirhall, Armadale; Joseph Carr, miner, Heatherfield; Margaret Harrower or Hunter, from near Russell Square, Armadale (there was smallpox in the family); Rosa Donnelly or Conner, wife of James Conner, Mount Pleasant, Armadale; Alex Reid, miner, Armadale, an Irishman; Daniel McDonald, was a drawer in pit near Armadale, he lodged with Thomas Pow, miner, at the Beeches; Jane Baxter, of Shotts Row, Armadale; and William Brock of Barbauchlaw Mains, died, (buried at Kirkton).

Armadale got its first Post Office. Barbauchlaw toll point stood at Woodhead. A Proxy acted for Alex Dennistoun of Barbauchlaw. Armadale had a Temperance Brass Band and a Flute Band.

Edinburgh to Glasgow Railway was operational and Armadale had a railway station.

Armadale Station

William Rennie owned property at Armadale and William Hunter lived in Armadale. Provisions were supplied to Peter Millar, Armadale. Ann Inglis was the widow of John Donald of Armadale. James Cunningham was an Armadale miner, as was John Gorman. Henry Duncan, miner, Armadale, joined the Dunbar Militia.

Isabella Mackay lived at Colinshiel. J. Gilchrist, miner, lived at Bathville. Geo. McIntosh lived in Armadale. Henry Wotherspoon and Mrs. Wallace were both of Armadale. Two Armadale orphans were William and Robert McPhail. Robert Young and Francis Cairns were Armadale miners.

Mary Cherry, wife of William Lees, labourer, Armadale, rejected the offer of the Poorhouse. Luke Haughney, an Irish navvy / collier, while passing through Armadale, got into a scuffle when his head was cut. An application for relief on his account was made by Sergeant Kerr. The Inspector brought a cart to his door where he lodged in South Bridge Street, Bathgate, to take him to the Poorhouse, but he refused to go. One pauper was an unemployed tambourer.

In 1855, the first Ordnance Survey map of West Lothian came out:

- About a dozen different blocks and rows of houses were clustered around the Cross (Toll Bar); around fifty houses in total. The map shows smithy, inn and school, also T.P. (Toll Point).
- Near Birkenshaw Mill was a mill lade, mill dam, footbridge and ford.
- At Woodhead (the 'White Hooses') was Barbauchlaw Check Toll Point, a road mileage stone (Edinburgh 21, Glasgow 21), Barbauchlaw Rows, a well, old shaft and coal pit.
- Armadale Store was near bowling green entrance to Wood Park.
- Bathville Row was to the west of Bathville Cross.
- Bathville House was about ½ mile east of Bathville Cross, on the south side of the road, down a drive.
- Down Mill Road was Barbauchlaw Farm and well, also Eastertoun.
- Barbauchlaw Mill was a corn mill, with mill lade and sluice, nearby were stepping stones and old quarries.
- Woodend Farm had a pond and mill lade.
- Whitockbrae had a footbridge, ford and stepping stones, while Woodbank had a footbridge, stepping stones, old shaft, well and quarry.
- Near Armadale Station stood Polkemmet Cottage, Polkemmet Rows and brick and tile works. Trees had a draw-well and standing stone.

1856

Thomas Bishop was a publican and grocer and John Calderhead was a publican, both in South Street. Brock farmed Barbauchlaw Mains while Thomas Harvie farmed Barbauchlaw Mill and Farm.

Here are particulars of some farms around Armadale in 1856, the estates they were on, and the name of the tenant farmer –

Estate	Owner	Farm	Occupier
Polkemmet	Sir William Baillie	Balgornie	Russell
		Netherhouses	Purves
		Springfield	Murray
		Tippethill	Walker
		Stanerig	Ruthven
		Tarrareoch	Miller

Estate	Owner	Farm	Occupier
Barbauchlaw	A. Dennistoun	Whitockbrae	Bell
		BarbauchlawMains	Brock
		Barbauchlaw Mill & Farm	T. Harvie
		Standhill	Jardine
		Cowdenhead	Sinclair
Torbanehill	Gillespie	Torbanehill Mains	Millar
		Drum	Brodie
Boghead	T.D. Weir	Boghead	Steven
Couston	Sandilands	North Couston	Tod
Torbane	W. Johnston	Torbane	Salmond
Trees	Shaw	Trees	Shaw

1857

John Wilson built property in the south-east corner of the Cross and Mathew and John Wilson operated licensed grocers there. Mr. Murray of Springfield built the Crown Hotel, James Bishop became publican and grocer at the Crown. Armadale got its first policeman.

South Street looking south

The first local authority to cover Armadale was the Parochial Board of Bathgate (Armadale was wholly within the ancient Parish of Bathgate). From 1846 till 1895, the Parochial Board saw to

Armadale's poor, etc. From 1857, the Bathgate Parochial Board concerned themselves with public health, social work, poverty, diseases, the sick, frail, widowed, single parents, mentally and physically handicapped and the like. Most of the people who were being helped financially were described as paupers. Of a list of 102 paupers on the Poor Roll of the Parish in 1859 perhaps ten or twenty lived, or came from, Armadale.

Here are particulars of applications for relief from Armadale people and the decision of the Parochial Board - John Leggat, an elderly miner from 2 Cappers Row was allowed 2/- weekly, Jane Smith also got 2/- weekly, Neil O'Donnell, an injured miner from Bathville, was given 2/- weekly, James Thomson, an Armadale miner with a sore leg, was offered accommodation in the Poorhouse - it was in Linlithgow.

Two years later, in 1859, Mr. Inglis asked the Inspector of the Poor, not to send any more children to Bathgate Academy from Armadale. Mr. Inglis was Rector of Bathgate Academy, the reason isn't given.

1858

Mr. William Edwards, pit oversman, bought Armadale Inn. Mr. Wilson bought the Crown Hotel, also Stanerig Farm on Polkemmet Estate. John Calderhead became manager of Stanerig Farm. James Beveridge built the Buckshead Tavern.

1859

The trustees of James McHardy sold Bathville Estate to John Watson for £10,500. Mrs. Mary Campbell built the Railway Tavern. c.1859 (according to Robert Blair), Armadale had few houses, a large plantation, toll-house, and no (passenger) trains. Trees were cut down and new streets created and houses built.

One morning Armadalians were wakened up by tap of drum, the inhabitants quickly prepared for a confrontation with Irish reapers (shearers), but a repeat of a previous encounter was avoided and the Irishmen passed through Armadale peacefully.

1860's

From 1851 to 1863, Armadale grew from a small village to a small town. During these 12 years, Armadale's population grew as never before, or since, from around 140 in 1851 to approximately 3750 in 1863.

1860

Armadale Free Kirk, later the 'East Kirk', building was started. Pre 1860, a probationer from Bathgate Free Kirk preached in Armadale. Armadale Free Gardner's Society, Thistle Lodge, was founded. Ironstone pits at Northrigg and Armadale were abandoned. Thomas Graham's widow and family lived at Buttries Row. Henry Cherry, miner, of Russell's Square, widow Elspeth Thomson or Hunter of Bathville New Row were recorded, Mary Kelly (orphan child) lived with her grandfather James Wyper near Buttries Row, J.T. was injured in Shotts Iron Co. Pit at the Cappers and widow Snedden of Armadale applied for clothing for five children.

South Street, or the Toll Brae, with Armadale East Kirk on the left

Andrew Barnard, poet, was born in 1860, a miner, he was injured. Other Armadale poets, past and present, included James Ballantyne, Francis Barnard, William Brock, William Cameron, J. Gorman, Davie Kerr, Thomas Learmonth, Liz Marcella, J. Morrison, Mrs. Mulvey, Mrs. Murgatroyd and Thomas Sharp.

Some inhabitants of Armadale - John Hunter, widows Haddow, Ballantyne, Cumming and Watson and widow Thomson or Wilson of Mount Pleasant. There was a Jeffrey's Row. William Hair was a teacher.

Joseph Jones, miner, was found lying badly at No.2 Buttries Pit with his two children - all three were sent to the Poorhouse. Alexander Russell of Slamannan owned property a little to the west of Armadale Toll Bar. David Lang was a miner, of Polkemmet Row. Archibald Wardlaw a carter, of Mill Road. Archie McCulloch, miner, lived at 28 Cappers Row. Persons in arrears with Parish Rates were listed, street by street.

1861

The 1861 census shows that about 50 families lived in Drove Loan, (South Street), 40 in Mount Pleasant, 6 in Store Row, 6 in Hardhill Row (south), 20 in Hardhill Row (North), 6 in Moor Huts, 9 in Jeffrey's Row, 3 in Brick Row, 3 in Wylie's Row, 3 in Beveridge's Row, 10 in Johnston's Row, c.50 in Russell's Row, c.22 in Turnpike Road, (East and West Main Street), 7 in Barbauchlaw Row, 9 at Woodhead, 11 at Eastertoun, 48 in Bathville Row, 46 in Polkemmet Rows (Cappers), 5 in Snab Row, 12 in Castle Poorie, 6 in Shotts Row and 12 in Buttries Row.

There were still about 10 families in Colinshiel Colliery village, as in 1851. With about 12 Pits sunk within 1½ miles of Armadale Cross by 1855, hundreds of men were attracted to Armadale mainly from other parts of Scotland, but some from Ireland.

Armadale had changed a bit since the 1851 census - about 120 new Armadalians were born in Ireland. Of these, about 50 lived near each other in Hardhill Row, Bathville. Several were born in England. Of

Armadale's 3,750 villagers, some 2,000 were born within 25 miles of Armadale, including Helensburgh, Bothwell, New Monklands, Kinross, Perthshire, Fife, Leith, Doune, Clackmannan, Tollcross (Glasgow), Cumbernauld, Penicuik, Denny, Stonehouse and Chapelhall. From further afield came people from Islay, Mull (Macmillan), Wigtownshire, Berwick, and Banffshire, a blacksmith was born in New Lanark and a day old girl was born in Armadale (i.e. she was born the day before the 1861 census was taken). Of the Murray family, the parents were born in Ireland, their oldest son was born in England and their two youngest children born in Scotland (two lodgers were also Irish born).

The census usually gave the shire / county followed by the town or village where the person was born in Scotland. Where they were born in a local farm or country cottage, the parish and farm, etc., name was given, e.g. John Purves aged 35 of Blackdub, was born at Blackdub.

Mrs. Ann Young built the Star Inn. The road from Armadale Cross to Whitburn, was called Drove Road. By 1861, the first 39 miner's houses had been built at Woodend. The railway through Armadale Station became part of the North British Railway Co.. 483 Armadale miners were in a local miners' association.

In 1861, Armadale had an evening school (possibly for young miners). The same year, visiting Inspectors gave Armadale's Subscription School a favourable report. Mr. Gardner was the Master. The Inspector was "much pleased with the manner in which the pupils acquired these subjects - grammar, writing, geography, arithmetic, English and Scripture history."

1862

On March 1862, James Liddell of Glasgow applied for a teacher's job at Armadale Subscription School. John Wilson sold the Crown Hotel and leased Whitockbrae Farm.

An historic meeting took place in Edinburgh on 19th November 1862 in the run up to Armadale becoming a Burgh.

1863

Armadale's first Police Station, in West Main Street, was described as a but and ben with cells. It appears that the but and ben built by John Russell in 1795 was converted into a Police Station. Armadale's first Co-op Society only lasted five years, from 1863-1868. It was built at the foot of Bullion Brae, later renamed Academy Street.

Armadale Parish Kirk

The parish Presbyterians of Bathgate Parish erected a kirk on Bullion Brae. The kirk became Armadale Parish Kirk. St Paul's Episcopal Church was built at the Marches.

c.1863, Robert Blair and family flitted to one of the new houses being built in Woodend. Helen Ramsay or Sinclair was deserted by her husband, Robert Baxter, a miner in Armadale. Donald Cameron, late of Tyree, was a miner in Armadale. Andrew Brown lived at 40, Bathville. Helen Russell, an orphan girl, resided with Mungo Brown at the Beeches. John Jackson, bricklayer, lived at Armadale. Bridget Cassidy or Taggerty lived at 22 Cappers Row and Robert Harvey, miner, lived at Davidson's Lane whilst Catherine Bathgate or Tulloch lived at Masons' Land. Robert Brown and Hugh Skellon lived in a hut at Mount Pleasant. J. Carmichael lived at Mount Pleasant. Address of J. Selvedge, miner, was Monkey Row, Mount Pleasant. William Marshall was a smith in Armadale. Alex Bell lived at Whitockbrae.

Robert Livingstone was killed while ascending the shaft of a pit at Armadale. Margaret Green of Armadale, wife of Robert Irvine, died giving birth, the child was cared for by the wife of Constable J. Crawford of Armadale. An Armadale miner requested £14 to go to America. Hugh Allan was killed at a pit at the Cappers. When a miner died at Bathville, the Board gave 5/- to the family and also provided a grave.

In 1863, there were 79 Paupers in Armadale, with 30 living east of the Toll, 35 lived west of the Toll and 14 lived south of the Toll - the streets having not yet been named. An Armadale miner got 8/- from the Cappers Society.

By 1863, Armadale had about 500 coal miners and around 200 ironstone miners, most were married men with families and some women and girls as young as 10 found employment down the pit. Many new Armadalians had occupations in the coal mining industry other than coal and ironstone miners e.g. pit shanker, pit road brusher, pit oversman or overseer, coal-weigher, pit-sinker, engine-keeper, engine-feeder, pit-headsman, mineral borer, blacksmith, pit-bottomer and coal-drawer.

Although mining had now replaced farming as the main industry in Armadale district, the growing town also attracted new businesses and new occupations to service and meet the needs of the growing population. Among the many occupations of Armadalians of 1861 were temporary watchman, midwife, dressmaker, general merchant, brickwork contractor, grocer, wool-spinner, seamstress, shoemaker, paper worker, mineral borer, toll-keeper, clerk in the Chemical Works Bathgate, carter, joiner, blacksmith and dressmaker. A scavenger lived at Moor Huts. Other occupations were baker, spirit dealer, barmaid, earthenware merchant, confectioner, tailor, tambourer, roadman, traveller, washerwoman, brick-maker, horse dealer, clothier, minister, ploughman, farmer, dairymaid, housemaid, servant, labourer, Police Constable, bookseller & stationer, flesher, gas-coal miner, domestic servant, pawnbroker, carpenter, milliner, carrier, colliery manager, lawyers' clerk, hawker, coachman, cook, farrier, grain merchant, professor of dancing, white seam flowering, linen cloth lapper, district missionary, merchant and paper finishers.

Among the more unusual entries in the 1861 census were these ones - Alexander Gardner, teacher and census enumerator, under Barbauchlaw Mill and Rev. Alex Rodger, boarder, minister of the Free Kirk. Of Armadale's two Police Constables, one was born in Ross-shire and one in Kirkcudbrightshire. At Torbanehill House, Elizabeth Gillespie employed a coachman, cook and housemaid. The 11 year old son of a widow woman was an ironstone miner. In one family, two sons aged 13 and 15 were ironstone miners. Another family had four sons aged 11 to 23 - all four were coal miners. A young unknown man, aged about 15, who slept at a Pit on the night of the 1861 census, was described as a traveller.

Application for Burgh Status for Armadale –

Some Armadale businessmen, professional men, contractors, property-owners and shop owners decided that it was time that Armadale became a Burgh now that it could be described as a "populous place". This was the term used in an Act of Parliament designed to encourage Scotland's fast growing mining towns to become Police Burghs.

About 22 prominent Armadalians prepared a Petition of Application for Burgh Status and arranged for a qualified person to prepare a map showing the proposed Burgh Boundaries, along with a description defining the Boundaries.

The Boundary changed direction at eight points and the boundary line ran through these places - Lands of Barbauchlaw, Beech Plantation, Mill Road, Armadale Toll Bar, Linlithgow Road, ditch or water course, lands of Heatherfield, Estate of Barbauchlaw, lands of Hardhill (owned by the Earl of Hopetoun), Episcopal Chapel (recently erected), Bathgate to Northrigg / Shotts Road, lands of Bathville, Stanerig farm steading, watering pond, lands of Stoneridge (property of William Baillie of Polkemmet), lands of Barbauchlaw, farmhouse of Stanerig, plantation corner where lands of Barbauchlaw, Hopetoun and Polkemmet meet at a point, Barbauchlaw Plantation and the Edinburgh to Glasgow Turnpike Road.

Bathgate's Registrar was engaged to find out Armadale's population - which was 3,750. The Petition being successful, nine Commissioners were appointed (or elected) after a total of nine meetings had been held in Edinburgh, Linlithgow, and Bathgate.

East Main Street

1864

In 1864, Peter Muir, of the Cappers, was a miner. About 100 Armadale people were in arrears of rates. Thomas Johnston lived at Barbauchlaw Quarry. Addresses were given as north, south, east and west of the Toll. Monkey Row seemed to have been an 'official' address - Monkey was probably an abbreviation of Monklands Company who owned the houses. Alex Lauder, a miner, lived at 12 Polkemmet Row. Robert Beattie, of Edwards' Land, was a miner.

The first meeting of the Commissioners of the Burgh of Armadale was held at the schoolhouse on 18th April 1864. James Clark was appointed Chairman, or Preses, for this meeting. (J. Clark was manager for J. & J. McLelland). Robert Thomson, baker, was elected Senior Commissioner, Archibald MacDonald, merchant, and Mathew

Donaldson, merchant, were appointed two Junior Magistrates of Police. George Sinclair, solicitor, Bathgate, was appointed Clerk to the Commissioners. Thomas Wilson was appointed Treasurer to the Commissioners. William Forrester, bookseller and stationer, was to be Burgh Collector of Rates.

At the second meeting of the Commissioners, the sole business before the Commissioners was the provision of a water supply, the water supply to come from the Moss on Barbauchlaw ground.

At the third meeting, A. Turner, owner of Barbauchlaw Estate, to be asked if he has ground suitable for construction of water works (ground to be leased). The meeting appointed a Glasgow civil engineer to superintend the water works.

At the fourth Meeting, Airdrie Water Works Manager to be invited to Armadale.

23-08-64: The Commissioners awarded two contracts - John Pollock to make the pond and John Boyd to cut the drains and lay the pipes, T. Wilson to supervise the works at 4/- per day.

10-10-64: Arrangements to be made with Mr. Simpson, banker, Bathgate, for loan to finance the water works. (£100 needed right away to pay for work already done)

31-10-64: First rates assessment to be prepared, a loan to be obtained and total water works costs to be estimated.

10-11-64: Estimate of total loan needed to finance the water supply was before the Commissioners - £570.

1) Formation of pond or tank, £175.
2) Pipes to conduct water throughout village, £212.
3) Valves and scour stopcocks, £25.
4) Erection of wells and stones etc., £35, other work, £123.

A statement giving the amount to be borrowed to appear in the local weekly paper, the Airdrie, Coatbridge, Bathgate and Wishaw Advertiser. The Clerk to make up a book or roll of assessment (re rates) from the valuation Roll.

In 1864: the Burgh Commissioners (Town Council) were meeting at the Subscription School schoolhouse.

1865

The Armadale Methodist Church / Wesleyan Chapel was open. At first, it shared a minister with Airdrie Methodists. Armadale Roman Catholics were holding religious services in the school - many Roman Catholics had by now arrived from Ireland, mainly to work in the pits.

In 1865, William Jarvie, of Hardhill Row, was a miner, James Paterson of 20 Cappers Row, was a miner, Grace Neish or Gallacher lived in Armadale, and Jane Graham lived at Episcopal Place, Armadale.

09-01-65: The Burgh Commissioners held their meeting in the Subscription Schoolhouse. The Collector of Rates to get £20 per annum and 5% commission, a cautioner for the Collector was appointed. A Burgh Roll or Book of Assessment was approved, rates were fixed at 9d in £1. The first vote was taken - on the cost of supplying water to private properties.

14-06-65: The householders of Armadale held their first elections, three Commissioners to retire, three to be elected. Only nine householders attended including James Clark, who was now the manager of Monklands Iron and Steel Co.. Among three successful candidates was Rev. Teape of the Episcopal Church.

14-06-65: A second pond, south of the first one, to be constructed, to increase the town's water supply.

26-06-65: A three-man committee was formed, to take decisions between full meetings of the Commissioners on minor matters connected with the water supply.

10-07-65: Public notices to be displayed regarding arrears.

31-07-65: Summary warrants to recover unpaid rates to go out. £2 maximum to be allowed to convey water from McKinlay's ground to the middle of Gillespie Street.

21-09-65: £60 maximum to be spent on filter and tank to improve water.

26-09-65: Approval had been given by owner (Mr. Turner) and neighbouring tenant (Mr. Harris) re piece of ground for water tank measuring 30 feet by 50 feet at south side of Mount Pleasant.

09-10-65: Two contracts were awarded re water tank for cutting, puddling, and embankment, also for brickwork.

04-12-65: Several payments were authorised re water tank, £100 more to be borrowed.

1866

08-01-66: Mr. Bryce, Blackridge, was awarded the contract to take gravel from Barbauchlaw Burn to the tank (to filter water). Each of the Burgh's 10 Public Wells to get an iron sole plate, with malleable iron gratings (to replace stone seats), Shotts Iron Co. to supply plates and gratings, to be delivered to Armadale Railway Station.
06-03-66: The Commissioners confirmed three of their number would retire by rotation (three were to be elected "in room of" three who were retiring), three others were to be elected to replace the three who were co-opted.
14-03-66: A 6 feet fence to go round the filter and tank, the fountain-head well to be enclosed in brick. A Glasgow plumbers' merchant supplied the faucet, stopcock and brass cranes. An account from Peter Smith, tacksman, for Tolls to be paid, 10/2. Water arrears were discussed.
11-04-66: Annual elections by householders - proof that statuary notice of elections was shown in the form of a copy of the local weekly paper and a handbill containing the advert, certified by John Arthur, Town Drummer, Bathgate, of proclamation. 3 Commissioners, retiring by rotation, were elected. Six people were nominated for the three other places. The voting seemed to show that only 13 householders attended the meeting. Thomas Harvie got 10 votes, Mathew Wilson 9, George Brown 8, J. Aitken 7, James Donaldson 3 and James Finlay 2.
28-05-66: The Commissioners to enquire at Bo'ness of the cheapest method of obtaining sand from Blackness for filtering.
04-06-66: Water not to be conveyed to Bathville Row.
18-06-66: The Commissioners considered the Nuisances Removal (Scotland) Act of 1856. The Provost of Leith to be asked for his opinion of this Act.
09-07-66: A letter was considered from the Inspector of the Poor, Bathgate, informing the Commissioners of "a nuisance existing in the yard and premises belonging to William E., innkeeper, viz. two privies, a dunghill and a great accumulation of filth." The Commissioners decided to take no action until the Sheriff decides against them. The paling at the filters to be tarred and the embankment to be sown with

grass seeds. A Payment of 10/- was authorised for a japanned tin box for holding Burgh documents.

Local Authorities Powers and Responsibilities –
The Commissioners at first believed that, as they had adopted only the Police and Improvements Act of 1862 when they agreed to become Commissioners, they felt that they did not legally require to implement the Nuisances Act of 1856, which they hadn't adopted. By 30th July 1866, they accepted that they had also to act as Local Authority for the purposes of the Nuisances Act. They attempted, unsuccessfully, to get Bathgate's Inspector of Nuisances to perform the same duty for Armadale. Armadale stationer W. Forrester agreed to fill the position of Burgh Inspector for a six month period. Handbills to be circulated asking townsfolk to co-operate with the Inspector.

14-08-66: Dr. Kirk of Bathgate was appointed Medical Officer for Armadale.
21-08-66: Commissioners decided to send the town crier through the town calling upon the inhabitants to cleanse and whitewash their dwellings previous to an inspection being made of the same by persons appointed by the Local Authority.
23-08-66: Commissioners met the feuars of property in the street leading from Armadale Toll Bar to the south-most well. The purpose of the meeting was to devise the best means of improving street drainage. A gutter to be made. A letter to go to Mrs. Y. of the Star Hotel calling on her to remove her pigsty and dung-stead within 24 hours, otherwise legal proceedings will follow.
27-08-66: Commissioners considered Mrs. Y.'s refusal to remove pigsty, dung-stead and privy. The Inspector of Nuisances to take appropriate steps.
04-09-66: The Commissioners considered communications from the Parochial Board re a Cholera Hospital.
08-10-66: Part of Drove Road (or Loan), later called South Street and Toll Brae, to get an open gutter, causewayed, one yard broad, without a kerb stone. After taking this decision, the Commissioners decided to incorporate a gutter, at 6d per yard, additional; feuars to meet the whole cost in proportion to frontage.
16-11-66: Rates were fixed at 9d in £1. The Commissioners considered an offer by the Road Trustees for improvements of the channels of that part of the Turnpike Road within the Burgh.

28-12-66: A letter was read from the Board of Supervisors to the effect that Armadale's domestic water supply was found to be so tainted with impurities as to be poisonous and dangerous, calculated to promote and aggravate choleric or other diseases. In future, water to be certified by a chemist and Medical Practitioner, contaminated wells to be shut up.

1867

Armadale Bowling Club formed. Permission for a bowling green was granted by the Laird of Barbauchlaw, on south side of estate, behind Monklands Cottages.

Armadale Bowling Club

14-01-67: 30/- to be paid to Subscription School to cover the cost of holding meetings in the school and gas - the Burgh Commissioners (Town Councillors) were meeting in the Subscription School.
14-02-67: An account was passed regarding the repair of wells. A further £600 to be borrowed. Because of the Royal Bank's interest rates, the Clerk to advertise, in the first instance, an advert to go into the Glasgow Herald, then the Scotsman, then the North British

Advertiser. Summary warrants to go to rates non-payers. Alex Hutton, tinsmith, to look after the wells.

11-04-67: Elections of five Commissioners by householders - Thomas Robertson, Town Crier, confirmed that a proclamation had been made giving notice of election. George Brown was elected Chief Commissioner. John Aitken and James Walker were elected Junior Magistrates.

15-04-67: Payments were made to Thomas Harvie for land occupied by the South Pond and by water filters.

06-05-67: The Commissioners considered how to pay back private loan of £100.

27-05-67: £139.10/- collected in Rates for year 1866-67.

01-07-67: The Commissioners visited filters and the North and South Ponds. Filters to be cleaned and pointed and gravel spread.

08-07-67: The drain between the South and North Pond to be improved. A reward of £1.1/- to be given to any person giving information to police that leads to a conviction of persons found guilty of damaging the Burgh's wells. The Town Crier to give notice.

15-08-67: Following water complaints from inhabitants, work to be done to the South Pond embankment and 30 tons of sand purchased from Blackness to filter water, the sand to be carted to Pardovan railway siding and taken by train to the line of rails close to the filter (south of Mount Pleasant).

12-09-67: The contract to clean the filters and raise the South Pond embankment was awarded to a contractor from Clarkston, Airdrie.

14-10-67: The South Pond to be enclosed by a railing.

20-10-67: Water rate fixed at 1/- in the £.

16-12-67: Mr. Hutton, tinsmith, to keep well and filter in proper repair. Permission was given to Archibald Gall to lead water into his premises on condition that he pays his water rates. Commissioners considered a letter from solicitor for Bathville Estate, seeking information on rates assessment on part of estate within the Burgh, also questioning the Commissioners decision not to supply water to the Bathville estate tenants who live within the Burgh.

1868

Excerpts from the Bathgate Parish Valuation Roll of 1868 relating to Armadale (John Donaldson was the Registrar) –

Allan Davie was a contractor at Mossend. Mr. Barclay was a store-keeper. Mr. Mungall was stationmaster. Mr. Hutton was described as an ironmonger and he was given contracts for work for the Burgh as a tinsmith. McGinty was a baker, Thomas Stewart was a currier and Robert Stewart was a flesher. Armadale had a Working Men's Institute. Adamson and Aitken were grocers. Loanhead seems to have been at Bathville. J.W. Meek of Armadale was an inventor.

Robert Gillies, brick-maker, occupied a house in Armadale owned by John Aitken, grocer (annual rent was £7). Rev. James Anderson occupied the Free Church manse in Armadale. Beveridge owned 14 houses. George Brown, shoemaker, owned several houses - occupants included Torrans, Thom, Snedden and Hailstones. Brown, blacksmith, owned several houses. J. Calder, oversman, owned two houses. Robert Leiper, baker, was owner / occupier of a shop, house, stable, byre and garden, the rent was £17. Barclay occupied the Crown Hotel and stables. James Russell, pawnbroker, Armadale owned three houses. Peter Scott, ironmonger, owned 18 houses. Mrs. Shaw owned four houses. Joseph Syson owned 17 houses. Rev. Teape owned the Parsonage and four houses. James Thomson owned three houses - Baxter, Gray and the Police Commissioners occupied them. Thomas Wilson, mineral borer, owned four houses and one washing house. J. Alexander owned eight houses. Esau Edwards owned fifteen houses.

William Motherwell, timber merchant of Airdrie, owned 60 houses in Armadale including eight houses at Eastertoun (total rent was £192). J. Alexander, ferryman, Glasgow, owned eight houses in Armadale. James Somerville occupied a house owned by a Bo'ness banker. Property investment company, New Provident, owned houses in Armadale. Rev. McLachlan of Torquay owned about 18 houses in Gillespie Street, Armadale, including several in Milligan's Land. W. Rennie, carter, Bathgate, owned several houses, a wright's shop and a byre. Alex Russell, farmer, Slamannan, owned five houses. Thomson of Glasgow owned three houses and house / shop / bake-house. William Wilson, miner, of Mossend, owned three houses.

Wilson of Whitockbrae occupied Stanerig and Smith occupied Tarrareoch, both paid feu duty to Sir William Baillie. Salmond (who farmed Torbane) paid £10 rent for Cappers grazing, (Cappers was originally next to Tippethill then). Trustees of the late William Shaw owned house, garden, grass parks, and minerals at Trees. Peter Salmond of Torbane owned houses and land at Snab occupied by Shotts Iron Co..

Shotts Iron Co. paid £80 rent on Netherhouses and Westfield Farms (on Northrigg road) - the feu duty went to William Baillie of Polkemmet. Shotts Iron Co. also owned six houses. Coltness Iron Co. owned Woodend Colliery and four houses. There was a lime quarry at Standhill. The rent on the minerals of Torbanehill was £2,775 per annum. Fraser, miner, owned five houses. Hamilton, miner, owned 14 houses. Three miners (Davidson, Carruthers and Finlayson) either owned or occupied their houses. William Naysmith, miner, owned three houses. Peter Ramsay, miner, owned three houses. David Russell, miner, owned four houses. Hugh Simpson, miner, owned eight houses. John Tweedie, miner, owned six houses.

The Earl of Hopetoun owned about eight farms in Bathgate Parish, including Middlerigg and Hardhill. He also owned six occupied lands near Middlerigg. James Russell owned 63 houses in Armadale and 20 on Hardhill land. Lewis Sandilands of Chelsea, one of the Sandilands of Mid Calder, owned Couston Estate, which included several farms including North and South Couston, Colinshiel, Balmuir, Muirhall and also Colinshiel Colliery, occupied by Shotts Iron Co.. Shotts Iron Co. owned c.50 houses near Armadale Station and Tarrareoch, feu duty to William Baillie of Polkemmet. Farms owned by Baillie to the south of Armadale - Balgornie, Netherhouses, Springfield, Tippethill, with mill lade, Stanerig and Tarrareoch. The late Alexander Turner, owner of Barbauchlaw Estate, owned five farms - Whitockbrae, Barbauchlaw Mains, Barbauchlaw and mill, Cowdenhead and Standhill, also the minerals at Barbauchlaw and 32 houses. J. & J. McClelland paid rent for working the estate minerals.

Armadale Gas Light Co. paid a rent of £95 on the gas works. William Edwards owned Armadale Inn, also land, shops, and houses. Mary Campbell was owner / occupier of a public house. Elizabeth Young owned a public house and three houses. James Beveridge, publican, owned fourteen houses. Thomson, wood-merchant, owned a house and shop. James Verrier, merchant, owned seven houses, two shops and a stable. T.W. & D. Watson, coal-masters, Glasgow, owned Bathville Farm and minerals, rent was c.£1,930 per annum. They also owned two firebrick works, pit office, paraffin oil works, store, 61 houses and two houses at No.1 Pit and six at No.2 Pit. John Wilson of Whitockbrae owned a house, shop and bake-house and several other houses. Mathew Wilson, grocer, owned several houses and two shops. James Wylie, grocer, owned eleven houses and one shop.

13-01-68: A letter was read from Mr. Hutton, tinsmith, offering, for 5/- per week, to keep the town's wells in repair, also to watch over the ponds and filter and clean water basin, in order that a clean water supply be kept in the wells.

17-03-68: Ratepayers in arrears to get four days notice, after which a penalty of 1d in £1 is added and expenses of recovery. Permission was given to the Free Kirk to lead water into the new manse.

11-04-68: Elections of three Commissioners "in room of" - paper advert in the Advertiser and handbill re proclamation certified by Alexander Fleming, Town Crier. James Verrier, John Aitken, John Simpson, David Sneddon and James Finlay all nominated, first three named elected.

08-06-68: Sanitary condition of Armadale discussed. £148.8/4 was collected in water rates. Liquid lime to be got for scouring the water pipes.

01-07-68: Because of dry weather, private water supplies were to be cut off and public wells supply cut off at night.

13-07-68: The Clerk to write to Sir William Baillie of Polkemmet asking the privilege of quarrying a quantity of whinstone from his quarry near Armadale Railway Station. Part of South Pond embankment to be lined with whinstone to withstand wind and weather.

03-08-68: The Commissioners agreed to repair the South Pond by turfing and pinning down the same with saugh willows. Five business men of the town were to be penalised for opening the cock, which supplies their premises with water in contravention of the orders of the Commissioners.

12-10-68: The Board of Supervisors in Edinburgh ruled that the Parochial Board of Bathgate was the appropriate body to execute the Public Health (Scotland) Act in Bathgate and Armadale.

28-10-68: Water rate was fixed at 1/- in £ upon all occupiers of lands or premises within the Burgh of Armadale. Handbills to be circulated.

1869

11-01-69: Each January, Thomas Harvie is given ground rent on account of pond and filters being on his ground. Mr. Hutchison, manager of the gas works, to be asked his terms re supervising and repairing street wells. Wells to be refitted on a stronger, more approved, principle. The Commissioners were considering combining the offices of Collector and Treasurer.

02-03-69: An account was passed, 5/4d for refreshments supplied to workman engaged at the Moss.

16-03-69: The Clerk to draw out a water specification for repairing wells, also superintending filter and ponds, regulating supply of water, scouring pipes, etc..

24-03-69: Glasgow plumber to supply and fit new valves to the Burgh's nine wells. South Pond embankment to be planted with saugh willows.

12-04-69: Householders meeting, i.e. householders of yearly rent or value of £4 or upwards. Commissioners censured R.M., manager of Armadale Colliery, for using water during drought when supply was for domestic use only.

28-04-69: The contract to repair wells and superintend water supply was awarded to Peter Scott, ironmonger, for £4 per annum.

29-04-69: The drought continued, private water supplies were cut off.

09-06-69: £8 was claimed from the Burgh by Armadale Colliery manager to cover cost of alternative private water supply when the town supply was cut off. Commissioners decided to lift the pipes from North Pond along the north side of Blaes Hill. Mr. Martin sought the privilege of taking supply of water from pond as he needs it. Simpson, banker, Bathgate, suggested that part of the £500 debt be paid annually, £100 to be paid when collected.

01-11-69: Water assessment 2/- in £1, a charge of £1 annually on bakers to cover water used by them, all parties keeping cows, horses, machines let for hire and steam engines within Burgh, to be charged 5/- for each cow, horse, machine let for hire, or steam engine.

1870's

c.1870, a second storey was added to the Police Station in West Main Street. c.1871 – c.1881, John Moffat was owner of Barbauchlaw Estate. There was a fireclay mine at Bathville in the 1870's. The 1870's saw the start of organised football in Armadale.

1870

10-01-70: The cost of Commissioners meetings in the school for the past year was 10/-. It was felt that, the school being public property, meetings should be free (coal and gas charges excepted). A vote was taken and the account was paid.
17-01-70: A special meeting was held in the Crown Hotel (Mr. Walker's Hall) to consider the refusal by the school committee to allow the school to be used free of charge. Commissioners agreed to pay 10/- annually. (The meeting in the hall cost 5/-)
04-03-70: £190.10/6 was collected in water rates. Peter Scott was given permission "to operate one of the wells in a principle of his own".
01-04-70: Four railway sleepers to be got for each well, 32 in total.
11-04-70: Elections of three Commissioners to replace three retiring - Robert Gartshore proposed Archibald Gall, Joseph Syson and John Mallace, seconded by Robert Love, 5 votes; Duncan McDougal proposed Mathew Donaldson, Mathew Wilson and George Brown, seconded by Thomas Harvie, 6 votes; John Mallace proposed William Edwards, Maurice Thomson and Robert Love, seconded by Hugh McKinnon, 7 votes. The last three named were elected.
18-04-70: Mr. Shanks, smith, Bathgate, to be invited to repair wells.
28-04-70: Letter before the Commissioners - "I am instructed to act for Mr. J.W. innkeeper, Armadale in reference to a charge made by the Commissioners upon him, for assessment for water purposes in respect of certain horses & carriages kept by him". Hugh McKinnon, cow-keeper, offered to pay the water charge for his two cows.
09-05-70: James Hynds, factor for McLachlan's property, to be given four days notice re payment of water rates. Each public well to get a new cran.
27-05-70: Water rates collected, £261.6/3.

06-09-70: A special meeting was called to consider relief of sick and wounded in the Franco-Prussian war, a public meeting to be arranged.

07-11-70: Water rate to be 1/6 in £1. Bakers to pay an additional £1 and 5/- to be paid for each cow, horse, steam engine and machine let on hire.

28-02-70: A special meeting to consider appeals and proposals re water charges –

1) Mr. Teape claimed that his horse and cow drink water out of the burn that flows past his premises.
2) Mr. Hynds pointed that he takes water out of the same burn for his two horses and cow. He expressed willingness to pay 2/- for horses or 2/6 if water supply guaranteed for the whole year.
3) Mr. McKinnon would give 2/6 for each head of cattle.
4) Mr. McDonald said his machine was not in use at present.
5) John Aitken said he washes his machine with rain water.
6) The charge on George Simpson, baker, to be reduced by half as he had only one oven while other bakers had two.

1871

20-02-71: Collector to write to Wishaw Building Society re payment of water rates on properties of theirs. The Clerk to arrange the purchase of eight patent wells, without ladles, from an Airdrie plumber to replace the old wells. Clerk was to get the length of time he will guarantee them.

01-04-71: Annual householders' elections (restricted to male householders whose property has a yearly rent or value over £4). Commissioners by now were responsible for Police, lighting, cleansing, paving, draining, supplying and improving wells; also public health. Formalities were gone through re arranging an advert in the Advertiser, also handbills certificate signed by Hugh Brown, Town Crier. Three elected were Messrs. Simpson, Eason and Elder.

20-04-71: Over £197 came in from rates.

10-07-71: Burgh debt to be reduced.

12-09-71: A letter before Commissioners from Bathgate Burgh who objected to the Parochial Board of Bathgate being the Local Authority for Bathgate Parish (including Armadale) responsible for public

health. Armadale Commissioners were satisfied with the Parochial Board.
09-10-71: Armadale's water, on being analysed, was found to contain carbonate and sulphate of lime and magnesium, chloride of sodium, oxide of iron, phosphate, organic matter and silica, also a small quantity of floating vegetable matter; slightly yellow, insipid taste, decidedly mossy or peaty, suitable for domestic use, mawkish flavour, poor compared to spring water. The lime and magnesium makes it hard water and not suitable for washing operations where soap used.

1872

John Moffat of Barbauchlaw owned 943 acres, Peter Salmond of Torbane had four acres, William Honeyman Gillespie of Torbanehill had a 709 acre estate, John Gentleman of West Craigmarry had 50 acres, Thomas, David & William Watson owned 145 acre Bathville Estate, 50 acre Trees Farm was administered by the trustees of the late William Shaw.

08-04-72: Over £100 came in from rates and £6 from cattle etc..
11-04-72: Robert Gartshore and John Paterson were commissioners elected.
08-08-72: Walter Adamson was appointed to regulate the water, scour the pipes and clean out the filter yearly, with an assistant.
21-10-72: The Commissioners considered a copy of the new Ballot Act. Commissioners accepted the offer of £1 from William Edwards, manager of No.7 Pit, Barbauchlaw, for the supply of water to the pit.

1873

On 23rd October, 1873, the Trustees and Manager of Armadale's third Subscription School, paid for by all of Armadale's wage earners, met to discuss a letter from Bathgate School Board who described Armadale's school as 'The General Assembly School in Armadale'.

The school Trustees were Thomas Harvie, farmer, Thomas Wilson, mineral borer, George Brown, shoemaker, John Jeffrey, contractor,

Robert Jamieson, manager of Shotts Co. and James Clark, manager of McClelland.

Armadale Co-operative Society Ltd. was established in 1873. Hunter's Land and Scott's Land, which were both on Barbauchlaw land, were sold by roup in the Crown Hotel. Also sold by roup, a tenement occupied by Drummond and Wilson, also a house occupied by Mason (John Mallace was house factor).

Woodend Village

There was smallpox at Woodend. Two boys were injured while playing with gunpowder at Drumbowie. T. Brown and A. McCullough drowned in Barbauchlaw Burn near Standhill Farm. M. Donaldson (tea, wine and spirit merchant) retired. T. Bisset, joiners and cabinet-makers, started up in Russell Square. The Thistle Lodge of Free Gardeners had its annual procession through Armadale. Members of Armadale Bluebell Cricket Club and team players - Marshall, Syson, Russell, Bisset, Morris, Halbert, Johnston, Watson and Donaldson.

Drunkenness was a problem in Armadale. c.1873, the Scotch Gothenburg Licensing Bill (Parliament) was seriously considered in Armadale. The Goth system allows no private gain from spirits. Members of Jessie o' the Dell Lodge of Armadale Good Templars - Brothers Calder, Cowan, Martin, McMillan and Moffat.

03-01-73: Account for 6/- passed to Jane Easton, Bathgate, for cement.

06-03-73: Thomas Dodds, Bathgate, solicitor, explained new elections procedures under the Ballot Act, namely that nominations to be submitted so many days before an election, then election held. The Commissioner agreed with Mr. Dodds that the expense of an election could be saved if the householders nominated a number of people equal or no more than the number of vacancies. The notice of election, as required by law, fixed to the door of the established churches in Bathgate and Armadale, also advertised twice in recently started West Lothian Courier, later notices fixed to doors of certain buildings announcing as only four nominees for four vacancies, no election needed. The Returning Officer's notice declaring names of four new Commissioners also fixed to certain doors.

14-04-73: The Commissioners elected John Aitken as Chief Commissioner / Senior Magistrate of Police. John Simpson was described as elder Baillie.

28-04-73: Henry Murray of Bathgate applied for supply of water to No.7 Barbauchlaw Pit. He was unsuccessful, owing to scarcity of water. Messrs. Barr and Higgins of No.7 Pit Barbauchlaw were to be told to lay pipes to their own pond.

30-06-73: Archibald McMillan, miner, co-opted to replace J. Simpson who had left Armadale.

13-10-73: An account for £1.6/6 was passed from Robert Smith for repairs, time and lime. The Clerk to get a copy of the book on law and practise of municipal elections for Police Burghs. A small house to be built to hold the Burgh implements. (The first offer to come from a Contractor was for £12.10/-) Notices of assessments to go out –

1) To Barr and Higgins, coal-masters, on rental of pit.
2) To Monklands Iron and Steel Co. on £5 rental on minerals within Burgh
3) To Messrs. Watson re Bathville Row.

1874

James Wood bought Bathville Estate and built a large mansion house (Woodlands) on the estate as his own residence.

Bathville House

The Local Authority took over responsibility for education and Armadale's third and final Subscription School was taken over as Armadale's first BLEB School between 1874 and 1877. (Bathgate Landward Education Board)

Andrew Jameson, miner, of Cappers, had nine children; two girls were in domestic service, two boys in the pits and he was given school fees for three children. Widow of John Baxter was given school fees and books for sons William and Robert.

17-02-74: £1 reward was offered for information on malicious person who destroyed the wells. The manager of Barbauchlaw Pit No.7 to be rebuked for uncoupling pipes and wasting water.
14-05-74: Rates collected amounted to over £88. A letter came from Linlithgow proposing a joint water analyst for the County.
22-06-74: The well at Buttries Row to be kept in proper repair.
13-07-74: Placards to be printed cautioning parties against throwing any filth, dirt or animal in the Burgh ponds. Rifle Volunteers applied for the use of the South Pond embankment for a shooting range.

From a school log dated 22nd May, 1874 - Commenced duty as Headmaster of the school on Wednesday May 20th, 155 attended Junior Department. One week later there were 290 on the roll, four assistants; by June 5th, 334 on roll; and on 12th June, 360 on roll. 25th June was a school holiday on occasion of Bathgate Parish Fast Day. On July 3rd, only half the pupils attended, the rest are attending the Mission Sabbath School annual excursion. July 17th, 21 cases of measles. Two weeks summer holidays only, restart 7th August. 14th August, there was a low attendance due to the reopening of the Monklands Iron and Steel Co.'s school at Mount Pleasant. One teacher off, at the coast with her family. Nov 13th, an assistant teacher was absent without leave; he sent a notice giving his reason - "from a disinclination to follow the profession of teacher, I think it better to give up at once. This is the cause of my absence". On the 9th December, the Headmaster resigned.

Station Road, later South Street

1875

In 1875, there were a few cases of scarlet fever and measles in Armadale. Sanitary conditions were very bad, scarlet fever was prevalent. A scavenger was recommended.

Daniel MacDonald, Registrar, resigned his post from Whitsunday. Henry Edwards was allowed school fees and books for two children. William Simpson was allowed fees and books for his two children. Helen Malcolm was allowed school fees and books for two children. James Thomson, teacher, became Armadale's Registrar. Three Armadale men applied for the privilege to carry on the business of slaughterer of cattle. They were John Aitken, Gilbert Stewart and Mathew Wilson.

11-01-75: Mr. Motherwell's Factor apologised for missing the Appeal Court hearing, but he had missed the train.
01-04-75: About twenty householders met to nominate for vacancies in advance, to save the cost of an election.
12-04-75: In his notice re elections, reference was made to the Acts of William IV, Victoria 1862 and 1868, the Municipal Amendments (Scotland) Acts 1868 and 1870 and the Ballot Act 1872. Five nominated included a minister, a farmer, a miner, a draper and an innkeeper. Three declined, leaving Duncan McDougal, draper, and Robert Leishman, innkeeper, as new Commissioners.
17-05-75: The new Collector / Treasurer to be James Beveridge, collector of Armadale Gas Works Co..
27-05-75: Robert Smith's duties - to look after filter, ponds, fence, water-boxes and wells. A deputation from the Parochial Board recommended that Armadale Commissioners be responsible for cleansing.
21-06-75: The Commissioners considered the Petroleum Act of 1871. They passed an account due since 1870 of 1/- due to the Bathgate Foundry Co..
11-11-75: Water rates were 6d in £1; cow, etc., 2/-; and 5/- per baker's oven.
02-12-75: Appeals considered –

1) Monklands Iron and Steel Co., unlet houses.
2) Six unlet houses belonging to John Linton.
3) Robert Stirling charged for two cows, he only possessed one.
4) John Hynds said that his cows drink from the burn.
5) Maurice Thomson had four unlet houses.
6) Mrs. Norris had one unlet house.
7) The School Board of the Parish, re Subscription School.
8) Mrs. Summers, widow, residing in Gibb's Lane.
9) Robert Dryburgh, fruit merchant, shop not occupied the full year.

10) R. Dryburgh had his horse and machine for 3 months only.

1876

Widow Gordon, or Chalmers, lived at Bathville. Mr. Thomson was allowed £2 for the use of his room as the Registrar's Office. Widow Agnes Lafferty, or Smith, lived in Armadale. Helen Ramsay had palsy. Widow Roberts, or Edwards, was offered the Poorhouse. Widower Richard Nisbet was destitute. Jane Lock was the wife of Abraham Smith. Five year old Andrew Jamieson (son of a widow) to be allowed an education. Vaccination of children to be enforced.

10-01-76: Three new wells were fitted up.
03-04-76: Five new Commissioners - William Edwards, Thomas Elder, Maurice Thomson, Joseph Syson and William Orr.
15-05-76: Postage stamps for circulars calling a meeting of ratepayers were 6/- i.e. 36 @ 2d = 72d = 6/-.
08-06-76: The new auditor to be James Aitken of Clydesdale Bank, Bathgate.
14-07-76: The Commissioners considered offers from eight contractors to repair embankment of the South Pond. Esau Edwards was cheapest, but James Hailstones accepted.
24-07-76: Four new wells to be ordered.
23-10-76: Rates 4d in £1, no charge on cows, etc., or ovens.
09-10-76: Appeals considered –

1) Mr. Wood, coal-master, appealed that minerals assessment (Barbauchlaw) should be less than previous year.
2) That Bathville Row be assessed by a half because of distance to the nearest well.
3) Mrs. Douglas, Midwife, residing in Verrier's Land (inability to pay).

1877

On 27th February, many subscribers of Armadale Subscription School agreed to the transfer of the schoolhouse and school to Bathgate (Landward) School Board, with conditions.

On 8th December, four men fighting in the Crown Hotel started a riot. The crowd were incensed at one of them (a local popular soldier) being taken away by the police. Police reinforcements from Bathgate were also attacked. There were plenty loose stones handy as West Main Street was newly resurfaced. The Police sought shelter from the mob in a butcher's shop. It was battered with stones.

In 1877, James Wylie was a merchant in Armadale. Several cases of fever appeared in Armadale. Mrs. Kerr was given an allowance to cover her children's school fees. A stagnant gutter at the end of Russell's Row to be attended to by Road Surveyor of the Bathgate / Airdrie Turnpike Road. Mrs. Sneddon of Armadale was recorded. Widow Boyd and Widow Aitken, were both of Armadale. Armadale had a Homing Club, i.e. homing pigeons.

12-03-77: An application came from Wood, coal-master, for water for Pit No.12.
02-04-77: Nominees for vacancies included a spirit merchant, mason, joiner, clothier and two labourers, (there were nine nominees, and five vacancies.). The system being used for voting, several votes were taken, the bottom man dropping out each time.
23-05-77: Only £41+ collected in rates. Hailstones account was paid re drain between ponds.
09-07-77: Chairman / President of meeting was described as "Preses of Meeting".
08-10-77: Meeting of Commissioners received a letter from Mr. Rankine, Road Surveyor (which came via Inspector of Poor) requesting Parochial Board to open drains in Armadale so as to abate a nuisance. (The Commissioners learned that the Uphall Authority employed a man to sweep and clean the streets of Uphall and Broxburn) Mr. Rankine maintained that a thorough system of drainage was needed in Armadale. Mr. Rankine expressed doubt as to who was responsible for enforcing the cleansing of streets and drains. (i.e. the Burgh or the Parochial Board, or even the feuars). He offered to put drains across the Turnpike Road but is not at liberty to make sewers for drainage without the authority of the Roads Trustees. The Commissioners decided that they were powerless to deal with the nuisance. The Commissioners approved a new well opposite George Brown's property. The Commissioners considered a complaint from Torphichen Parish Local Authority to the effect that Armadale sewage

was polluting streams in Torphichen Parish. The Commissioners again felt they were powerless to deal with the complaint.

15-11-77: A letter came from the Inspector of Poor, Bathgate, regarding the polluting of Couston by Armadale sewage. He proposed that Bathgate and Torphichen Parochial Boards and Armadale and Bathgate Burghs should meet to consider a remedy. Armadale Commissioners declined, claiming that Bathgate Parochial Board is the appropriate authority.

03-12-77: The Commissioners considered appeals against water rate assessment, James Wood appealed against Bathville Rows being fully assessed, Mr. Gilmour of Bathville Store and a teacher, James Thomson, also appealed. Robert Leishman, Star Hotel, claimed exemption for two unlet houses. William Naysmith, miner, and Mr. Balderston, baker, of Airdrie, both appealed.

14-12-77: The Commissioners considered steps re the preservation of peace and order in the District in view of the recent riot, which occurred in Armadale on Saturday. The Commissioners expressed willingness to help the police by organising 40 or 50 special constables who should be supplied with batons.

In 1877-78, Armadale's first Local Authority purpose built school was built at the top of Academy Street.

Public School and Parish Church

1878

In 1878, Armadale was found to be in a "most unsanitary condition" and a serious epidemic could develop. There was a delay in removing a nuisance at Russell's Row and it prompted the Board to urge Armadale Burgh Commissioners to adopt the whole of the Police Act. There were several cases of fever at the East end of Armadale and two died,

14-01-78: A letter came from the Procurator Fiscal regards recent riot. A letter was considered from the school Board of the Parish of Bathgate asking if the Commissioners were willing to lead water to the new school that was in course of erection in Armadale. The Commissioners decided against.

05-03-78: A letter came from the Parochial Board enclosing the report from Dr. Kirk, Medical Officer, complaining of unsanitary conditions of Armadale. The Commissioners were urged to adopt the remaining clauses of the Police Act.

02-04-78: At the annual meeting of the electors called to pre-select candidates for the two vacancies (to avoid the cost of an election) Duncan MacDougal, draper, and John Russell, fruiterer, were selected from seven who were judged fit to be Commissioners. Again, no election would be needed.

08-04-78: The School Board (who had previously offered to make connection of water supply to new school) said they would connect to mains supply at entrance to the Established Church. Mr. P. of Crown Hotel to have water cut off unless he got his leak seen to.

08-07-78: Letters to be sent thus –

1) To James Russell and Son, proprietors of Russell's Row, to clean drains and remove filth and refuse.
2) To Road Surveyor of the Parish of Bathgate re state of road from the Toll Southwards.
3) To Mrs. Murray of Royal Hotel re flooded footpath.
4) To Shotts Co. re open drain in front of Shotts Row and dirt heap.
5) To all proprietors on the south side of Toll westwards re drains.
6) To Gilbert Stewart, grocer, and Walter Brown, blacksmith, re drains.

31-03-78: All proprietors of property east of Russell's Row to open up their enclosed drains, i.e. John Johnston, miner, John Russell, fruiterer, James Wylie, grocer, James Wood, coal-master, etc. Owing to drought, several wells to be cut off, also water supply to No.12 Pit.

07-08-78: The Commissioners learned that -

1) Conduit led into main drain running from Toll past Buttries Row,
2) Overflow from Toll well led into same drain.

Clerk to write Trustees of the late Mathew Wilson for Mr. Thomas Wilson to clean thoroughly the drain behind his property leading to the field of Whitockbrae Farm.

14-08-78: The Commissioners considered eight offers from contractors to improve South Pond, their estimates ranged from £4.5/- to £14. Road Surveyor to be asked what distance should be in front of house, i.e. to gutter. A civil engineer to be appointed to prepare a Burgh drainage scheme. Mr. Copeland, civil engineer of Glasgow offered to prepare a map of the Burgh of Armadale and to mark on the course of water, gas, and sewer pipes, all for 20 guineas, and to prepare a set of levels for guidance, for 10 guineas.

15-04-78: A small house to be built at filter for holding tools, lime etc. (9 feet by 7 feet by 9 feet high, slated, with wooden floor) and to cost £12.11/4. Mortar to be two parts sand, one part lime. Commissioners to hold a special meeting to consider adopting the remaining clauses of the Police and Improvements Act to cover public health, cleansing, and drainage. Water rates brought in £49.3/-.

10-06-78: Resolution before Commissioners - "That taking into consideration the correspondence between the Local Authority of the Parish of Bathgate and the Commissioners of the Burgh of Armadale anent the sanitary of the said Burgh, and paying special heed to the report of the Medical Officer of the said Local Authority in which he says that the Burgh is in an unsanitary state, the Commissioners of the Burgh of Armadale hereby resolve to adopt the remaining clauses of the General Police and Improvement (Scotland) Act 1862 as a remedy against the increasing evil and instruct the clerk to report the resolve to the Sheriff.

1879

Armadale Football Club was founded. A woman from Cappers went into Larbert Asylum. A letter came from the Board of Supervision dated 6th February, 1879, separating the Burgh of Armadale from the other portion of the Parish as a local Authority under the Public Health Act. Alex Black lived in Armadale. A child, Masterton, died at

Bathville Row and Armadale Burgh was instructed to pay burial expenses. Widow Baird lived at Hamilton's Land. John Mighton, Bathville, died. James Spalding lived at Bathville. An ill man, William Smith, was conveyed from Heatherfield to the Bathgate Sick Room by cart, he died soon after.

14-02-79: Armadale Brass Band asked Commissioners to be custodians of the band's instruments, etc. Inspector of the Poor asked Commissioners to meet the funeral expenses of Mrs. Susan Cairns or Paterson, who died in Tweedie's Land (under the Public Health Act).
05-05-79: A Commissioner who took out sequestration was barred from attending meetings.
20-05-79: Armadale streets that were without kerb and gutter were to get them on both sides of the street, also some sewer pipes to be laid, the Engineer to prepare specification. Mr. Moffat, proprietor, Ardrossan, was asked permission for part of sewage to go into Colinburn, also to alter sewage to run into fields lying on north side of the Turnpike road, east and west through Burgh. £104.17/9 from rates. The Burgh to charge Mr. Gordon, mason, 7/6 and Mr. Linn, plasterer, 5/- for water used in the erection of Police Buildings in Armadale.
16-06-79: Board of Commissioners in Edinburgh and Chief Constable of Linlithgowshire both asked what Commissioners were going to do re sanitary condition of Armadale and the existence of scarlet fever.
20-06-79: The Clerk to write Mr. David McNair, mason, Torphichen, charging 5/- for water used for building purposes in Armadale.
07-07-79: Specification re Armadale footpaths – footpaths, formed of quarry shivers 4" deep; altered to, formed of burnt blaes 3" deep; whinstone causeway kerb 9" by 5" in length 10" to 15", laid on a bed of riddled engine ashes (½" riddle) not less than 3" deep.
10-07-79: Burgh to consider appointing a Medical Officer, Sanitary Inspector and Scavenger under Public Health Act.
14-07-79: Circulars to go to proprietors and others, to be delivered or posted to owners or factors of all properties on Main Street, Woodend Road and road leading to gas works re footpath with kerb stones. Footpath on south side of main street from Crown Hotel westward to be 23" in breadth, if trustees of the Turnpike agree. Dr. Langmuir to be asked to be Medical Officer for the Burgh, at £7.50 per annum. Police Constable Robert Chalmers to be invited to be Sanitary Inspector at £5 per annum. A man to be engaged to do scavenging work at Crown Hotel and Toll.

28-08-79 & **10-09-79:** Mr. Simpson, banker, Bathgate, would only give £300 overdraft if the Commissioners accepted personal liability.

03-10-79: The Commissioners paid 2/6 for digging a grave for the illegitimate daughter of a lady hawker of Holt's Land.

10-10-79: Water to be laid on both sides of the Branch Road leading to Linlithgow.

13-10-79: Russell and Aitken of Falkirk to be told to improve the footpath at Russell's Row and the tenants to be cautioned against throwing dirty water on the footpaths. Clerk to write to the proprietors of houses on each side of the Parish Road requiring them to level up the footpaths with burnt blaes. Commissioners were shown a printed bill from Linlithgow Local Authority showing scale of prices for the adjustment of weights and measures. Public Health rate 2d in £1.

28-10-79: Of 18 persons considered for three vacancies, there were a colliery manager, clothier, grocer, flesher, merchant, miner, spirit merchant, joiner, blacksmith, carter and draper; also John McKenzie of Wilson's Land. As more nomination papers came in than there were vacancies, an election took place. Candidates were William Gibb, flesher, of Murray's Land, Alexander Mallace of Balderston's Land, Archie Robertson, manager of Bathville Colliery, Gilbert Stewart, grocer, of Stewart's Land, Robert Love, miner, of Love's Land, Archibald McDonald, merchant, Thomas Pow, clothier, of Anderson's Land, John Simpson, joiner, of Rennie's Land, Maurice Thomson, merchant, of Thomson's Land and James McDonald, spirit merchant. The three successful were Robert Love, miner, 29 votes, Thomas Pow (27), John Simpson (24). This was probably the last year that the town's electors attempted to predetermine candidates and thereby save the ratepayers the cost of an election.

17-11-79: The annual meeting for hearing appeals against assessment was held. Bathville Store owner appealed against water rate on grounds that they didn't use any.

24-11-79: The Commissioners learned of account in from Bryce, contractor, for work done on Burgh footpaths including kerbstones of whin, blaes, pipes, etc.. The branch railway in Armadale belonging to North British Railway Co. to be assessed.

09-12-79: The Burgh to advertise for a scavenger to sweep the gutters, attend to filter pond, make himself generally useful and keep the Burgh in all aspects clean, for 10/- per week. Carters to be told not to cross kerbstones. All persons to be cautioned against throwing refuse or anything other than water into gutters. £2.10/- rent of pond and filter ground paid for the year from Martinmas to Martinmas.

19-12-79: The duties of Burgh Scavenger to be –

1) To regulate water supply, keep pipes and wells in good order and doing all the work in connection with same except where tradesman needed.
2) To clear the ponds, drains and filters when required.
3) To keep cesspools and gutters clean and remove refuse to nearest depot.
4) To remove, or help to remove, any special nuisance pointed out by the Commissioners.
5) To open and, if need be, to put on a fire in the Subscription School for Commissioners' meetings.
6) To deliver, or post up, any bills required by the Commissioners.

Scavenger to take and give a months notice, wages 10/- per week to be paid every Saturday evening by the Treasurer. Of four applicants, William Simpson was appointed, a barrow and tools were to be supplied.

North Street showing the remains of the Pale House on the left and the Toll House on the right

1880's

c.1881 - 1893, George Readman owned Barbauchlaw Estate.

1880

1880, Bathgate Football Club beat Armadale 2 – 0.

Armadale Thistle Lodge of Free Gardeners' Friendly Society

12-01-80: Armadale Thistle Lodge of Free Gardeners' Friendly Society offered a loan of £300 to the Burgh at £5 per annum payable in three years - the offer was accepted. The Commissioners learned that 1,842 yards of new footpath had been laid in the Burgh in the recently completed contract. Accounts re footpaths given to the proprietors of the Burgh then challenged by owners of these properties - Wishaw Building Society, William Thomson's property, Drummond and Gartshore's Land, Amelia Burns' property, Thomas Hamilton, Henry Mungall, Alexander Beveridge, Mrs. Mason's, Rev. Hickman's for Trustees of Wesleyan Chapel, Johnston's Land,

Joseph Syson / Balderston's Land, and William McGregor, factor for James Verrier's property.

12-03-80: A miner applied for the Burgh to meet cost of burying his wife. The Commissioners agreed, but arranged for 2/6 per day to be deducted from the wages of the husband and sons to repay costs. The Commissioners considered a suggestion that Armadale Burgh should pay a share of building a hospital for the treatment of infectious diseases. The Commissioners decided that more privies should be built, all of an improved construction. They also considered drafting rules re Lodging Houses, there was only one in the district.

12-04-80: The Medical Officer reported 38 deaths in Armadale, including 17 less than five years old. Only one of the 17 died of scarlet fever, seven of the 38 were over 70 years old.

22-04-80: James Wood to be told to gutter Bathville Row and remove other nuisances.

10-05-80: The Commissioners considered a complaint that water from the Burgh Pond overflow was flooding a farmer's field, they decided "that no attention would be paid to it".

17-06-80: Rates collected, water, £64+, police, £122+, and public health, £21+.

10-08-80: There was a lengthy correspondence between the Burgh and the owner of Barbauchlaw Estate over the ground that Armadale water supply ponds and filter sits on. Mr. Moffat of Ardrossan was owner. The Commissioners offered £1 per annum as nominal fee for ground. On 18th August, Mr. Moffat to be given a plan showing ponds, filter, access roads and water runs that feed ponds.

On 23rd June, Mr. Moffat had offered to sell the pond's ground at £2 per acre to the Burgh. The Burgh offered £2.10/- all in, which was the annual sum they had given the farmer since c.1865.

On 11th July, Mr. Moffat declined £2.10/- and proposed an Airdrie estate factor as arbiter. The Commissioners proposed John Waddell of Southrigg as arbiter (he had been arbiter re Bathgate ground).

25-08-80: The filter to get pebbles and charcoal, the clean water filter to be cemented with Portland cement. Invitations to make offers for a water supply contract to be placed in two windows (Crown Hotel and Calderhead's). While renewing an old pipe track laid in 1865, the contractor drained a pond that supplied a pit owned by Uphall Oil Co.. Drainage work approved including kerbing and guttering at Mr. Verrier's property and for a cesspool at Bathville Co-op Store and Wilson's.

08-09-80: Hugh Brown to keep possession of the Burgh Bell and to allow no-one to use it except himself or a depute appointed by him or the scavenger of the Burgh.
11-10-80: The scavenger was given one months notice, the Burgh to advertise for a scavenger on wages of 13/- per week.
22-10-80: Five applied for the scavenger's job, including David Craig of Wilson's Land, John Walker of Buttries Row and Robert Gillon, Mount Pleasant. Mr. Moffat willing to arrange for the Burgh to get title to pond ground on condition that his tenant, Uphall Oil Co., get their water restored. The Burgh to increase their offer for ground to £5.
28-10-80: Rates fixed - water, 6d; police, 8d; horses, no change; cow, 2/-; oven, 5/-; steam engine, 10/-; and public health, 2d.
15-10-80: Some people appealed against assessment for the following reasons - inability to pay, three cows now sold, two cows outside Burgh.
06-12-80: Burgh got certificate of valuation of the portion of lands and heritages belonging to or leased by the North British Railway Co. situated within the Burgh. A valuation was sought on railway within Burgh belonging to, or leased by, Monklands Iron & Coal Co.

1881

Office-bearers and committee of Armadale Football Club were - Sprott, McKenzie, Russell, Goldie, Scott and White. A game was played at Mayfield ground. C Coy. 8th Volunteer Battalion, Royal Scots moved their H.Q. from Torphichen. They used a hall in South Street bought for them by Colonel Hope of Bridgecastle. They also used the Volunteer field. Captain Stewart offered the park to Armadale Star on condition that the team players joined the Volunteers and nine did. The Star became the 'Volunteers'.

Soon, the Senior Armadale F.C. started using the Volunteer Field and the Rifle Volunteers moved to Heatherfield.

There was a nuisance at the Beeches. Woodend School received 7/10½d. Kirk elder Robert Blair placed robes on the new Armadale Parish Kirk Minister Rev. Cameron. Armadale Parish Kirk got a bell from Durham Weir of Boghead.

523 attended school, Miss Crabbie was one of the teachers. Summary of Report by HM Inspector: Mixed school - very good / satisfactory / very creditable, writing and arithmetic remarkably good. Infants' school - very good, instruction very satisfactory except arithmetic. The staff in 1881 - Arthur Livingstone, Kenmure Blair, Elizabeth Dougal, Martha Fleming, Joanna Crabbie, Elizabeth Robertson, James Meek and Elizabeth Chalmers. April 21 was a Sacramental Fast Holiday.

10-01-81: The Sanitary Inspector, in his report, said 9/- expenses were incurred in burying a tramp's child, Alex Vaughan, who died in Holt's Lodging House on 29th December 1880. The Burgh later paid the burial costs of 2/6. The Burgh replaced the scavenger and paid the next scavenger, William Storrie, 14/- a week.

25-01-81: The Commissioners considered leasing the Subscription School for 10 to 15 years at a nominal rent of 1/- a year. The erection of eight new lampposts to be costed, notepaper headed "Burgh of Armadale" to be purchased. The Commissioners decided that the scavenger gets a barrow with two wheels. Rates brought in £196+.

12-05-81: Mr. Stewart claimed 30/-, 6 years at 5/-, for the right-of-way through his field to the filter.

16-06-81: Drains were discussed –

1) Hamilton's Yard at west end of Burgh.
2) Mrs. Wilson's park.
3) Side of Branch Road.
4) Below Buttries Row.

A letter, re smallpox, was read from the Board of Supervisors. The Sanitary Inspector's report referred to the want of privy and ashpit at certain (named) proprietor's property.

11-07-81: Account for laying kerb gutter in front of Pale House to go to Thomas Harvie, Chairman of Pale House Committee.

26-08-81: Burgh wells to be causewayed.

25-09-81: Contractors were invited to give estimate for the erection of 15 lampposts - Muir, Robertson and Dougal, Bathgate, Hutton, tinsmith, Armadale, and Stevenson, Bathville. The main streets of Armadale were given names - East Main Street and West Main Street were east and west of the Toll Bar. North Street was formerly Branch Road, South Street was formerly Drove Loan. The road to Woodend was named Mill Road, the street at the eastern boundary was to be 'Marches' - a March being a boundary where estates met. The street where the new Public School was built was to be Academy Street, formerly Bullion Brae - bullion was old Scots from the Gaelic word for a bubbling well or spring. All the Rows of, mainly, miners' houses to retain their name except Monkey Row to be renamed Thomson Street. (Monkey Row was probably from Monklands Iron and Steel Co. who owned the houses)

10-10-81: The Clerk was instructed to write to Mr. Joseph Syson to remove his wooden jaw box. The Clerk was to write the trustees of the Parish Road complaining of the disgraceful condition of the road between Armadale Toll Bar and Bathville Store causing carters to use footpaths. The Sanitary Inspector to get a quantity of disinfecting powder.

27-10-81: Water, 4d; police, 6d; lighting, 2d; public health, 2d; cow, 2/- per annum; oven, 5/-; Co-op steam engine, £1; horse, 1/6; pigs above three months, 1/-; and slaughterhouse, 5/-.

27-10-81: A letter from William Roberts stated that the dungsteads and privies attached to Rev. McLachlan's properties would be attended to. Gilbert Stewart, grocer, to remove the cesspool and wooden jawbox opposite his door.

07-11-81: Mr. McDougal, Returning Officer, offered to use his Returning Fee to erect a lamppost (pillar lamp) between the parsonage and the railway crossing. The following were asked to erect lampposts on their properties –

1) North British Railway Co. at level crossing at station.
2) Commissioner of supply for County at Police Station.
3) James Wood, coal-master, at level crossing leading to No.12 Pit.

Mr. Wood refused on grounds that the engine that crossed the road belongs to the North British Rail Co..

15-11-81: Sewerage drain at Quality Row discussed.

24-11-81: Annual appeals against assessment came from Monklands Iron & Coal Co., Mrs. Jean Smith appealed against assessment on water for two pigs, Mr. John Marshall, three horses, Mr. Alex Borrowman, slaughterhouse, John Walker, nine cows, Joseph Syson, three pigs, Mrs. Muirhead, three cows and one pig, and Robert Russell, six cows. Mr. Wood appealed against assessment on minerals at Hopetoun on grounds that Pit No.8 is outwith Burgh, also re coal at Barbauchlaw because part was outside Burgh.

1882

Robert Muir owned Barbauchlaw Fireclay Works. Dr. John Anderson came to Armadale as resident doctor. Mrs. Rushford lived in Armadale, Mrs. Lillias Marshall or Aitken died and left four children orphans and Mrs. Neil or Drysdale lived in Armadale. Many Armadale parents defaulted over compulsory vaccination of their children. J. Wilson received aliment, Robert Finlay of 33 Simpson's Land, Armadale, was granted school fees and books for three children and P. Linnoch, of 23 Bathville Row, was refused school fees and books. James Simpson lived in Johnston's Land. Fireclay works were started by Robertson and Love.

09-01-82: A sum of £1.4/10 was given to the Parochial Board being Poors' Rates (for relief of the poor).
14-02-82: The Commissioners offered £1 reward after two street gas lamps had been broken.
21-02-82: Two privies with ash-pits to be erected at Moffat's houses in North Street.
13-04-82: The kerbs and gutter between Stirling's property and the Toll was to be in a continuous line. The Burgh was to buy two padlocks and hasps for boxes at the bing.
05-06-82: £3.2/- was paid to Mr. Reid for lighting and putting out street lamps. The Commissioners asked the Parish Board to make another entrance to Bathgate cemetery for the convenience of the western part of the parish.
10-07-82: Reference was made to kerb and gutter from Toll Bar to Shairp's Land.
27-07-82: Pipe joints to be clay puddled at 4/- per chain.
21-08-82: Barbauchlaw Estate had a new owner, George Readman. (There had been lengthy negotiations between the Commissioners and Mr. Moffat, previous owner, over the sale or lease of the Barbauchlaw ground used since 1865 for water supply purposes) Paid to Robertson Love for pipes, 5/6.
12-09-82: Hugh Brown to leave the town bell with James Beveridge.
09-10-82: John Black's offer accepted to cart and lay 25 carts of blaes on footpaths from Shairp's Land to Verrier's. Clerk to write William Edwards requiring him to remove the water barrels from front to back of his property and to get the property properly rhoned.

27-10-82: Water, 4d; police, 6d; lighting, 2d; public health, 2d; (from Whitsunday to Whitsunday) cow, 2/-; horse, 1/6; pig over three months, 1/-; oven, 5/-; steam engine, £1; and slaughterhouse, 5/-.
13-11-82: Returning Officer offered to apply his fee to put a new well at the Toll if the old one was transferred to opposite his dwelling house.
23-11-82: Appeals came in against water rates, etc. that showed that many Armadalians kept farm animals within the Burgh. Appeals concerned two pigs, one horse and seven pigs, four cows and two pigs, nine pigs, one horse and six pigs.
13-12-82: The Burgh paid £1.3/4 in Poor Rates. The Water Committee was authorised to get two boxes for water works and the Lighting Committee to get sponges and shammy leather for cleaning lamps.

1883

Education - preparations took place in June for a Public Exhibition, additional time was given to crayon, drawing, painting, printing, illuminating sepia, map drawing, singing, sewing, spelling, recitations, etc.. Two dux medallists each received a silver medal, being a gift from the Superiors of the Parish. Among those who attended the Public Exhibition were several church ministers, Sir William and Lady Baillie, Dr. Kirk, Dr. Stevenson and Dr. Anderson, and Mr. Maxwell Durham.

In May 1883, 604 pupils attended Armadale School. Reasons given for a reduction in attendance in June –

1) Not fully recovered from the shock of two holidays the previous week.
2) Monday was the annual Term Day.
3) Wednesday was Bathgate's yearly Fair.

Francis Logan of Bathville, died. Mrs. Logan lived at Bathville. Charles Baird lived at Armadale. James Wilson died in Mrs. Holt's house. Widow Rachel Forrester or Brown was granted school fees and books for her daughter Rachel Brown. William Martin was allowed 2/6 weekly. Widow Ann Littlejohn or Kerr applied for education of her nine year old daughter Mary Kerr. Mrs. Catherine Easton was allowed 2/- a week for her 12 year old son Nesbit.

17-01-83: The Commissioners agreed to co-operate with the Brass Band Committee in raising funds and framing rules and regulations.

18-01-83: At a special meeting of all town ratepayers, the Feu Charter, re water Works, was finally accepted.

12-02-83: Two Burgh men (R. and A.) were each to pay 3/- for breakage of globe lamps by their children.

23-02-83: Monklands Iron & Coal Co. were asked to provide a horse and cart to lay ashes on footpath between railway crossing and Bathville Store, the Burgh Scavenger to assist. Bathgate Town Clerk to advise Commissioners if they have power to compel builders of new buildings to keep in uniform line.

05-03-83: An account for £12.12/- from the solicitor to pay his fee for work done in connection with Burgh Water Works Feu Charter was challenged and returned, back came a revised account for £17.2/2. (The Commissioners quickly authorised payment of the original Bill)

14-03-83: For use of town bell, charges thus - merchants, 3d, others, 6d, and announcements in public interest, free.

01-05-83: Shotts Iron Co. to remove, as a nuisance, the jawboxes in front of Buttries and Shotts Rows.

21-05-83: The Commissioners to take steps to replace Dr. Longmuir by Armadale doctor, John Stevenson, as Town Medical Officer.

08-06-83: Feu Charter re water works ground signed by George Readman, now in Clerk's hands.

09-07-83: Archibald McDonald claimed damages when his child injured two fingers by falling over Burgh Sewer grating. The Cleansing Committee to meet Mr. McDonald and express sympathy for the misfortune, which happened to his child. A cash box to be got for the Treasurer.

16-07-83: Charge for supplying water used by mason and plasterer at new building operations varied from 2/- to 12/6. The new work was at West Main Street for W. Edwards, North Street for Mr. Verrier and South Street for McLean. One mason appealed, saying that he didn't use the town's water.

23-07-83: Lettering and numbering of the streets now complete. Commissioners met two representatives of Armadale Brass Band. They decided to appeal to the public to subscribe towards the purchase of instruments.

30-07-83: Resident Dr. Stevenson to replace Dr. Longmuir of Bathgate as Medical Officer.
29-08-83: Gas street lamps to be lit on Sunday evenings.
05-09-83: Nine additional street lamps to be erected at old Toll Bar, Subscription School gate, five from Mr. Brown's property South towards Bathville Store and two at Bathville Row.
14-05-83: Account passed re laying of new water supply and new pump at Bathville Row, £7.0/9.
28-09-83: Dispute with Armadale Gas Co. re supply pipe for two proposed street lamps for Bathville Row.
08-10-83: Mr. Reid, lamplighter, resigned through ill health arising from rapid change from hot to cold temperature, a written notice advertising for a lamplighter to be put in window of Crown Hotel. The Water Committee to inspect the pumps. Rennie's Land to get an ash-pit.
15-10-83: John McLory was new lamplighter at £4 per annum.
12-11-83: Committee chosen for water, lighting, cleansing and finance. Election expenses' accounts were passed - printing, £2.3/7; Returning Officer's fee, £2.2/-; two clerks at 1 guinea each, £2.2/-; list of voters, 6/6; and polling booth, 7/6. A letter from the County Road Surveyor claimed that a drain on the road between Armadale and Bathville Store was choked up and damaging the road.
19-11-83: The Commissioners decided to buy globes wholesale.
22-11-83: Appeals were from three owners of pigs (5, 3 & 2 pigs).

1884

Armadale Gas Light Co. was in business. Shotts Iron Co. owned minerals at Cappers, James Wood of Paisley owned the minerals at Tarrareoch, Coltness Iron Co. owned houses at Barbauchlaw and Eastertoun, William Edwards owned 20 houses in North Street, James Forsyth, Fraser, Gillon, Monkland Iron Co. and Rev. MacLachlan were all owners of local property. Armadale Parish Kirk in Academy Street was elevated to Quoad Sacra, Parish Kirk status. Coltness Iron Co. held the right to extract iron on Barbauchlaw Estate. William Martin suffered from lung disease, widow Chalmers of Bathville got 1/6 a week. David Gray, miner, was granted books for his sons Thomas (12), Joseph (8) and David (10). From 1884 to

1921, the Infant Department of Armadale Public School kept a log book.

14-01-84: The Burgh sent two representatives to a joint meeting in Edinburgh of Scotland's Royal and Parliamentary Burghs and Police Burghs of Scotland. The representatives were William Marshall and Robert Russell, who received 5/- expenses each. The Burgh asked the County Road Surveyor to remove the Toll House. A great nuisance at Rennie's Land to be removed.
23-01-84: It was made known that the demolition date for the Toll House was the Wednesday after 17th January.
04-02-84: Account for £1.12/10 was passed to cover funeral expenses of William Kelly, a destitute shoemaker who resided in the Burgh.
20-02-84: Minute of the joint Edinburgh meeting was read, then a form of petition for a separate Department of State for Scotland was read, then signed, by the Chairman. John Russell was authorised to sell the old Bathville water pump for 8/- or whatever he could get.
27-02-84: Account passed for seven gas lamp pillars at 15/6 each, £5.15/6. It was agreed that the convener of any of the committees be empowered to pay a sum not exceeding 10/- for any small job or give 10/- in part payment of any account.
14-04-84: It was agreed to erect a pillar lamp at the most convenient place at the curve of the old Toll.
21-04-84: The Water committee were authorised to see Mr. Verrier as to his toby (one of several decisions at a time of drought). Clerk to write William Edwards to get his water closet sorted out at once. Clerk to write William Gibb, flesher, as to waste of water at Mr. Combie's stable door. Clerk to write Syson and Beveridge as to waste of water at their washing houses, requiring them to put new crans at pipes.
30-04-84: Account passed to William McFarlane, Glasgow, for bucket, 17/6.
26-05-84: The Commissioners to meet at Toll one evening, thereafter to inspect two reported nuisances.
02-07-84: A letter from Mr. Beveridge's solicitor, claiming that the four man water committee had illegally entered private property and smashed his client's lead pipe. In a lengthy reply, it transpires that the water committee could not find the toby.
14-07-84: The health of the Burgh was very satisfactory. An account was passed to Mr. Holt, lodging house keeper, 10/-.

01-08-84: The Commissioners learned of the threat of an epidemic of cholera.
18-08-84: The street lamps to be painted.
09-09-84: It was agreed to extend the dyke at South Pond as far southward as the stones will go.
30-09-84: Court case re water issue, Beveridge versus Burgh.
13-10-84: Court case - decree announced in favour of Burgh. Three South Street proprietors objected to paying 3/6 per yard for kerb and gutter. Contractor to give price for rubble stones instead of flats.
22-10-84: Russell and Wood to be told to remove the nuisances at their property. Burgh to investigate nuisance between Shotts and Buttries Rows.
10-11-84: Three newly elected Commissioners were John Russell (99 votes), Thomas Robertson (93) and A. Beveridge, publican, (87).
27-11-84: Appeals before Appeal Court included one from Young's Paraffin Light and Mineral Oil Co. on grounds that 44% of Barbauchlaw minerals are outside the Burgh. Others appeals were from Leckie (4 pigs), Marshall (7 pigs), Mrs. Watson (3 pigs) and Maurice Thomson (4 pigs). One appeal showed that the Free Gardeners' Friendly Society used the Hall at the Crown Hotel.
01-12-84: Crawford Jamieson appealed against his assessment on Barbauchlaw Moss.
05-12-84: Railway carters were informed of damage done to kerb and gutter, to east of Co-op Store, by loaded carts.
23-12-84: A letter came from Mr. Fleming, brick-maker, re right-of-way to South Pond through ground he had feued from Monkland Iron & Coal Co.. Accounts re new kerb and gutter in South Street to go to property-owners Stewart, McLean, Thomson, Anderson and Brown; also to Monklands Iron & Coal Co. and George Readman. The Burgh was asked to pay 2/6, the cost of a coffin for a child who died in Thomson's Land. Messrs. Brown, Hutton and Tweedie were told to provide ash-pits and privies for their tenants.

1884-1885, eight houses in Armadale were owned by James Alexander of Glasgow (his factor was George Boyd, draper). Armadale Co-op owned a house, shop and cellar at 70 West Main Street. Rev. Robert Cameron lived at the Beeches, at the manse. J. Ellis owned three houses in South Street. James Finlay, grocer, owned shop at 28 South Street, also house and shop nos. 30 and 32. Mr. Mungall was owner-occupier of 152 West Main Street. Robin Fleming, brick-maker, owned five houses in South Street, nos. 79 to

83. Houses in South Street nos. 42 to 45 were owned by James Forrester, labourer. The Free Kirk owned a house in South Street. Joseph Fraser, miner, owned five houses in Main Street; one was occupied by McAlpine. Mr. Lauriston owned seven houses in West Main Street whose occupants included Craig, McAlpine, Boyd and Dobie. Robert Martin owned 52 to 55 South Street. William Gibb was a flesher. Monkland Iron & Coal Co. Ltd. owned houses at Mount Pleasant. Adam McLean owned four houses in South Street. Archibald McDonald owned eleven houses. William Naysmith, traveller, owned nos. 55 and 56 East Main Street. Thomas Pow, draper, owned three houses in South Street.

Mrs. Anderson, whose husband was a spirit merchant, owned a public house and three houses. William Murray, farmer of Hill of Murdiston, owned the Crown Hotel and stables and other Armadale property including a hall. Alex Beveridge, publican, owned seventeen houses and a shop. William Edwards, contractor, owned Armadale Inn, twenty houses and two shops in North Street and West Main Street. J. Calderhead occupied public house and byre, South Street.

House and wright's shop, South Street, occupied by J. Simpson, joiner. J. Russell, fruiterer, owned nos. 19, 21 and 71 East Main Street. Mr. Russell also owned sixty-six houses and shop in West Main Street. Armadale had a new school and schoolmaster's house, the old school was owned by School Board of the Parish of Bathgate. Mrs. Simpson owned six houses. R. Stark, baker, owned three houses, shops and a bake-house, all in West Main Street. John Ballantyne, jeweller, had one shop. Gilbert Stewart, grocer, owned shops and houses at 60 to 66 South Street. Joseph Syson owned a shop and twelve houses. Rev. Alex Temple owned and occupied the parsonage. Maurice Thomson, grocer, owned twenty-six houses and one shop. The trustees of the Wesleyan Methodist Church owned Bathville Cottage and Field. John Tweedie, miner, owned six houses. James Verrier, Armadale, owned seven houses, two shops and a stable. Mrs. Mary Wilson owned a bake-house and a killing house. William Wilson, pawnbroker, owned houses at Mossend.

Falkirk Female Society owned five houses in Armadale. John Linton of America, owned twelve houses in Main Street. Rev. McLachlan of Guildford owned thirteen houses. McNair of Torphichen owned three houses in Eastertoun. Wishaw Building Society owned sixteen houses in Main Street. The Earl of Selkirk owned North and South Couston, Colinshiel, Balmuir and Muirhall. William Shairp of South Queensferry owned house and shops in Armadale. Shotts Iron Co. owned forty-five houses, a store, stables, office and a workshop at Cappers (on Polkemmet Land).

Armadale Gas Light Co. owned the gas works and street mains.. Armadale Police Commissioners owned a water-works, pipes, etc.. The Commissioners of Supply, Linlithgow, owned the Police Office. James Wood of Paisley worked the minerals of Tarrareoch. Shotts Iron Co. worked the minerals at Cappers.. Coltness Iron Co. owned three houses at Barbauchlaw and five at Eastertoun. William Thomson, Messenger at Arms of Wishaw, owned ten houses in West Main Street.

James Wood, coal-master, was owner / occupier of Bathville Mansion House. He also owned fifty-two houses, an oil store, brickworks, clay, waggon-works and a locomotive shed. Kopel Moritz, who lived in Bathgate, was a brick-maker at Bathville. Dickson & Mann occupied Bathville Foundry. T. Robertson was a brick manufacturer in Armadale. Young's Paraffin Light Co. worked Barbauchlaw minerals.

George Readman, owner of Barbauchlaw Estate, owned Whitockbrae, occupied by William Cochrane, farrier, Barbauchlaw Mains (Nisbet) and Barbauchlaw Mill (Thomas Harvie). Mr. Readman also owned twenty-nine houses, Barbauchlaw moss, Barbauchlaw brick and fireclay and freestone quarry. Hugh McKinnon, farmer at Stanerig, paid feu duty to Mr. Readman. Nisbet farmed Barbauchlaw Mains.

1885

James Williamson of Armadale died. David Craig lived in Armadale. John Simpson was paid 5/6 for a coffin (for child James Kinchella). Helen Ramsay recorded.

12-01-85: The right-of-way on Mr. Fleming's feu charter was changed. The Commissioners allowed the curlers of the District to use the South Pond for the remainder of the season for £1. A crossing at the

Co-op Store to be put in order, i.e. a drive-in for carts to be made. One case of scarlet fever was reported.

19-01-85: The Commissioners asked the North British Railway Co. if the people of Armadale could be given concessionary fares to Glasgow on Wednesdays - this was not given.

09-02-85: A note from Isaac Whitefield, clerk of Thistle Lodge of Free Gardeners' Friendly Society, intimating the expiry of bond on £150 loan. Commissioners requested a new bond without specifying definite date for repayment. John McLory to be told that he was employed to light and extinguish the lamps and not his boy. A painter to prepare five boards saying, "Carters are strictly prohibited from crossing the kerb and gutter except at the crossings. Offenders will be prosecuted. By order." Note from Medical Officer saying that James Watson of 30 Russell's Row has not an infectious disease, as was suspected.

04-03-85: Gilbert Stewart, shopkeeper, had complained at length to Commissioners that the state of the footpath at his shop was a hazard to his customers (the treacherous footpath was apparently next to a well). He was told to put up a wooden baluster inside the wall and that he would be responsible for any accident. The North British Railway Co. to be told to put up gates and fencing at railway level crossing in South Street to protect the public. James Wood to do the same at the crossing on East Main Street. Commissioners learned that North British Railway Co. in 1884 had reached an agreement with Bathgate Road Trustees over improvements at South Street crossing. Five boards warning carters against crossing kerb and gutter to go up - two opposite Adam Wilson's, one at head of Mill Road, one at Gilbert Stewart's and one at the Marches.

13-04-85: An appeal for financial support came from the International Exhibition of Industry, Science and Arts to be held in Edinburgh in 1886. Adam McLean of Mount Pleasant applied for permission to erect a fence as he intends keeping flowers. Commissioners told North British Railway Co. that safety gates were essential at South Street crossing especially as 200 children attended school within 100 yards. Account passed for wheelbarrow, £1.1/-.

20-04-85: Gilbert Stewart and Walter Brown both refused to pay for the kerbs and gutters laid in front of their property. Mr. Hailstones reported on filthy state of the necessaries in Russell's Row, Monkland's Row, Bathville Row, etc.. Water Committee to get India-rubber mountings for the pump. Uphall Coal Co. to be asked to put a connecting pipe between pond and engine to improve water supply during summer months.

18-05-85: A 2'6" or 2'9" cast metal railing to be put up at Stewart's well. James Wood to put up gates at East Main Street railway crossing but hopes they are not wantonly destroyed as formerly.

A letter from agent for the Convention of Royal and Police Burghs asking the Town Council of Armadale to petition Parliament in favour of the creation of a separate Department of State for Scotland which should embrace the administration of education and every other matter distinctively Scottish. Commissioners unanimously agreed to petition parliament accordingly.

25-05-85: Court summonses re non-payment of accounts for kerbs and gutters to go to Messrs. Stewart, Thomson and Dodds' solicitor. Commissioners decided to supply gas to a new lamppost at Bathville Row if J. Wood or gas company laid supply pipes.

01-06-85: The Commissioners received written notice from Young's Paraffin Light and Mineral Oil Co. to the effect that their coal workings are approaching the filter's site and that supply of water would probably be affected, possibly about October.

19-06-85: The offer from John Shearer, blacksmith, Armadale, to put up railing in South Street was successful. Constable Alex Neil replaced Thomas Chalmers as Sanitary Inspector. Carters of Armadale were invited to submit priced offers to cart away street sweepings on Saturdays.

30-06-85: The Commissioners were advised to move Bathville pump to a level nearer the fountainhead or install a force pump. Re the sweeping of the streets on Saturdays, the scavenger's price was lowest so his wages were increased to 17/6 per week.

13-07-85: A complaint came in re pigsties kept by Robert J. in East Main Street.

04-08-85: It was agreed that the Burgh barrow be in the keeping of the scavenger. North British Rail Co. refused to put up gates at South Street crossing. Commissioners threatened to apply to the Board of Trade for public protection.

17-08-85: Besides the complaint of nuisance caused by Robert J.'s pigs, the Sanitary Inspector reported the dirty state of privies in Russell's Row, Bathville Row and Monkland premises. Mr. Ferrier of Birkenshaw to put a cran on the pipe in the field at No.12 Pit. Adam Smith to repair the pipes in Mr. Elder's washing-house connected with bake-house.

31-08-85: Mrs. W. to remove a stagnant nuisance at back of her property. Water supply to Co-op and two pits to be cut off on two days notice because of drought.

31-08-85: A letter from North British Railway Co. stated that a guard will be on the train in front of the engine when it crosses the road at South Street crossing and that the train speed would be limited to 3 miles per hour to make the crossing safer.

07-09-85: John Ellis was appointed new lamplighter at £6 p.a.. A water tank now situated at Bathville to improve supply. Mr. Pow gifted to the Burgh two new street lamps with his Returning Officer fee. Bathgate Parish Sanitary Inspector to arrange to have the bridge at the Marches cleaned out, as it is a nuisance.

15-09-85: Water committee to see about putting the clack right to ensure supply to Bathville pump. Robert F., brick manufacturer, objected for various reasons to the cistern sunk in front of his property in Drove Road (South Street). Commissioners unanimously agreed to take no notice of the letter. Offer considered from James Wood to give three street lamps free of charge to light Bathville Row if Commissioners or gas company lay the pipes.

25-09-85: Letter to go to the gas company alerting them to the heavy escape of gas from pipes leading to Bathville. Clerk to write James A. re filthy state of ditch at back of Castle Poorie. Mr. F. of Birkenshaw to be censured for throwing the carcase of a calf into his ash-pit. The Medical Officer to visit the Burgh pigsties and report if he considers them injurious to public health.

05-10-85: The Commissioners learned that Mr. Orr of Torrance, while riding his horse, had stumbled into the unfilled drain and been injured. He threatened to claim damages of £12 (eventually settled outside court for £9).

15-09-85: An ash-pit with privy accommodation to be erected on property of the Falkirk Female Benevolent Society.

05-10-85: Bowling Green Society asked for a few tons of the Burgh's filter sand.

12-10-85: Water, 6d; police, 6d; lighting, 2d; and sanitary, 2d.

09-11-85: Thomas Pow re-elected Provost or Chief Commissioner.

26-11-85: Rates Appeal Court dealt with appeals from owners of one pig and ten cows; also from James Lane, brick manufacturer.

18-12-85: The Commissioners learned that the filters had sunk a little due to underground coal workings.

1886

John Wilson lived at Whitockbrae. A man who died at Heatherfield Pit was taken to the Iron House at Bathgate (the morgue). Mrs. Gillespie of Torbanehill House, died. Mrs. Frazer of Torbanehill estate Gatehouse had to leave her house. By 1886, James Wood, coal-master, owned mineral rights at Barbauchlaw Estate. Barbauchlaw Pit was near a rail crossing at Armadale.

11-01-86: Filthy property to be cleaned up – Rennie's property at Bathville, J. Woods' and also Monklands Iron & Coal Co. houses. Sanitary Inspector to inspect the various cowsheds, dairies and milk-houses within the Burgh. Bathville now has a water pump. Mrs. Livingston, property-owner, said Coltness Co. should provide ash-pit and privy accommodation as they have the lease.

03-02-86: The Commissioners passed payment of funeral expenses of a stranger who died in Armadale (£1.8/6). The Road Trustees and Gilbert Stewart refused to pay account re new railing, both parties to be summoned to court. Mr. Wood appealed against assessment claiming all coal worked at Barbauchlaw would be outside the Burgh but investigation found this claim to be false. The Edinburgh Carting Agency, whose lorry had damaged Stewart's railing and coping stones, were instructed to repair same.

12-04-86: Many issues and problems were discussed including –

1) Action to preserve water in the South Pond.
2) Gas lamps at Bathville Row.
3) Allegations from Mr. Wood, that South Pond water finds its way into workings of Pit No.9.
4) Kerb and gutter contract.
5) Gates for railway crossing.
6) Application for private water connection.
7) Right-of-way.
8) Damage to kerbs and gutters by carts.
9) Nuisances at Verrier's, Marshall's and Simpson's.

12-05-86: Right-of-way to North Pond to be eight feet wide and laid with six inches of deep ashes. The Commissioners accepted an offer from John Russell to put up a pump, at his own expense, east of the Toll Pump. Mr. Moritz's valuation was reduced to £49.

07-06-86: The Commissioners considered a circular, memorandum and plan to do with a proposed District Hospital. Archie McD., merchant, complained of language used towards him by the Sanitary Inspector in reference to a dungstead on his property. Mr. Ferrier of Birkenshaw complained of an accumulation of sewage in his fields and that one of his queys died in the mud. A three-inch cast-iron pipe is to lead sewage from bye-wash to burn at east end of the Burgh.

11-06-86: A Combination Hospital is to be built to serve Bathgate, Torphichen, Whitburn and Livingston Parishes. Mr. McD. to be instructed to convert the little house seen by the deputation into a water closet. Five property-owners agreed to share the cost of a 12" sewer pipe - Armadale Co-op, William Edwards, Verrier, Shark and Harvie.

21-06-86: A 12" sewage pipe to the north end of five feus between Thomas Harvie's field and the Burgh march dyke. Several property-owners to be written to –

1) Monkland Iron & Coal Co. re dilapidated state of their privies.
2) Mr. Motherwell, owner of Post Office property, re ash-pit and privy.
3) Mr. T. re ash-pit, privy and channel bank in front of his property in Monkey Row.

05-07-86: Co-op to build a temporary shed on the north side of West Main Street. Power was given to the water committee to get a tinny or ladle for the well at the Toll.

12-07-86: Mr. Verrier to make a drain from the killing-house to sewer. Armadale's death rate per annum was 19 per 1000. Among causes of death - diseased respiratory organs, 21; digestive, 8; heart, 1; measles, 1; nervous, 2; tonsillitis, 1; diphtheria, 1; and premature births, 3.

17-08-86: The Commissioners discussed boundary of Mr. Thomson's feu at Old Toll next to sleeper fence. Mr. McD. was criticised for building a house on the site of dungstead without planning permission.

25-08-86: David Steel to be lamplighter for a year at £6.

10-09-86: The Commissioners heard a critical report from Inspecting Officer of the Board of Supervisors –

1) The sanitary state of Armadale is imperfect and a more complete system of drainage is necessary.
2) One or two competent scavengers should replace the Burgh Scavenger, an old man.
3) An open gutter along the foot of North Road is in a very dirty state.

4) The Burgh's six slaughterhouses are sub-standard with no water and drainage arrangements, Commissioners should build a Public slaughterhouse with all modern improvements.

21-09-86: Issues on the agenda included McD.'s building, McNab's slaughterhouse complaint and South Pond defect.

11-10-86: Improvements had been made to ash-pit and privies at Russell's Row, Bathville Row and Mount Pleasant. A complaint had come in re gutter and drainage at Monkland's Row. The Commissioners learned that the ditch on the east side of North Street, which leads the sewage from the drain which empties below Mr. Walker's, is still very dirty. Mrs. Wilson complained of blood from Mc.N.'s slaughterhouse going through pipe that empties at the back of her shop. Mr. Verrier to be told, firstly, that he can take the sewage water from North Street any time he likes and, secondly, that he cannot make a water connection on East Main Street as he has already got a connection at No.12 Pit by putting on a cran. Complaint of flooding at Drummond's houses because of no road gutter.

22-10-86: Rates held at 1/4 in £1; cow, 1/6; horse, 1/6; oven, 5/-; slaughterhouse, 5/-; and steam engine, £1. (Recorded in the minutes is word / term "Thereanent")

08-11-86: Commissioners elected were Marshall, Stewart, and Russell; Thomas Pow was still Chairman.

25-11-86: Rates Appeal Court assessment re Young's Paraffin Light Co. to be £240. Leckie, miner, appealed re five cows, White, miner, re ten cows and Wood appealed re minerals at Hopetoun and coal at Barbauchlaw. The Co-op no longer uses a steam engine.

03-12-86: There was a lengthy entry in the Burgh Minutes on A. McD.'s building; the question was - was the ground occupied by the dungstead an encroachment on the Public Street? All Burgh tobies to be raised to the surface. The Sanitary Inspector had visited the dairies, milk shops, and cowsheds within the Burgh. (Reference was made to 'Provost' Pow)

1887

William Anderson died of miner's lung disease. James Love of Armadale had bronchitis. Mrs. Cunningham of Mount Pleasant successfully applied for books for her son Hugh. Thomas Dewar lived in Armadale. Dr. Anderson reported on the state of A.G.'s property in Polkemmet Rows.

10-01-87: The drainage in two byres was found to be defective.

17-01-87: Regards Mr. McD.'s recently built structure, a lengthy written opinion of Counsel had come from Mr. Strachan of Edinburgh. The Commissioners were advised to take the case direct to the Court of Session, thereby saving the cost of taking it to the Sheriff Court first. Mr. McD. was allegedly in violation of part of the Police Act by failing to give notice, with plan, to Commissioners. He thereby committed a wrongful and illegal act, which fraudulently deprived the Commissioners of power to exercise their right. Mr. Beveridge walked out of the meeting, claiming that Chairman Pow had no right to speak. Mr. McD. to be given fourteen days notice before commencement of full (legal) proceedings. Mr. Scott complained of the nuisance committed by curlers and skaters on the South Pond (one of Armadale's two reservoirs).

26-01-87: Mr. McD.'s solicitor said that his client could not afford to contest the litigation. He now offered the Commissioners not only that part of his feu that they found fault with, but also the whole of his feu and the buildings at a fair valuation.

28-01-87: Mr. McD. offered to pay the cost of Commissioners seeking Counsel's opinion, if no more than £6. He also apologised for evading their authority.

15-02-87: Barbauchlaw Estate was told to lay kerbs and gutter in front of empty space between No.9 Pit and railway crossing as the Monkland Iron & Coal Co. are about to kerb and gutter in front of their property and to lay a crossing at entrance to right-of-way to South Pond at the north end of Fleming's feu. A complaint came from the gas company on loss of gas due to inefficient keys or stop-cocks on several street lamps. Queen's Jubilee - a letter came from the Secretary of the 'Women's Jubilee Offering to the Queen' through Mrs. Durham of Boghead House. The Commissioners resolved that, as a Commission, they would not interfere. A. McD. was told to remove a building in Mill Road Street. (He lived at 141 West End, Armadale) Plans were before Commissioners from James Wilson re proposed buildings in East Main Street.

21-02-87: A letter from James Wood stated that it was the duty of the Commissioners to sort the defective drain near Bathville Store.

25-02-87: A letter came from Mr. McD.'s solicitor (referring to the written advice given to the Burgh from Counsel) "we would be glad to be favoured with a perusal of it and the memorial on what the opinion proceeded". The Commissioners decided to act at once when Mr. Wood complained of want of water at Bathville and he was informed that the pump there did not get "fair play" from his tenants in the Row.

01-03-87: Mr. Hutton, tinsmith, submitted plans for a two-storey building between Police Buildings and his own premises. Mr. McD. to be given a 48-hour ultimatum, to apologise and pay expenses, or alter the building, or face a court case.

07-03-87: The Commissioners considered registration of dairies, milk shops, etc. within Burgh. A fence to be erected at South Pond, six feet high larch stobs, burned and charred, with four lines of galvanised wire. Mr. McD.'s solicitor acknowledged the 48-hour ultimatum and expressed regret that his previous letter was not answered. The Commissioners instructed their solicitor, Mr. Dodds, to proceed with the court case. Provost Pow submitted plans for shop and dwelling house to be built on the west side of South Street.

13-03-87: Mr. McGregor, draper, replaced Mr. Marshall who resigned as Commissioner. James Balloch, miner, successfully appealed for rates exemption. (He had a certificate from Dr. Anderson, having been injured at work and having chronic bronchitis) Provost Pow was allowed to erect a barricade round his private building site and got the privilege of a gas lamp.

11-04-87: Complaint as to want of ash-pit and privy accommodation at Beveridge's. Mr. Motherwell wrote saying he would be getting railway sleepers, soon, to finish the work. Commissioners learned of a want of pressure in water supply from the Toll eastwards. Ten Burgh property-owners to be told to raise water tobies to the surface. Clerk to write William Louden of Beeches warning him against allowing his ducks to frequent the North Pond, thereby fouling the water used for domestic purposes or risk prosecution. Plan submitted from Thomas Gordon for a building in West Main Street.

02-05-87: The Commissioners learned that the cesspool in East Main Street was finished. Clerk to write giving ultimatum to ratepayers who were in arrears including Mrs. M. who had failed to pay for supply of water for cows. Mr. McD.'s ash-pit and privy were offensive to R. Russell and his tenants. A circular was received from the Convention of Royal and Parliamentary Burghs asked Commissioners to petition Parliament in favour of an extension of the powers of the Scotch Secretary and it was resolved to do so. Liquor Traffic (Scotland) Bill - a circular for the Scottish Permission Bill and Temperance Association, was considered. Water charges were fixed for water used by masons and plasterers in new building works at Hutton's, Gordon's, Wilson's and Pow's buildings.

27-05-87: John Russell submitted Plans for a killing-house and stable to be built at the back of old Co-op store. A circular was before the Commissioners on matters arising out of the Chancellor of the Exchequer's budget. Another circular about a new local hospital was considered.

06-06-87: A Glasgow contractor won the contract to lay kerbs and gutters in South Street. Water charges on future building work to be ½% of contract price. The Marches to get a well. Commissioners to see Mr. Verrier with a view to leasing or renting the Pale House. Commissioners offered £1 rental for the Pale House, Mr. Verrier wanted 30/-. Commissioners learned that underground coal workings now 70 yards beyond filter which should now be safe. Police Station to be supplied off the water mains.

21-06-87: South Pond reservoir to be enlarged.

01-07-87: R.'s filthy privy to be cleaned and disinfected. (R.'s factor claimed that outsiders, and not tenants, made the privy nuisance)

11-07-87: In his report, the Sanitary Inspector complained of piggeries kept in Mill Road and of old rags in bags stored in a back room by John Roberts, hawker. Clerk to write James Aitken, writer, to get the ditch at the March cleaned out as it emits a very offensive smell. During the first six months of 1887 within the Burgh, 29 deaths, 84 births and 12 marriages. The Medical Officer, in his report, suggested that disinfectant be liberally used in the drains, midden steads and urinals during hot dry weather.

01-08-87: A cesspool to be provided at kerb and gutter in South Street.

10-10-87: The Sanitary Inspector reported complaint as to want of ash-pit accommodation at Henry Thomson's Star Inn. For the third year in succession, rates were held at 1/4 in £1. Complaint as to dirty water, filth and offensive matter that flows from houses into ditch at east side of road opposite gas works. Account passed for payment, A. Davidson for bell, 11/6.

01-11-87: Six persons nominated for four vacancies - Alex Beveridge (spirit merchant), William Gregor (draper), Malcolm Mallace (miner), Thomas Robertson (brick manufacturer), John Cairns (miner's agent) and John Russell (fruit merchant). Messrs. Russell and Robertson withdrew, so no election needed.

14-11-87: Complaint that gas was getting into water pipes in North Street.

24-11-87: Rates Appeal Court - three exempt (inability to pay). M. Mallace, on behalf of Armadale Co-op, appealed against paying water rates for two ponies.
19-12-87: A case of typhoid fever in West Main Street, complaint of want of drainage at C.'s washhouse and complaint arising from two pigsties. Inspector of Poor wanted recompensed on financial assistance given to a typhoid fever victim. (The Commissioners disclaimed all responsibility) John R. was warned that, if his pigsties were not kept clean, they would be removed altogether. James Cruikshank to be allowed to keep his pig for one month and no more pigs to be kept thereafter.

1888

c.1888, a new football team, Armadale Star, played in Volunteer Field.

John McMillan of Northrigg had asthma. Mrs. McNair of Eastertoun shut up the farm well as its contents had probably been analysed and condemned. Thomas Hope of Bridgecastle was having the well at Colinshiel put right. The water in wells at Standhill and Cowdenhead on Barbauchlaw Estate was found to be impure.

Malcolm Torrie was dispatch clerk at Bathville. Armadale residents - Mrs. Wilson, Halbert, and Henderson, Messrs. Nisbet, Douglas, McAlpine, Forrester, Russell, Sneddon, Brown, Gilchrist, Muirhead, Chalmers, White, McDougal, Hunter and Mighton.

09-01-88: Case of typhoid fever has abated and the Burgh had only four cases of bad sanitation. There were dirty privies at Bathville Row and Russell's Row and two drainage problems. Sewage drain needed to go from back row at 80-86 West Main Street into drain at Daniel Archer's house. During the last six months of 1887, of 38 deaths in Armadale, 11 were due to diseased respiratory organs. Uphall Oil Co. Pit now discontinued, the pit pond to be fenced off or filled up. Curlers to get the use of the South Pond.
13-02-88: R.'s Land ash-pit and privy also Robert R.'s drainage and F.'s piggeries were all in a dirty state, Young's Oil Co. (who had apparently recently bought over Uphall Oil Co.) agreed to fill up their

pond at the pit in Burgh. Burgh appointed Mr. Wilson to represent Armadale as a Road Trustee. A Public meeting to be held in the Subscription Schoolroom to consider earlier closing of public houses, the public meeting to be intimated by bell.

20-02-88: At a poorly attended public meeting on early closing of public houses, a plebiscite to be taken, this was later deemed unnecessary.

27-02-88: Circulars on bake-houses and smallpox. A Courier advert announced that Sir William Baillie of Polkemmet to submit a motion at next meeting of the Licensing Justices to the effect that licensed houses shut at 10 pm.

19-03-88: An account from the solicitor who dealt with McD.'s case was considered excessive. It was reduced from £16.17/10 to £12.

11-04-88: A report from Public Health Inspecting Officer was very critical of sanitary state of Burgh. He was also concerned about the seven dairies and several milk shops in Burgh, two public urinals were not connected to drains and, in some parts of the Burgh, sewage goes into ditches and remains stagnant.

07-05-88: Dr. Anderson was appointed Medical Officer for Armadale. Parliament to be petitioned in favour of Burgh Police and Health (Scotland) Act and for the Secretary for Scotland to have Cabinet rank - petitions to go to Mr. McLagan, M.P. for county. In his report on Burgh sanitary conditions from Board of Supervisors, they maintained Armadale's Medical Officer was either ignorant of statute or incompetent. McAlpine's pool now empty and piggeries clean, also Mrs. Brown's piggery clean.

28-05-88: The Sanitary Inspector resigned. Reports on T.B. in cattle and shops belonging to Marshall, fruiterer, flooded. Street gutter at Marshall's to be lowered, paling at North Pond to be repaired.

12-06-88: Burgh engaged a new Dairy and Sanitary Inspector at £7 per annum. Constable James Simpson got the job. Building plans were submitted from Finlay, draper, South Street.

09-07-88: Sanitary Inspector reported causes for concern –

1) Nuisance at Lauriston's Land.
2) Ash-pits at McLachlan's Land.
3) Want of ash-pit and privy accommodation at Johnston's Land.
4) Privies at Russell's Row.
5) Want of drain at Livingstone's Land.
6) Privies at Bathville Row.

Medical Officer's report mentioned mumps, 61 births, 8 marriages and 38 deaths in first six months of 1888.

30-07-88: William Calder, tailor, was co-opted Commissioner to fill a vacancy. Letter from Mr. Beveridge's factor, "I am cited to remove a nuisance within four days which will cause me an awful lot of inconvenience". A nuisance at McLachlan's Land and a drain at Livingstone's Land were left in the hands of the Sanitary Committee.

27-08-88: Complaints included a near choked conduit and a burst public sewer. Robert Storrie was re-engaged as lamplighter at £7 for the season. Account for removal of manure at Laurieston's to be paid and claimed back from the proprietor - to O'Donell for wheeling out, 5/-; and to Jardine and Walker for carting away, 11/-.

14-09-88: Cost of supplying gas per street lamp was up from 7/6 to 10/- per year, after lengthy hassle with gas company.

22-10-88: Rates were pegged as last year at 1/4 in £1, cows and horses, 1/6 each, and slaughterhouses and ovens, 5/- each. Annual meetings of the electors arranged for nominating candidates at ensuing elections. Commissioners seem to have been so annoyed at the gas company's 33% increase in cost of supply to street lamps that they decided to charge £3 per annum to the gas company for "the privilege of supply of water".

06-11-88: The Burgh Treasurer / Collector was asked to resign having failed to produce the balance of money held by himself when visited by the Finance Committee. Four newly-elected Commissioners were William Calder, tailor, Thomas Pow, clothier, Thomas Robertson, brick manufacturer, and Adam Wilson, grocer. On 9th November, Andrew Graham, grocer, was appointed to fill remaining vacancy.

12-11-88: An account was passed for six planks, 19/6. The Burgh Treasurer / Collector to be told to hand over the balance (£14.0/9½) also cash box and his written resignation by the following Friday.

19-11-88: Mr. B. asked for a month to repay balance of Burgh money held by him, his cautioner to be asked to pay same.

26-11-88: Letter from Mr. B.'s cautioner telling the Commissioners to lodge information against Mr. B. with Fiscal.

28-11-88: The Commissioners appointed John Simpson as new Burgh Treasurer / Collector. Former Treasurer requested meeting with the Commissioners.

29-11-88: Rates Appeal Court - three appealed through inability to pay, James Wood appealed re minerals at Ballencrieff also coal at Barbauchlaw. (The Commissioners postponed decision until they had examined plans of workings)

24-12-88: Dr. Anderson and Mr. McCombe of Crown Hotel agreed to become security jointly to amount of £100 for Mr. Simpson. Bond of caution to be signed, moneys received by Collector to be lodged in the Royal Bank of Scotland, Bathgate.

From the Valuation Roll, 1888-89 - in this roll, Armadale Burgh properties were listed street by street. The streets of Armadale in 1888 were East Main Street, including Russell's Row, West Main Street, Academy Street, Back Street (6 houses off West Main Street), Mill Road Street, North Street, South Street and Mount Pleasant. Bathville properties within the Burgh were listed separately. East End, including the Marches, was listed.

At East Main Street lived Smith, Paul, McMillan, Shaw, Jones, Duff, Burn, McLay, Renfrew, Selkirk, Nealy, Duncan, Brand, Hutton, Williams, Wardrop, Brown, Morris, Simpson, Smart, Brown, McEwan, Rogers, Hamilton, Boyle, Finlay, Bennett, Black, Munro, Black, Pearson, Marshall, Johnston, Wood, Neilson, Neilly, Ronald, Neill and Brown.

In the forty-nine houses of Russell's Row (still East Main Street) lived Henderson, Baird, Greenwell, Bishop, O'Donald, Boles, Forrester, Sharp, Douglas, Middleton, McConnell, Stirling, Strang, Marshall, Mains, Cameron, Gillon, Craig, Gilchrist, Darroch, Freil, Edwards, Wilson, Brown, Watson McDowall, McKay, Newton, Marshall, Phillips, Brown, McCluney, Bennet, Smith, Bryce, Forsyth, Smith, Donaldson, Hall, Brown, Smith, Dow, Elliot and Anderson.

In nos. 3 to 78 East Main Street lived McNab, Anderson, Mungall, Wilson, Stewart, Dodds, Nimmo, Edwards, Brown, Baxter, Sneddon, Russell, Simpson, Shaw, Dickson, Smart, Steel, Johnson, Hempseed, Whyte, McGarrity, Black, McKinnon, Strang, Naismith, Galloway, Middleton, Greenwell, Holt, Frazer, Lawson and Wallace. McNab, butcher, had a killing-house in East Main Street. At nos. 22 and 23, the C. Company Royal Scots had an armoury store. John Kerr was publican of the Star Inn Vaults.

In West Main Street, McCombie was manager of the Crown Hotel. The Police Office was at no.14. Also in West Main Street lived Gibb, Graham, Jeffrey, Dougan, Geddes, Johnston, Gillon, Forsyth, Shearer, Peerson, Watson, Scott, Beveridge (postmaster in no.46), Kirk, Brown (no.49, killing-house), Daniel Archer (stationer), Smith, Drummond, Knox, Easton, Bishop, Drysdale, James Thomson

(Registrar no.70), Gorman, Jack, Marshall, Geddes, Sneddon, Wilson, Smith, Ramsay, Marshall, Kirk, Steel, Brown, Marshall, Baxter, Whitefield, Adamson, Gibson, Walker, Higgins, Thom, Semple and Syson.

West Main Street

Others who lived in West Main Street were Brown, Rankine, Storrie Dryburgh, Strang, Bows, Drysdale, Love, Easton, Ferguson, Hamilton, Thomson, Prentice, Calder, Bishop, Mackie, Higgins, Brownlee, Marshall, Stewart, Whitefield, Anthony, Weir, Jack, Donaldson, Strang, Stirling, Millar, Balloch, Gillon, Brown and Mair. Armadale Co-op Society occupied nos. 17-28 where they had a meat shop, a bread shop, flour lofts and bakery. In four Co-op houses lived Sneddon, Whitefield, Wilson, and Ballantyne (watchmaker). Also in West Main Street, were Stirling, Miller, Balloch, Gillon, Cruikshank (publican), Jones, Verrier, Brown and Mair.

In Academy Street was the Public School owned by the School Board of the Parish of Bathgate and schoolhouse, John Matheson, Headmaster.

In West Main Street - Pow, Bowie, Laird, Maxwell, McKay, Drummond, Harrower, Hill, Brown, Baxter, Pow, Boyd, McAlpine, Gough, Givan, Cosgrove, Robertson, Hunter, Love, Steel, Peden, Anderson, Marshall, McIntyre, Mungall, Smith Dougal, Gordon, Geddes, Fox, Williamson, Williams, Forrester, Rodger, Ellis, McNair, Stafford, Roberts, Davidson, Loudon and Lamond.

In Back Street (off West Main Street) lived Fleming, Hamilton, Baxter, Mallace, White, and Blair.

In Mill Road Street lived Linnoch, Kerr, Boyd, Middleton, Steen, Russell, Bonnar, Harrower, Gillies, Russell, Prentice, Drysdale, Smith, Dewar and Morrison. Also in Mill Road Street was a reading room, run by the Hopetoun Habitation of the Primrose League per Thomas Maxwell Durham of Boghead.

In North Street lived Livingston, Brodie, Thomson and Riddell (near them was the Burgh Store), Macdonald, Jones, Ross, Marshall, Allingham, Donaldson, Edwards, Jones, Hay, Brodie, Love, McLeish, Hunter, Anderson, Haldane, Donaldson, Wilson, Smart, Stewart, McAlpine, Hicks, O'Connell, Gillespie, Thomson, Boyd, Jack, Smith, Brodie, Smith, Simpson, Knox, Cook, Dunsmuir, Walker, Baxter, Spratt, Wright, Blades, Pow, McGarrity and Balloch.

In South Street lived Wilson, Dobbie, Ferguson, McLory, Simpson, Rankine, McArthur, Smith, Morton, Forrest, Brown, Marshall, Kerr, Tweedie, McDonald, Hailstones, Drysdale, Ritchie, Whitefield, Wilson (pawnbroker), Brown, Middleton, Ramsay, McFarlane, Wardlaw, Wilson, McMillan, Smart (Free Kirk House), Thom, Cairns, (The old school was owned by the School Board of Bathgate), Thomson, McCorrie, Baird, Cunningham, Anderson, Baird, Brown, Fullerton, Kerr, Duffy, Paul, McKay, Clark, Borrowman, Anderson, Stafford, Love and Wilson.

Quality Row / Dandy Row - Fleming, Hunter, Sneddon, Smith, McKenzie and Russell.

In South Street - Stewart, Henderson, Sibbald, Stevenson, Menzies, Hamilton, Conn, Neilly, Friell, Fisher, Francis, Thomson, Gallacher, Lambie, Lafferty, Bowes, Dowell, Marr, Rev. McDonald, Martin, Finlay, Kerr, Edward and Dr. John Anderson.

1-30 Mount Pleasant - Greens, Prentice, Mighton, Smart, Smith, Wilson, Burnett, Thomson, Rodgers, Mathieson, Strickland, McCabe, Wilson, Hamilton, Sneddon, Cunningham, Dowall, Watson, Mowbray, Hutton, Burnett and Muir. Armadale Bowling Club owned the bowling green - it was on Barbauchlaw Estate land, owned by George Readman.

Part of the farms of Hardhill, Whitockbrae and Barbauchlaw Mill were in the Burgh. Kopel Moritz, brick-maker, extracted fireclay from Barbauchlaw lands. Dickson & Mann steel-founders were tenants of Bathville Foundry, owned by Peter Stevenson. William Dickson of Armadale and W. Robertson Mann of Edinburgh were partners. In the part of Bathville estate within Armadale Burgh Boundary, James Wood owned a house occupied by A. Robertson. At Bathville Row, McAra occupied a house and store.

James Wood owned 3-66 Bathville Row, where the occupiers were Scott, English, Livingston, Mark, Brown, Johnston, Mitchell, McIntosh, White, Pollock, Brown, Bowes, McNamee, Mighton, Martin, Young, McLachlan, Fisher, Fagan, Cross, Rorran, McIndoe, Wardrop, Sinclair, McInulty, Logan, Mullen, Ross, Casey, Barclay, McCue, McPhillip, Russell, Chalmers, Johnston and Walker.

East End - in seventeen houses lived Rev. Temple, Gracie, Livingston, Shaw, Cartwell, Watson, Thomson, Scott, Duff, Nimmo, Bowes, Holt, Wylie, Brand, Muirhead and Halbert.

Here are some people who lived in Armadale outwith the Burgh –
West Main Street - Gillies, Ramsay, Gibson; Fraser, Earl, Donald, McAlpine and Dryburgh;
Eastertoun - Thomson, McQuiston, McGirvan, Stevenson, Anderson, Tennant, Wallace, Gunn, Ross, Campbell and Millar;
Mossend - Beveridge, Storrie, Smith and Cunningham;
The Beeches - Rev. Robert Cameron;
North Street - Gillon, Chalmers and Gas Works House, Reid;
Bathville - Simpson, Sykes, Wardlaw, Baxter, Hunter (stationmaster), Leckie, Foster and Gunn;
Bathville Mansion - Wood (coal-master), Robertson (manager); Gatehouse - Beaton; Oil Store - D. Watson, tenant; and Brickworks machinery and house – tenant, Robertson and Love and Co.. (Thomas Robertson of Armadale, James Eaglesham of Kilmarnock

and James Love of Mossend, Armadale) Potter lived in company house.

Brickwork, clay, etc., Robert Fleming and Co, Brick-makers. (R. Fleming of Carnbroe, J. Wood of Bathville, W. Cochrane Ferrier of Birkenshaw and Robert King of Bathville)

In company house lived David Kerr (foreman) and Wallace (fireman) also Paul and Duncan Richmond (joiner).

J. Wood owned a locomotive shed and workshop, wagon works and machinery were tenanted by Dickson & Mann, wagon-builders, a house occupied by King.

1889

c.1889, Armadale Volunteers were a Junior Football Club. In 1889, Kopel Moritz was a brick-maker using fireclay from Barbauchlaw. Gillies Bros owned Boghead Fireclay Works. James Gunn of Eastertoun was a van-man. Thomas Harvie was farmer in Barbauchlaw Mill (he may also have been a miller). W. Ballantyne of Northrigg had bronchitis. Mr. Ward, mining engineer, Bathville, prepared plans and specification for Bridgend drainage scheme. William Lawson, grazier, was in Whitockbrae. Mrs. Holt got 13/6 for food and lodgings to tramps sent to her house by Armadale Police.

William Cruikshanks of Barbauchlaw Mains became registered under the Dairies Act, as were Leckie, miner, who lived at Heatherfield, Smith of Tarrareoch and Sinclair who was in Cowdenhead.

On 29th March 1889, a photographer visited the school and took photographs of all the children. On 2nd April, 1889, the Inspector called and reported on three schools - Mixed (Junior Standard), Infant and Evening. Mixed school subjects - arithmetic, dictation, reading, mental arithmetic, sums, handwriting, composition, pronunciation, reading, Latin, French, German, agriculture, physical geography, domestic economy, history, geography, grammar, music, needlework and drawing.

14-01-89: James Wood appealed; one appeal refers to Hopetoun Coal (and Ballencrieff). Hopetoun estate seems to have bought over Ballencrieff estate. Mr. X.'s ash-pit and two privies in filthy condition and not cleaned out for eight or nine months. Burgh death rate down from 19 to 14 per 1000 population. The Burgh's bellman to go through the Burgh giving notice to ratepayers of the appointment of a new Collector; Burgh Rates to be paid to him without delay. Burgh to meet cost of a funeral of a girl, Caroline Black, who died in North Street (the Inspector of the Poor was involved). The Burgh paid Poor Rates of £1.4/2.
11-02-89: The Clerk to order a wagon of sand from Musselburgh for filter for £1.1/-.
12-03-89: Balance of debt paid by Mr. B.'s cautioner.
01-04-89: Building plan submitted by Henry Mungall of West Main Street.
08-04-89: The Sanitary Inspector reported that a few back premises need attention, several ash-pits need cleaned, footpaths need ashes and level gutters, where water lying stagnant, need re-laid to fall.
13-05-89: Account from gas company passed for supplying 28 lamps at 9/- each, £12.12/-
10-06-89: Duncan Livingstone's cesspool now satisfactory. Laidlaw, pavior, to start work at Armadale Station.
08-07-89: Complaint re offensive smells from two cesspools in North Street and T.'s Land needs more ash-pit and privy accommodation. There was an epidemic of scarlet fever. Lodging house in state of cleanliness, cowsheds in fair condition. During first six months of 1889, 85 births (including 8 illegitimate), 28 deaths and 10 marriages. During May and June, c.30 cases of scarlet fever (2 died). A cutting had been made from South to North Pond. Plans in from Co-op for two-storey tenement. Collector to call on owners of property for payment of water supply in Mill Road Street, North Street and Beeches, all outwith Burgh.
29-07-89: Rates brought in, £98+ (water), £95+ (police), £31+ (lighting), £29+ (sanitary). Total expenditure, £257.0/3. Total income, £255.17/6.
12-08-89: Circular from Edinburgh Merchants' Association re dormant and unclaimed bank accounts, Parliament to be petitioned. Robert Storrie of Drummond's Land appointed lamplighter at £7.10/- per annum for one season only. Account passed to Dr. Anderson for disinfectant, £2.6/6.

16-09-89: Circular from National Society for Prevention of Cruelty to Children.

24-09-89: Gas supplied to street lamps to cost 9/6 per lamp. The manager of the National Telephone Co. Ltd. asked permission to erect a line of poles along the south side of Main Street, poles to be removed on three months notice. Commissioners rejected request and suggested that poles be erected at back of feus. Summons to be served on W.M., dairyman, Marches, re supply of water for his cows for the past four years.

14-10-89: Assessment to be 1/4 in £1, same as previous year, cows, etc. as before. New Bathville water pump to cost £4.

28-10-89: At electors meeting, six were nominated for four seats.

11-11-89: Account passed for election ballot papers, £1.2/6. The Finance Committee were given powers to borrow £30 or £40 to tide them over till the assessment came in.

21-11-89: Rates Appeal Court - Mr. Mungall said he does not use the water for his pony, several claimed inability to pay. The question of the ability of the scavenger to do his work properly, through old age, was delayed for further consideration.

West Main Street
looking west from Armadale Cross

Kerr family of Armadale taken in 1900 - the author's ancestors

1890's

Robert Muir and Co. owned Barbauchlaw Fireclay Works from the 1890's until 1939-45, makers of building bricks.

1890

c.1890, Hibs were guests at Armadale.

Volunteer Park

13-01-90: The road leading to the Marches was considered dangerous to foot passengers. The Sanitary Inspector's report was very favourable although a number of footpaths needed ashes. Dairies and cowsheds were clean and cattle healthy, the Lodging House was fairly clean. One case in the Burgh of scarlet fever, several cases of influenza. Of 63 deaths during 1889, 26 were under one year, and 12 between one year and five years old.

10-02-90: Top of well at Cross was knocked off, also a pipe in the slaughterhouse was running night and day. Burgh water analysed, found to be not too hard, free from iron and lead, very pure, suitable for domestic use.

07-03-90: An assistant scavenger at 12/- weekly was to be considered. It was agreed to lay the south part of Academy Street (Bullion Brae) with blaes. Plans submitted for buildings in North Street by John Russell, fruiterer, and in Academy Street, by Blades and Stirling.

01-04-90: The scavenger and the man offered the assistant's job, both at 12/- weekly, demanded 14/- per week. The Commissioners decided both were to be offered 13/- and, if they turned job down, Burgh to advertise for a new scavenger at 22/- per week.

14-04-90: One case of measles in Burgh. Rev. McLachlan, owner of property at or in the Marches, to be told to get his road repaired. James Wood explained to the Commissioners the scheme proposed by Airdrie and Coatbridge concerning the diverting of Forest Burn and its tributaries. Mr. Forrester, tinsmith, was engaged to do repairs at the pleasure of the Commissioners. Four applications for position of scavenger (at 22/-weekly) the Burgh engaged two who offered to work together at 13/- each. They were Messrs. Storrie (former scavenger) and Donnelly. Plans were submitted from Robert Fleming for building at Quality Row.

12-05-90: Four Mossend residents (who lived outside Burgh) were warned that, as they refuse to pay for water, they will be prosecuted if they are found using it.

05-07-90: The Commissioners met Mr. Hope of Bridgecastle and the County Clerk re submission of Petition to the House of Lords opposing the Airdrie and Coatbridge Water Bill.

14-07-90: The Burgh was advised to find a proper place for depositing rubbish. In the following properties in the Burgh ash-pits were found to be too full and filthy - Jeffrey's Land, McLachlan's Land, Russell's Row, Balderston's, Wilson's, Russell's Square, White's, Marshall's, Livingstone's Land, Scott's Land, Anderson's Land, Alexander's Land, Laurieston's Land, Tweedie's Land, Pow's Land, Martin's Land, Brown's Land and Edward's Land. Mrs. T. refused to move her pigsty, which is too near an adjoining house. Two cases of scarlet fever reported and several cases of whooping cough. Death rate down to 16 per 1000. The County Clerk asked the Commissioners if they would co-operate with other local authorities in Linlithgowshire in getting a water supply with pressure to rise to highest parts of the Burgh and with enough water to extinguish a fire. Burgh account to be transferred from the Royal Bank, Bathgate to the recently opened Commercial Bank in Armadale.

23-07-90: Other places found to be unsanitary were Hutton's Land, Rennie's Land, Holt's and McDonald's. Commissioners agreed to ask James Wood to represent them in the House of Lords in opposition to the Airdrie and Coatbridge water scheme. (Commissioner Andrew Graham dissented saying he was to appear as a witness on the other side)

28-07-90: A public meeting was called to learn the views of the inhabitants on the Airdrie and Coatbridge water scheme, there was near unanimous opposition to the scheme.

11-08-90: Rev. Joseph Druce of St Paul's Episcopal Church attended meeting to discuss the problems at the Marches - the Earl of Hopetoun, as superior of land to east of burn, had offered 18" pipes to culvert in the whole length of the burn and Mr. Druce requested two additional street lamps. As the burn was the March (boundary) between Hopetoun and Barbauchlaw, Mr. Druce was advised to approach Mr. Readman of Barbauchlaw re sharing cost of culvert, etc.. There was a scarcity of water in Burgh on account of a plug having been taken out of a pipe at the filter and a sluice taken away from South Pond. The Burgh to offer £1 reward for information leading to a conviction. Clerk to ask the Gas Board - cost to supply gas to 28 lamps, cost to supply an additional nine lamps and cost per meter and discount.

25-08-90: Nine new street lamps to be erected.

01-09-90: Two offers in for erecting nine street lamps complete with globe fittings and seated on a whinstone block – A. Hutton, £2.13/6 and A. Forrester, £2.7/6. Two lamplighters engaged for the season at £10.10/-.

10-09-90: Captain Hope of Bridgecastle and James Wood of Bathville met Commissioners re proposed new water scheme. All Commissioners were agreeable to get the Forestburn water provided water rates wouldn't exceed 6d in £1.

29-09-90: Mr. Russell apparently couldn't get any farmer or carter to take away the contents of his ash-pit at Russell's Row. Account passed for broom-heads, 10/2.

13-10-90: Sanitary Inspector and Medical Officer reported several problems needing attention - several proprietors were unable to get anybody to take away ashes, scavenger needed a depot, there was a cesspool in North Street, seven gutters were very filthy, there were too few privies, the Medical Officer recommended a slaughterhouse and Burgh butchers were to empty their dungsteads more frequently as very bad smells were allegedly dangerous to public health. A request came from R. Flemington asking Commissioners to point out track for cribbing and a right-of-way for his sewage.

29-10-90: The Commissioners decided not to send a deputation to Edinburgh re roads and streets of Police Burghs of Scotland. Rates were fixed as previous year, 1/5 in £1.

24-11-90: The Commissioners concerned how appointment of County Sanitary Inspector would affect position of their own Inspector.

04-12-90: Rates Appeal Court - one from Rev. Druce re parsonage, six people exempt including five widows and four ratepayers from Bathville appealed on grounds they had no water. Postmaster to pay for premises occupied by the Volunteers, £3 to be taken off rental for Armoury.

1891

Inspector reported that a large number of vagrants reside at No.8 (Heatherfield) Pit.

12-01-91: Midlothian, West Lothian and Peebles were considering the same medical officer. Lodging Houses fairly well kept.

09-02-91: The School Board proposed erecting a new infant school after which the Subscription School would be sold. Automatic delivery machine for the sale of postage stamps and cards to be fixed at Bathville and at the Cross. County Road Surveyor was told of heaps of dirt on the street of Armadale lying for weeks.

18-03-91: The Commissioners decided not to use or pay for the service of the newly created Sanitary Inspector for the County as they have a Sanitary Inspector of their own. James Wood represented the Burgh on the County Council. Mrs. Thomson to move her pigsty court to the west side of her property. The County Council to be asked to take over Academy Street as a highway.

13-04-91: Whinstones in front of the pall-house to be removed as they are dangerous to foot passengers after dark. As ash-pits overflow and owners are unable to get farmers to drive them away, the Sanitary Inspector recommended that some other method of cleaning be adopted. The Burgh to look for a place to deposit ashes and to meet the following evening at the Wee Burn.

11-05-91: The convener of the Sanitary Committee reported that a coup for ashes had been obtained at Barbauchlaw Road leading to No.15 Pit. Ash-pit owners to be given seven days to clear away their ashes. County Road Inspector to be asked to remove the scrapings from the street at North Street.

09-06-91: Estimate to be obtained for kerb and gutter in Academy Street and elsewhere.

19-06-91: During a time of scarcity of water, water to be sought from No.17 Pit.

13-07-91: The Medical Officer reported that, considering the unsanitary state of the Burgh, the death rate (18.2 per 1000) is low with one case of scarlet fever; new water track to convey water from No.17 Pit to South Pond by pump; and Clerk to find out the cost of a Clyde Steam Pump with steam throttle and also a 12" suction pipe.

10-08-91: Cost to Burgh of new water supply from No.17 Pit, £86.9/7. Burgh received £8.5/6 as residue tax under Local Taxation Act of 1890.

08-09-91: An advert for a lamplighter to go in Courier and two notices in shops. Issues dealt with included - cost of gas supply to street lamps, South Pond water and supply from No.17 Pit, Mill Road improvement, sewage pipes, footpath blaes, kerbing and guttering.

14-09-91: Thomas Sanderson became the Burgh's new lamplighter. Filter to be fenced in with railway sleepers.

12-10-91: Several cases of measles, one of typhoid fever. Burgh to get a new hand bell.

20-10-91: Mr. Wood explained that the new county water scheme would result in Armadale getting a good supply of water. Commissioners agreed to apply to the County for the supply of water on condition that rates are no more than 1/- in £1 or 4d per 1000 gallons.

21-10-91: Meeting attended by Messrs. Hope, Stuart, and Wood of the District Committee of the County Council - Mr. Wood said filter and tank would be erected at Stanerig Farm, cost to Burgh to be no more than 4d per 1000 gallons or 1/- in £1. Burgh Rates as previous year - 1/5 in £1.

26-10-91: Letter from James Wood of Bathville House - "During my residence here I have observed the want the town of Armadale and neighbourhood has of a field for recreation and a hall for lectures, concerts and other public entertainment. With a view to remedying this want, I give the field west of the bowling green for the purpose of a Public Park and recreation ground". That same evening, the ratepayers of Armadale (who probably knew beforehand of this generous offer) met and received the news with applause and a vote of thanks was tendered to Mr. Wood and Lord Hopetoun.

09-10-91: Messrs. McNab, Marshall and Sneddon were elected Commissioners, Adam Wilson became Provost / Chief Commissioner, Grant Chalmers became Senior Baillie and Andrew Graham became Junior Baillie.

09-11-91: Measles and typhoid fever prevalent, parts of the Burgh were unsanitary - Marches ditch, gutters, privies and a ditch to the north of East Main Street. A large accumulation of cow manure was in front of Muirhead's dairy.

03-11-91: Rates Appeal Court - six widows were exempt from rates, nine other applicants mainly exempt. A letter came from Independent Order of the Good Templars Excelsior Lodge requesting that licensed premises close on New Years Day. Burgh water analysis showed no lead, a little oxide of iron and was judged fairly good.

1892

The Burgh of Armadale's coup was at No.15 Pit, Barbauchlaw, opposite the entrance to Barbauchlaw Mains Farm. Brown Brothers' shop was broken into. James Brown of Polkemmet Rows had chronic bronchitis. David Dunn died. In January, ash-pits were reckoned to be injurious to public health because they were close to houses. Cow manure at the Marches has not yet been removed.

One case of typhoid fever and a few cases of influenza. A report by Inspecting Officer of Board of Supervisors was very critical as there were several serious sanitary defects to be remedied without delay. Apparently, one scavenger had died and the other was laid up. James Douglas was appointed scavenger at 15/- weekly. The Burgh got £13.12/6 from the Government towards Medical Officer and Sanitary Inspector for 1891.

08-02-92: Drain running into field between McAlpine's and Mill Road needs piped as ground to be built on.

14-03-92: Marches ditch to be filled in for about £100, the cost was eventually shared between the two March estate owners i.e.

Hopetoun and Barbauchlaw Estates and the Burgh (also possibly the Parochial Board or District Council).

28-03-92: Culvert at the Marches to be cleaned out.

11-04-92: An advert for a Burgh Scavenger, whose wages to be 25/- a week to go into the Herald, Scotsman, Courier and Airdrie Advertiser. Bathville water tank problem, new wells to be erected at Mill Road and Academy Street. Burgh got a cheque from Secretary for Scotland for £18.18/11 being a grant towards rates. Burgh Clerk's salary increased by £5 per annum.

22-04-92: Three applications for post of Burgh Scavenger - Joseph Paul, Armadale, Alex Lister, Musselburgh, and George Milne, Midlothian Asylum, Roslyn Castle, Edinburgh. All three to be interviewed, the two from the east to get 5/- expenses. Steps taken for road at Marches (to St Paul's Episcopal Church) to be added to the list of highways. Account paid for supply of gas to 37 Burgh lamps, £18.10/-.

02-05-92: Joseph Paul new scavenger. Cleansing committee to see Mrs. Thomson of Thomson's Land about relaying kerb and gutter and ascertaining what she intends to do about the matter. Application to erect a new building at North Street (from Mrs. Smith) turned down because a drain runs under site.

09-05-92: Burgh to lay pipes and cesspool at Thomson's Land at Mrs. Thomson's expense. By letter, A McD. told the Commissioners to do their duty in removing of dust, ashes, dung, rubbish and privy matter (in terms of the Burgh Act). The Clerk, in replying, referred Mr. McD to nuisances' clauses of an Act of Parliament. A property-owner, Mrs. Marr of South Street, threatened to evict her tenants if the commoners didn't organise the removing of their ashes. She was told that ashes removal was her responsibility. A representative is to meet Messrs. Wood and Hope re site for promised hall.

13-05-92: Burgh to consider providing an isolation hospital because of typhoid fever in Armadale. Apparently, three members of the same North Street family were down with typhoid fever and two of them died, this family thereafter received 8/- per week of Poor Relief. Commissioners were annoyed at being told by Bathgate Parish Board to build an isolation hospital when they hadn't one to cope with their own cases of typhoid. They agreed for Mr. Wood to represent the Burgh and meet the County Clerk to make arrangements re hospital accommodation.

13-06-92: George Plant and his wife went down with typhoid fever and received 10/- relief per week.

11-07-92: The Sanitary Inspector reported that M.'s byre at the Marches is a complete wreck. Two families in East Main Street are affected with measles and scarlet fever. Commissioners learned of a jump in the death rate to 26.3 per 1000 largely due to large mortality rate of infants under one year. Several cases of scarlet fever, influenza, whooping cough and measles. Mr. Wood produced plans of a Public Hall to be erected by him on west side of South Street.

01-08-92: Eight Burgh property-owners to be told to kerb and gutter their footpaths - Messrs. Weir, Anderson, Love, Sprott, McGarrity, Wilson, Bishop and Mrs. Martin. Kerb and gutter to be laid in North Street from Walker's to entrance of No.12 Pit. Commissioners were warned of a countrywide outbreak of cholera and told to promote cleanliness.

22-08-92: The Commissioners learned of Allotments Act by which persons belonging to the labouring population who are desirous to hold land for cultivation may receive facilities, etc..

05-09-92: It would appear that Dr. Anderson has been overworked lately because he is said to be considering resigning as Medical Officer. Constable Malcolm Corsie was appointed new Sanitary Inspector at £7 per annum, Thomas Sanderson new lamplighter at £10.10/- per annum.

10-10-92: Committee chosen to look into the question of a new slaughterhouse for the Burgh; a square lamp to be erected at the Cross, the old one being transferred to Academy Street; a Public Steelyard to be considered for the Burgh; rates were fixed, as before, at 1/5 in £1, cows, etc. as before.

07-11-92: After annual elections, committee elected for planning applications as well as for finance, sanitary, water and lighting. John Frew, Sanitary Inspector for the County, to also be Sanitary Inspector for the Burgh at £3 p.a.; County Clerk to be asked for up to date position re new (Forestburn) water scheme; and roads trustees to be told of disgraceful state of Burgh roads.

01-12-92: Rates Appeal Court - six people were exempted through inability to pay, twelve other applicants were refused including the occupiers of Etna Cottages, Bathville. (Several ownerships and tenancies had changed hands during the year and rates assessments amended accordingly)

02-12-92: Account passed to T. Brown and Co., shoemakers, leather for pump at Bathville, 10/3.

1893

c.1893-1906+, George Readman owned Barbauchlaw Estate. Thomas Harvie was occupier of Barbauchlaw Mill. Meetings of the Commissioners took place in the Subscription Schoolroom. George McCallum, a tinker in Perth, was born in an old quarry near Armadale. Robert Martin of Bathville died. In 1893, when a rail line was laid in Western Australia, a carpenter from Armadale (Ishmael Rodgers) named the rail stopping-place 'Armadale'.

09-01-93: The Provost / Chairman was Adam Wilson, Junior Baillie was Robert McNab, the Senior Baillie was William Marshall, the other six Commissioners were John Russell, William Grant Chalmers, James Hailstones, Thomas Snedden, Thomas Robertson and Malcolm Mallace. During the last six months of 1892, there were 76 births, 13 marriages and 28 deaths (17.55 per 1000). In the Burgh, there was little sickness and no infectious diseases. A map of the Burgh, showing drainage, to be revised by a Burntisland civil engineer; the Burgh got a grant of £7.14/5 from the Government to go towards cost of Medical Officer and Sanitary Inspector; A. McDonald's kerb and gutter account was reduced; and two defaulters were told to pay accounts re kerb and gutter or face additional expenses; Hugh Smith of Bathville Row was exempted from paying Burgh rates on grounds of inability to pay.
13-02-93: *(meetings were now being held monthly)* The cost and site of a public slaughterhouse were being looked into. Thomas Harvie of Barbauchlaw Mill complained about Burgh sewage discharging on to one of his fields. In response to a call for cholera precautions recommended by the Board of Supervision, the Burgh to arrange temporary accommodation in case of epidemic. Account passed for payment to John Shearer, blacksmith, Armadale, £2.3/-.
13-03-93: Dewar of Armadale won contract to remove sewage at 2/6 per chain of 22 yards (the Burgh to holdback 10% retention).
13-03-93: Mr. Ferrier of Birkenshaw complained to Sanitary Inspector re water and sewage running on to his field from East Main Street.
27-03-93: Burgh to pay Mr. Verrier £2.12/- for the use of the old Pale House as a tool house.
10-04-93: Mr. W to be told that his ash-pit and privy at Mount Pleasant are in a filthy state; as are the privies in Quality Row; Mrs. T. to put doors on her privies; and James M. to erect necessaries and

dungstead for his tenants in South Street. Other problems before the Commissioners - footpath at Mossend Cottages, Dr. Anderson's water closet drains were choked and a piped drain to be laid on north side of East Main Street for £67.6/4.

08-05-93: John Black, teacher at Public School, to audit Burgh accounts; Commissioners learned that Police Burghs of Forfarshire and Lanarkshire do not contribute to County Officials' salaries; account passed for gas supply to 37 street lamps, £18.10/-.

18-05-93: James Thomson was reappointed Clerk with John Simpson Treasurer and Collector and John Black, Auditor; Dr. John Anderson, Medical Officer; John Frew, Sanitary Inspector and Joseph Paul, Scavenger. The Provost and Baillie Marshall were authorised to sign cheques with Treasurer countersigned by the Clerk. A meeting is to take place re supply of water from Forest Burn. Philip Kerr and Walter Ross to pay half year's assessment only.

22-05-93: James Wood as District Councillor and C. Allan, solicitor, attended meeting regarding water supply. Meeting discussed –

1) Powers to lease supply.
2) Collecting of water assessment.
3) Existing Burgh plant and piping.
4) Length of contract.

27-06-93: Mr. Allan, solicitor, to draw out a draft agreement on water supply for Commissioners to consider. Accounts passed for legal costs of a prosecution case, £1.13/8, purchase of a book on the Government of a Burgh, £1.5/-.

10-07-93: A pump well was erected opposite Love's property in South Street; the Burgh bought a truck of Arran sand for filter. During the first six months of 1893, 93 births, 11 marriages and 34 deaths (death rate 21.2 per 1000 population, down from 26.2 in 1892), two mild cases of scarlet fever; ash-pits, privies and streets fairly clean. A circular came from Govan Town Clerk re licensing of public houses. Clerk to seek information from James Wood re gift of public hall he promised two years ago. Dickson & Mann of Bathville Steel Works to be told they could be fined up to £5 for starting to build houses before they had been given planning approval. John Sinclair, farmer, Cowdenhead got £1.5/- damages.

14-08-93: Dungstead and privy on south side of West Main Street attached to Joseph B.'s property were declared a nuisance and dangerous to health; R.'s property in South Street was filthy; Mr. N., grocer, South Street, to provide ash-pit and privy and to stop the practise of throwing straw and rubbish over the railing on to the public street; Mrs. T. to put doors on privies at once or build a blind wall; John M., fruiterer, West Main Street, to clean out his privy and ash-pit more regularly and the dungstead in connection with the slaughterhouse which was a very offensive nuisance. Several proprietors to remove the rank grass growing in front of their properties; Burgh lamps and globe to be painted; Burgh to look into the cost and site for a Public Steelyard. A committee to consider draft document on supply of water from Forestburn. James Wood, by letter, stated that it is unsafe to build a Public Hall on the proposed site until the ground has settled after coal is worked out. He is communicating with Lord Hopetoun's agent re Public Park.

14-08-93: A complaint came from Mr. Wood saying that sewage from Bathville and Etna Cottages is discharging into pond at Mr. Robertson's house; Burgh to be constantly vigilant in case of epidemic of cholera.

11-09-93: The bond of agreement re the Forestburn water scheme on the following provisions - supply was for domestic, trading, manufacturing and other purposes, 25 gallons per head could be supplied, County Council to be responsible for upkeep of Burgh's pipes and street wells, Burgh be given the value of existing wells and pipes. Gas supply to street lamps for next year to cost 10/- per lamp. Six offers came in for position of Burgh Lamplighter, Thomas Sanderson was given the job of lighting lamps and cleaning globes for season for £10.10/-. The Burgh received two Government grants - one of £11.2/10, the other (for education) of £49.17/7. (The total, £61.0/5, was to be applied for relief of local rates) A No.6 burner needed for lamp at the Cross. During scarcity, the Burgh water supply to be augmented from Pit No.17. Provost Adam Wilson resigned, being unable to give the duties the attention they require. This year's annual meeting of ratepayers was to be advertised in the Courier and by hand bell.

30-10-93: The rates assessment from Whitsunday 1893 to Whitsunday 1894 to be - water, 6d, police, 6d, lighting, 3d and sanitary, 2d, giving a total of 1/5 in £1.

10-11-93: First meeting of the Commissioners after annual elections. The three new Commissioners elected included two of the same name - Robert Smith, (one was a miner of Boyd's Land, the other was a miner of 58 West Main Street) the third elected was James Bryden, draper. The new Provost to be Thomas Robertson; Senior Baillie, James Hailstones and Junior Baillie, Thomas Snedden. Committees were appointed on water, cleansing, lighting and finance. An account was passed to Robert Edwards, tinsmith, £5.6/8. Lamps were needed at Etna Cottages and Mill Road Street. Robert A., spirit merchant, to be told to wash his machine elsewhere as water used flows down in front of houses in Martin's Land and causes a nuisance. Commissioners to visit Forestburn.

29-11-93: Issue considered by Commissioners - four new lamps at Etna Cottage and one at Mill Road, Marches street lamps, slaughterhouse and West Main Street drain; bank overdraft of £100. The Burgh agreed to meet part of the cost of the Court case re licensing powers with conditions.

14-12-93: Account to Mr. Hutton, tinsmith, for five new Burgh street lamps, £16.1/-. Dungsteads needed for John A., flesher and others. Right-of-way to slaughterhouse required; and the Burgh Scavenger made application for a waterproof coat. The Burgh considered the provision of a steelyard. Five appeals against rates were exempted on the grounds of inability to pay, four were refused and a decision on a further seven was delayed.

1894

Mr. Readman of Barbauchlaw Estate sold ground to Armadale Burgh to build a slaughterhouse.

08-01-94: A letter was sent from the Sanitary Inspector to Mr. Anderson anent his property. There was a case of whooping cough. Three Armadale fleshers made recommendations re proposed slaughterhouse; Balderston's trustees were approached re entrance to slaughterhouse; and Commissioners to visit slaughterhouses in Linlithgow etc.; Commissioners met an Airdrie architect to discuss slaughterhouse; privies and ash-pits need increased attention; non-domestic water rates were pegged at previous years prices, i.e. 1/6 for cows etc.; Commissioners, in reply to an enquiry from the Secretary for Scotland, said there was no demand for allotments in Armadale; Armadale Coal Co. received £11.5/8 for pumping water into town's reservoir; Commissioners were authorised to put up a steelyard in the Burgh; Dickson & Mann to give a list of occupiers of their new dwelling houses (Etna Cottages) and William Stewart, flesher, to pay for six month's supply of water to his cows. Widow Steel's assessment also reduced to six months.

12-01-94: The Burgh received £20 from District Committee of County Council towards drain in East Main Street. The Commissioners were not happy with the proposed Forestburn scheme agreement. To Robert Edwards, tinsmith, £1.1/-. All houses in Armadale to get their street number fixed to each house costing the Burgh 8d per dozen letters. Slaughterhouse to cost £700 to build; it was discovered that the proposed Burgh slaughterhouse would be outside the Burgh Boundary, the building was to go ahead and the Commissioners later to arrange to extend the northern boundary. Muir, Armadale, won the contract to build the slaughterhouse brickwork, and other contractors were from Airdrie, Chapelhall and Whitburn. Burgh to appoint a Burgh Surveyor; £700 to be borrowed for Slaughterhouse, upon the Security of the Burgh General Assessment.
09-04-94: Mr. Baird, architect, Airdrie, was appointed Burgh Surveyor. His first duties were to survey new drain for Bathville and add on to the plan of the Burgh all houses built since 1879.
12-04-94: Sinclair of Cowdenhead claimed £6.3/4 damages to his fields from Burgh pond overflow, settled for £4.10/- after a dispute.
15-04-94: Account passed for gas to 40 lamps, £20.
07-05-94: Scottish Legal Insurance Society to lend £700 to Burgh at 3¾% repayable over 25 years. Dr. Anderson, West Main Street, submitted a building plan.
22-05-94: Mr. Aitken, solicitor, Glasgow, attended meeting as law agent for Barbauchlaw Estate and re loan. Commissioners heard the slaughterhouse ground feu disposition read out giving description of ground needed for slaughterhouse, ground area was 1 Rood, 39 poles, and 23 square yards. The ground was sold to the Burgh by Mr. Readman, owner of Barbauchlaw Estate, with burdens including –

1) Ground for slaughterhouse only (and nothing else);
2) Reserving rights to ironstone, freestone and other minerals;
3) Burgh to erect a brick or stone wall or sleeper fence round feu;
4) £8 feu duty, £4 paid at Martinmas and at Whitsunday;
5) Burgh to pay a penalty if feu duty not paid punctually;
6) £4 to be paid every 21 years;
7) Tenant of Barbauchlaw to get a right-of-way access to horse park.

Mr. Aitken also produced a bond and assignation re £700 loan, the bond describes the slaughterhouse buildings as "shambles and slaughter-house", loan to be paid back in twenty-five annual instalments of £43.12/8. Provost Robertson, who was leaving Armadale, resigned.

05-06-94: William Marshall became the new Provost. Mrs. R. to clean her ash-pit and privy.

11-06-94: An Edinburgh firm to supply crans and ironwork at slaughterhouse, Burgh to ask North British Railway Co. to grant the same privilege to Armadale (as Bathgate) in respect or reduced fares to Glasgow at weekends.

25-06-94: A job of superintendent for slaughterhouse at 10/- per week to be advertised; Sanitary Inspector's salary increased to £8 per annum.

02-07-94: Steelyard to be erected and a five year agreement entered into with Daniel Brownlee as weigher to be paid 1d for each cartload weighed.

09-07-94: James A. to remove the refuse he put into the Burgh magazine at once; drains (in future) to be shown on plans of all proposed new buildings; death rate of 14.54 per 1000 was reckoned to be the lowest ever recorded in the history of the Burgh and sheep racks and sheep stools to be supplied to slaughterhouse. A defective drain opposite Daniel Archer, stationer, was reported.

27-07-94: From this date, the Burgh minutes were now recorded in different handwriting after thirty years of the same handwriting. The Burgh got a government grant of £55+. A grievance complained by Mill Road Street tenants to be remedied by party complained against. Enamelled name plates to be fixed at Burgh street corners; the Crown Hotel got 10/6 for providing dinner to witnesses at a court case.

06-08-94: All hides and skins to be removed from slaughterhouse twice a week in summer and weekly in winter; Burgh to join with County Council in providing a Combination Hospital (to isolate cases of cholera etc.); all new drains to incorporate traps; and public weighing-machine established at Daniel Brownlee's dairy premises in West Main Street.

17-08-94: John Frew, Sanitary Inspector, to be appointed inspector under Food and Drug Act; five tons of moss to be bought for slaughterhouse bedding purposes.

10-09-94: John Rankine new lamplighter at £9.10/- for season. Rob Edwards to supply and fix street nameplates for £3.

08-10-94: Mr. Verrier's offer to put up a gold street nameplate on his property was accepted; Bathgate District Committee of the County Council offered to take Armadale cholera patients in temporary hospital for a small weekly charge. John Forsyth, joiner, to erect weigh-house for £7.4/7. Water to be charged for in new buildings - Infant School, Academy Street, Dr. Anderson's, Adam McLean's and

William Drummond's. The Cross to get two incendiary lamps to replace two square lamps. Account paid to Pooley & Son for weigh machine, £19.10/-. Agreement between Bathgate District Committee of the County Council and Burgh Commissioners re new Forestburn water supply in a 99 year agreement; ratepayers to pay through rates, interest and annual instalments of borrowed sum. The District Committee to take over the Burgh's street wells and water pipes for £150, up to 25 gallons per head per day, provision was made for supply during times of scarcity or future excessive demand or for manufacturing or trading premises; Burgh reservoirs to be taken over by District Council and Burgh relieved of feu duty, agreement signed by representatives of each local authority, also by Thomas Hope, M.P. and chairman of Bathgate District Council.

22-10-94: Problem kerb and gutters at North Street and West End; Bathville drainage problem; scavenger to get overcoat (17/6).

26-10-94: Provost Marshall to represent the Burgh at a conference where the number of County Councillors for each Parish and Burgh to be fixed.

09-11-94: New elected Commissioners were William Hunter, William Grant Chalmers, William Marshall and John Forsyth. Committees were appointed for water, sanitary / cleansing, gas / lighting, slaughterhouse, building plans and finance. Hides to be removed from slaughterhouse within 48 hours in summer and twice a week in winter; a fairly extensive Bathville drainage scheme was being considered; Burgh to buy five tons of German litter from Leith for the slaughterhouse.

12-11-94: First water rate, imposed by the County Council, to be 3d in £1 which would bring in £62.2/- less collection charge. Annual rates - water, 6d, police, 7d, lighting, 3d and sanitary, 2d, total 1/6 in £1.

26-11-94: While the meeting held on 12th November was described in the minutes as meeting of Commissioners, the meeting of 26th November did not mention Commissioners, the minutes said meeting in Subscription School. The Burgh to send three councillors to the meetings of the County Council and, from about this date, the Commissioners of Armadale were designated Councillors, the Burgh claimed four Councillors instead of three (on basis of population). There were delays in newly built houses in the Burgh getting an occupation certificate, allegedly because the Burgh Surveyor lived in Airdrie. One Councillor was to propose that the Burgh Surveyor should live in Armadale but he withdrew the motion. Account passed to Bathgate Foundry Co. for street gully, £2.10/-; another to J. Shaw for renumbering houses, £4.4/9.

10-12-94: Two more gullies to be ordered from Bathgate Foundry Co.; Amelia B.'s ash-pits and privies in East Main Street were in a deplorable state. A lighting rod to be bought for the lamplighter; traps to be added to drains at Beveridge's and Calder's.

14-12-94: An Inspector of Works to be employed to supervise Bathville drainage contract. Accounts passed to Armadale Coal Co. for pumping water, £4; also to Mr. King, farmer, for privilege of taking sewer drain through his land, £3.

26-12-94: Of nine offers received re Bathville drainage contract, six came from Airdrie, one each from Motherwell, Bo'ness and Uphall. Armadale was successful in applying for four Councillors on the County Council to represent Burgh.

1895

Councillor John Wilson of Armadale was a member of the new Parish Council, which replaced the old Parochial Board; a five man Landward Committee was formed.

16-05-95: There were several Armadale people on the seventeen person Parish Council, these Armadale councillors were transported to Bathgate meetings by hired 'machine'; Jane Pake, or Morgan, East Main Street, Armadale, suffered from paralyses; Agnes Brown, or Young, who was James Livingstone's housekeeper at the Marches took pneumonia and went into the poorhouse.

14-01-95: James G., dairyman, to stop the practise of pegging the handles of the pump and thus allowing water to run waste. During 1894, 162 births, 23 marriages and 50 deaths, 15.67 deaths per annum per 1000 (18 of these deaths were under one year old, 31 of the 50 deaths were under 15 years old).

17-01-95: Rates Appeal Court: seven people were exempted from paying rates - Mrs. Baxter, Boner, Russell, Duncan and Simpson, also Messrs. Simpson and Middleton; Thomas Dobbie, baker, to pay for one oven instead of two; bye-laws concerning the new slaughterhouse arrived from London.

21-01-95: Meeting held within the Clerk's room. Slaughterhouse to open on 28th January, fleshers who continue to slaughter cattle elsewhere than in the "said slaughterhouse" would be under penalty of £5. James Gillon was appointed Inspector of Works re Bathville drainage at 4/2 per day; secretary to write Secretary of the Thistle and Olive Lodges for terms of a £200 loan on security of Burgh Rates; a notice of Commissioners' decision to go in the Courier.

28-01-95: A. McD. pleaded ignorance in respect of a hall that he had converted into two houses without the consent of the Commission; the Treasurer to square with the superintendent weekly, re slaughtering dues.

05-02-95: New slaughterhouse superintendent resigned.

08-02-95: Alex Fulton became new slaughterhouse superintendent at 12/- week.

18-02-95: The Clerk to write to the Secretary of the Olive Lodge of the Free Gardeners requesting loan of £150 at 3½% in place of £400 at 4%; Clerk also to write Secretary of the Thistle Lodge of Free Gardeners about proposed changes to a current loan interest; account for Burgh map passed for payment, £1.1/6; a meeting of the elders of the Burgh to be held to consider the provisions of the Parish Council Act.

22-03-95: Mr. Neil, contractor for District Council of the County Council agreed to erect additional wells at Mossend, West Main Street and East Main Street; a Burgh committee is to meet with the Landward School Board re state of the road in Academy Street; the Commissioners are looking into the provision of fire plugs. Account passed to John Shearer, blacksmith, for sharpening picks, 10/5.

01-04-95: Mr. Weir's building in West Main Street approved. One of Armadale's fleshers was censured for removing a beast from the slaughterhouse contrary to rules.

03-04-95: Three Commissioners resigned (two later withdrew their resignations); the Inspector of the Poor for the Parish of Bathgate was notified of the four Parish Councillors elected to represent the Burgh, the four elected were J. Archer, J. Beveridge, J. Simpson and J. Wilson.

10-04-95: The meeting was attended by J. Wood of Bathville who explained the site, probable cost and construction of the proposed Combination Hospital. £1.8/- damages were paid out for one sheep that drowned in the South Pond.

24-04-95: Gas bill for supply to 44 street lamps was paid, £22.

03-05-95: It was agreed to hire a brake for the conveyance of the Commissioners to the opening of Forest Burn Water Works; an account approved was re an addition to the Burgh ballot box, 5/-;

James and Christina Thomson, as witnesses, signed a bond re loan of £150 from the Olive Lodge of the Free Gardeners Friendly Society at 3½% interest.

13-05-95: The Clerk to write the Town Clerks of Airdrie and Falkirk for information on butchers who slaughter cattle outside the Burgh boundary; the first account from the new Water Authority to the Burgh was for £58.7/5 for 1894; slaughterhouse manure to be offered for sale, John Baxter of Woodbank to cart it away at 3/- a ton, for a year.

12-06-95: The urinal in Academy Street to be maintained in good order; Mr. A., spirit merchant, South Street, to remove the urinal at his property as it is a nuisance; Commissioners want the new water authority to give three or four hours notice when water being cut off.

12-07-95: The kerb gutter now complete from Currie's to the Beeches and from MacAlpine's to Livingston's. The Medical Officer reported 94 births, 15 marriages and 48 deaths during the first six months of 1895; the 48 deaths included 17 who died under one year; many filthy privies and road gutters, sewers and ash-pits.

02-08-95: An indignation, 'greetin', meeting of the ratepayers is to be held unless the quality of the town's water supply improves.

03-08-95: The Clerk to inform John Baxter of Woodbank Farm to cart the slaughterhouse dung directly home and he doesn't need to go through the town to the weighbridge; the lamplighters wages fixed at £12 for season; J. Wood gave £15 towards Bathville sewer.

10-09-95: The slaughterhouse superintendent was dismissed, John Cook became the new superintendent. A cemetery for Armadale is being considered, also cholera precautions.

14-10-95: The Burgh was given £150 from the new water authority for the Burgh's wells and pipes, ponds, etc..

25-10-95: 1895-1896 rates set - water, 1/2, police, 7d, lighting, 3d and public health, 2d, total, 2/2 in £1. It was learned that the School Board is to sell the Subscription School.

07-11-95: The three new Commissioners elected were - James Archer, 55 South Street, James Beveridge, 2 Mill Road Street, and William Parker, Woodville Cottages.

08-11-95: Five committees were appointed - sanitary, slaughterhouse, lighting, finance and water.

11-11-95: A meeting was called to consider the purchase of Armadale Subscription School as a Town Hall and Council Chamber; the Commissioners decided to purchase the school; a notice to go in shop windows seeking offers to lift the metal pipes between Armadale Coal Co.'s No.17 Pit and the South Pond.

14-11-95: The Clerk to write the School Board asking if they would "consider the propriety" of kerbing and channelling the pavement in front of the new Infant School.
25-11-95: Six contractors who submitted offers re lifting metal pipes were Walker, Smart, Roberts, McGarrity, Dewar and Sprott; Mr. Sinclair agreed to accept 35/- for surface damage in connection with lifting of pipes from No.17 Pit to South Pond; Clerk's salary to be increased to £22 per annum; James Hailstones, property-owner, to get £2 for way-leave to slaughterhouse over his land.
18-11-95: Rates Appeal Court - an appeal came in re dwelling house connected to the Armoury Store belonging to the Volunteers on the grounds that the Volunteers, being servants of the Queen, the house and store should be exempt. Five widows and a widower were exempt from paying rates, four others were given relief. Thomas Brand flitted to the Marches.

1896

A patient in an Asylum to be boarded out in Bathgate; police to be asked to put a stop to vagrancy lying about Robertson and Love's brickwork and 'begging' the Parish; Council to convey Armadale members to future meetings. Alex Mitchell was a tailor and clothier, of 155 East Main Street. Armadale Daisy reached the County Juvenile Final. Mr. Readman of Barbauchlaw bought the old school in South Street and gifted the building to Armadale Burgh to be used as a Public Hall.

13-01-96: Contractor to get 7/6 extra for conveying pipes to No.15 instead of No.17 Pit. An advert to go into Glasgow Herald re sale of metal pipes and engine, a Motherwell company bought them. Mr. Dickson to be told that all pigs must be slaughtered in the slaughterhouse. Medical Officer reported that during 1895 there were 173 births, 32 marriages and 68 deaths, the death rate was 20.6 per 1000 population. During the year the Burgh "had been visited" by diphtheria, whooping cough and measles; many privies are dirty. The Clerk to write a town butcher asking him to send a written apology for his conduct in the slaughterhouse and for the abusive language to the Provost (the butcher complied); the Subscription School was offered to the Burgh for £150. An engineer was sent for to repair the travelling crane.

29-01-96: A claim was lodged from John Alexander, butcher, against the Commissioners for 4lb of mutton suet value 2/- that was taken from the slaughterhouse.

10-02-96: The Commissioners agreed to buy the Subscription School for £150; the Burgh Architect to produce plans for a Public Hall.

24-02-96: The Burgh no longer needs Mr. Verrier's Tool Room (the old Pale House). Four people, including two farmers, to be told they must use the slaughterhouse for slaughtering all beasts.

09-03-96: In future, plans of all new building work (stone, brick, and wood) to get Commissioners' approval; Messrs. Muir and Co., brick-makers, to submit a plan of a new brickwork in East Main Street; after complaints being considered from tenants who live near slaughterhouse, the manure pit there to be emptied weekly. The Subscription School is falling into disrepair.

20-03-96: The floor to ceiling height of Mr. Wardrop's new building to be 9'6"; superior's approval to be sought re conversion of the old Subscription School into a Public Hall with offices.

24-04-96: James Wood has to submit plans of new scullery and washhouse at Quality Row.

05-05-96: Mr. Wilson of South Street to submit plans of his new attic. A circular was read from the Scotch Education Department.

11-05-96: A new drain to be laid in South and North Streets to take road water; account to Robertson Love for pipes, 11/8.

20-05-96: Water meters being installed. A cow at the slaughterhouse was found to have T.B., so the carcase was burned; £10 set aside for lectures. George Readman, owner of Barbauchlaw Estate, by letter, pointed out that the Subscription School had been built about a generation earlier by subscriptions from mineral tenants, feuars and others on the estate, then was later conveyed to the school board of Bathgate. George Readman then told the Commissioners that he would buy the building and convey it, free of feu duty, to the Commissioners, to be used as a Public Hall, the offer was accepted with sincere thanks.

29-05-96: A farmer to the north of Armadale objected to the new drain taking water from South and North Streets discharging, with town sewage, on to his fields.

09-06-96: Andrew Graham, butcher, was to pay slaughterhouse dues on the beast he slaughtered at Northrigg. The Burgh Engineer was to enquire into the purchase of a fire extinguishing hose similar to the one Carluke Burgh recently acquired. Commissioners decided to pay up to £300 to convert the Subscription School into a Town Hall.

21-07-96: Estimate cost of conversion of Subscription School to Town Hall was £472.12/4; £6000 to be borrowed over 20 years at 3⅛% ; an ornamental malleable iron railing to be erected in front of the Town Hall.

29-07-96: Medical Officer reported 84 births, 9 marriages and 45 deaths during first six months of 1896, 10 died of whooping cough; at a public meeting, it was decided to object strongly to the old road between Mossend and Woodend being shut off.

24-08-96: The offer from Mr. Harvie of 2/3 per cart of slaughterhouse dung was accepted; the Burgh objected to the valuation on the Steelyard being £3.7/-.

15-09-96: The Town Hall floor was lowered by one foot, the vestibule to be tiled.

06-10-96: A scale of charges for use of Public Hall was set; William Stirling applied to use the hall for a Mission Sabbath School.

04-11-96: James Thomson, Clerk, organised the annual elections, handbills to be circulated throughout Burgh. As only three people were nominated, no elections were needed; the three men elected unopposed were Malcolm Mallace and the two Robert Smiths.

06-11-96: A Building and Hall Committee was appointed for the first time; rates were fixed – water, 1/2, police, 5d, lighting, 3d, sanitary, 2d and owners, 2d. It was planned that George Readman open the new Town Hall on 4th December 1896. The position of hall caretaker to be advertised, wages, £10 per annum, house and garden provided; Burgh to provide all material for washing and dusting the hall. Patent burners to be got for street lamps.

17-11-96: The first hall let recorded - a Poultry Show was held on 19th December 1896 at a rent of 42/-, eventually paid in instalments; the hall opening luncheon cost 4/- per head; a Grand Concert and Ball was held on 4th December, opening day.

18-11-96: The Rates Appeal Court allowed fifteen exemptions and several people had payment reduced.

23-12-96: Butter from a town grocer was alleged by the analyst to be sub-standard and the dairy owner was charged £10.

1897

Barbauchlaw Brickwork dates from 1897. By 1897, a second school building was in use on Academy Street. The right-of-way between Mossend Cottages and Woodend was in dispute.

Armadale people recorded this year - James Simpson, of 12 Cappers, John Anderson, miner, of 22 Cappers, John Brand, miner, of 185 East Main Street, Pat McInulty, 41-42 Bathville Row and John Casey, 50 Bathville Row.

James Archer was one of Armadale's Representatives on the Council. He resigned and was replaced by Mr. John Gordon, West Main Street, Armadale.

From map of 1890's, area to south of Armadale - Bathville Row (Upper Bathville) and draw well, smithy, brick and tile works at Tarrareoch, Polkemmet Cottage and Polkemmet Rows, several Cappers Pits (No.1 and No.2) Cappers Plantation (near Tippethill Hospital), Torbane Pit No.1 and Torbanehill Pits.

From 1897 O.S. map - Woodend Village consisted mainly of five stone rows of miner's cottages owned by Coltness Iron Co., 50-60 houses in total with several cases of two houses combined into one, the rows were School, Stable, East, West and Office Rows; site of Ogilface Castle on map, between village and Barbauchlaw Burn. Also on map - Academy Street, kirk, schoolmaster's house, Senior School and Infant School. There were houses between top of Academy Street and South Street. Binny's pond / former town reservoir unnamed, with smithy nearby. Armadale Colliery (Buttries), Parish Kirk, manse at Beeches, gas works, slaughterhouse, football ground (Volunteer Park), smithy at Dougan's Square, Police Station near Cross, Mount Pleasant Row (c.30 houses), also Monkey Row (c.16 houses officially probably Monklands Row), brickworks in South Street south-west of level crossing, Wester Hardhill Cottage (at back of Atlas Foundry), Hopetoun Colliery, Methodist Chapel (Wesleyan), brickworks (Barbauchlaw) and St Paul's Church (Episcopalian).

11-01-97: The Medical Officer, Dr. John Anderson, reported that during the last six months of 1896 there were 99 births, 9 marriages and 22 deaths, with only one person dying of whooping cough and one of diphtheria. The Burgh's analyst admitted faulty analyses of the Burgh dairyman's sample of butter; the Sanitary Inspector recommended that the Commissioners do not disclose this latest finding as the dairyman could sue. The annual premium on fire insurance policy on new Town Hall was 26/-, this sum covered occasional theatrical and scenic performances; the £600 Town Hall loan was at 3¼% over 20 years (mortgage).

29-01-97: An advert to appear in the Herald, Scotsman and Courier that Armadale Town Hall is open for concerts and theatrical performances, applications to go to John Fraser, hall-keeper; the Armadale Gas Co. offered to sell the gas works to the Burgh.

03-02-97: Town Hall mortgage - the Burgh to pay £41.5/4 annually for 20 years to the Royal Liver Friendly Society.

10-02-97: The Town Hall was booked for a concert and readings; two Commissioners and two fleshers were to select weights for the slaughterhouse from Glasgow; the Burgh was given over £75 government grant for rates relief.

26-02-97: Burgh to be extended; the Commissioners learned that the gas works was valued at £350 and that £1000 was needed to improve its efficiency.

29-03-97: A letter to go to Secretary for Scotland seeking powers to purchase the gas works; a report was received on Technical Education.

26-04-97: Washhouses and closets to be built at the Town Hall.

12-05-97: The slaughterhouse now had a weighing machine and the scavenger a new wheelbarrow.

24-05-97: The architect to be notified that a basin stand in one of the Town Hall lavatories was broken by a worker, also the present grates cannot be tolerated; during its first six months, the Town Hall made £23.8/9.

10-06-97: All Armadalians who attended a public meeting supported the purchase of the gas works by the Burgh.

12-07-97: The Commissioners passed plans re a dairy and porch for Douglas, East Main Street; a butcher and his accomplice were to pay dues for bringing a pig into Armadale for sale and killing it outside the Burgh (at Wester Hardhill). The Medical Officer reported 79 births, 8 marriages and 30 deaths, the health of the town's inhabitants was pronounced very satisfactory. The Burgh got over £74 government grant for rates relief. A letter was received from Lord Bute requesting information on any crests or seals in possession of the Burgh.

26-07-97: Two Burgh representatives to attend a meeting within the Sanitary Inspector's office re hospital.
09-08-97: The Commissioners learned that a Combination Hospital to be built during 1898; after the Town Hall is upgraded, public lectures to be organised.
13-09-97: Commissioner Grant Chalmers resigned (emigrating); the Burgh now has the title to the Town Hall and two houses in South Street; a circular was received from Dr. Craik on secondary education.
17-09-97: Armadale gas works in liquidation.
22-09-97: A waterproof coat to be provided for the scavenger.
01-10-97: Daniel McKenzie and sons were new lamplighters for season at £12.
01-10-97: The Commissioners learned that James Wood had bought the gas works.
11-10-97: An application to build a hall for band practice was approved subject to the outside doors opening out and in.
05-10-97: Five new committees were appointed - sanitary, slaughterhouse, lighting, hall & building and finance.
08-11-97: Rates were set - water, 1/-, police, 4d, lighting, 3d and public health, 2d, total, 1/9 in £1.
24-12-97: An 18" diameter drain to be laid at Horse Park; appeals against rates assessment - thirteen townsfolk were exempt, and four reduced by half.

1898

The Thistle Lodge of Free Gardeners in Armadale was made to pay aliment in respect of an inmate in a lunatic ward of poorhouse. William Martin lived at South Street, Armadale. The hire of a conveyance to take a sick Armadale pauper to the Sickhouse in Bathgate cost 5/6. The four Councillors who represented Armadale Burgh on Parish Council were - William Parker, 2 Lower Bathville, John Simpson, 50 East Main Street, John Shearer, 49 West Main Street, and William Marshall, 50 West Main Street. Armadale Marr, joiner, lived at 30 South Street; Mrs. Alison Douglas lived in Armadale.

10-01-98: The Medical Officer reported during 1897 there were 132 births, 22 marriages and 57 deaths, giving a mortality rate of 17.3 per 1000; the Commissioners challenged the accuracy of the North British Railway Company Armadale Branch measurements submitted for rates assessment (this was the start of a lengthy dispute).

17-01-98: Wester Hardhill was again mentioned, it stood near Mayfield Drive or Atlas Foundry; the Provost, Baillie Hunter and Adam Wilson were appointed to look for a place for deposit of refuse.

14-02-98: Another five townsfolk (mainly widows) were exempt from paying rates, being in receipt of parochial relief. All nine Commissioners were to inspect the Colinburn drain. A deputation to call on Dickson & Mann to discuss their offer of a manual fire engine for use in Burgh when required; the Town Hall platform to be heightened by two feet.

07-03-98: Dickson & Mann agreed to give the Burgh the use of their fire engine with all appliances and brigade, when required, for the sum of £5 yearly and the Burgh to take steps to get fire plugs installed.

21-03-98: Three Commissioners to represent Burgh on the Brass Band Committee. A letter was received from Thomas Hope, Colonel commanding 8th O.B. of the Royal Scots re training of Volunteers at Aldershot during week of Edinburgh Trade's holidays, the Clerk was to inform Mr. Hope that the workers in Armadale get Glasgow Fair holidays.

11-04-98: Plans were submitted for a Mission Hall on the east side of South Street, adjoining the nearest feu to south side of the level crossing.

09-05-98: The Commissioners to meet and fix site for refuse depot; the Combination Hospital to be built on a three acre site.

13-06-98: Plans submitted from William Love of North Street for putting a storey on his building; Clerk to write Mr. A Ure, M.P. for County, supporting bill to prevent Vexations Legal Proceedings. An account was passed re brooms for scavenger, £1.18/-.

11-07-98: During previous six months, 95 births, 20 marriages and 25 deaths; annual rates relief grant c.£89.

12-09-98: Tippethill to be site of hospital to serve Burghs of Armadale, Bathgate, Whitburn and Bathgate Parish; local authorities to pay initial expenditure and upkeep and cost of patients from each authority; scavenger, Joseph Paul, to get an extra 2/- a week to cover extra work.

10-10-98: Joseph Paul was appointed lamplighter at £12 for season; in future, Parish Councillors to be elected by voters at annual elections.
04-11-98: Three new Commissioners elected were William Parker, John Shearer and James Hailstones; rates were set - water, 1/2, police, 4d, lighting, 3d, public health, 2d and sewers (paid by owner), 2d. Commissioners approved plans for a two storey building in South Street for Adam Wilson; the Brass Band are considering holding concerts in the Town Hall.
18-11-98: In future, owners and occupiers each to pay half of assessment; rates now to be as follows - owners to pay water, 7d, health, 1d, sewer, 1½d, total, 9½d; occupiers to pay, water, 7d, health, 1d, sewer, 1½d, general, 6d, total, 1/3½. Rates Appeal Court - eight persons exempt, four to pay half of assessment; Robert Lambie, who occupies a garret, was to pay on £8 of annual rent.

1899

There was in Armadale a Thistle Lodge of Free Gardeners and Olive Lodge of Free Gardeners, each subscribed over £20 towards upkeep of one of their members who was in an asylum. James Hailstones of South Street was offered a seat on Bathgate Parish Council but declined. Sarah Gregory or Given, was a widow residing in Armadale. Rev. Robert Cameron of Armadale was offered a seat on the council and accepted. William J. Clark, head salesman, Co-operative Society, Armadale, became Assistant Registrar for Armadale.

1899-1900, Armadale Burgh Commissioners – Provost, William Marshall; Senior Baillie, James Gillon; Junior Baillie, Adam Wilson; Commissioners James Hailstones, George Greig, Robert Smith, John Shearer, Richard Morrison and John Duncan. The four Committees were - slaughterhouse, finance and building, Town Hall and lighting and sanitary. At the end of the 19th Century, Armadale's Commissioners were not yet called Councillors and there was not a Town Council, by name.

The Burgh had a slaughterhouse, weighbridge, Town Hall, between 20 and 30 public water pumps, over 40 gas street lamps and two Public Schools in Academy Street.

09-01-99: All Burgh proprietors to be instructed to lay hard ashes on the footpaths fronting their properties; the District council to be told to cease reusing the clawtings off the streets for blending the road metal. The Medical Officer reported that of the 59 deaths during 1898, 32 were under one year old; Armadalians health satisfactory beyond a few cases of mild types of measles imported from Bathgate.
13-02-99: Account passed to Dr. Anderson, for notifying to the Sanitary Inspector 14 cases at 2/6 each, £1.15/-; to Registrar, for returns of births and deaths in Burgh for 1898 at 2d per entry, £1.19/10.
10-03-99: Armadale Co-op got permission to install an additional oven in their bakery.
10-04-99: Plans for a chapel in South Street were passed, on condition that external doors open out and in; two felling ropes to be bought for slaughterhouse.

Tippethill Hospital

The Commissioners were informed of a recently held meeting of the Linlithgowshire Southern Joint Hospital Board re Tippethill Hospital; they learned that the total estimate to build the hospital was £6,594.18/5. This included extras for terracotta bricks and keenes cement. Local contractors involved were G. Gillon, Whitburn, carpenter and joiner, and James Easton, Bathgate, slater and plasterwork; an Edinburgh firm was installing electric bells for

£17.11/1. The estimated cost of heating apparatus, disinfectant, drying store and steam boiler was £430. A total of £7,000 was to be borrowed, Armadale's share to be £766. The site of the hospital (approx. three acres) was bought from the trustees of the late Sir William Baillie of Polkemmet.

01-05-99: The Burgh to borrow £800 from the Public Works Loan Board, payable over 30 years, to meet the Burgh share of hospital cost. The District Council to be asked to provide another well in North Street as there was only one well for c.50 tenants.

08-05-99: The Commissioners considered plans from James Wood for a block of houses opposite Dickson & Mann's houses; also plans from John Archer for addition to premises at 8 West Main Street.

08-05-99: The railway crossings at South Street and East Main Street were considered unsafe and dangerous. An account from Armadale Coal Co. for £3.0/8 was passed.

26-05-99: Plan of a boiler submitted by Mr. Thomas Neil of South Street was approved; plan of stable, submitted by Alex Mitchell, tailor and clothier, was approved; an Edinburgh engineer was asked to send a chain wheel for the slaughterhouse travelling crane as soon as possible.

12-06-99: William Stewart was allowed to build a new house in West Main Street; McNair, contractor, got £1.3/10 for repairs to the hall.

19-06-99: Town Hall ceiling to be whitewashed, walls painted and woodwork to get one coat varnish; rhones and railings to get two coats paint; D. Brownlee allowed to erect stable in West Main Street; a Burgh property-owner to be sent a statutory notice to get her jawboxes cleaned out.

26-06-99: Rates arrears for 1896-97 amounting to £25.1/9 were wiped off, being irrecoverable.

14-08-99: Barbauchlaw Fireclay to be assessed at £410.8/8; one case of typhoid fever was reported; gutters, privies and ash-pits of the Burgh were unsatisfactory; Mr. Small of Masonic Arms was told to submit a plan of his proposed cellar; the Commissioners were shown a deed made between themselves and Robert Philpot of the Public Works Loan Offices in the City of London re loan of £800, payable over 30 years, in respect of the new Tippethill Combination Diseases Hospital.

25-08-99: An Airdrie manufacturer's bakery van had struck a street lamp in North Street and broken it in two.

11-09-99: James Wood and a Burgh deputation had met; three meters to be put on lampposts to register gas consumed. Plans passed included Robert Knox's house, South Street; John Edward's house, South Street; and Michael Muirhead's house in South Street; also improvements to interior of the Crown Hotel, owner Adam Wilson. A mutual fence of railway sleepers to be erected between the Volunteer Hall and Town House.

09-10-99: A stove was installed in the slaughterhouse; emptying the Town Hall ash-pit cost 4/-; Robert Smith, Political Agent, of 87 South Street was one of the retiring Commissioners; a meeting of the Burgh ratepayers to be called by bell.

06-10-99: Three cases of typhoid fever were reported. Most ash-pits and privies are filthy and also a number are inadequate. The Medical Officer recommended that properly constructed water closets replace privies as soon as possible. The town's water supply had been analysed and found satisfactory for domestic purposes. Four new Commissioners elected were - John Duncan, George Gray, Richard Morrison and Robert Smith.

10-11-99: Public meeting in Town Hall to organise a fund on behalf of wives and families of sailors and soldiers sent to war in South Africa.

20-11-99: Burgh to organise the cleaning of the Burgh streets in future; rates fixed; water, 7½d, health, 1½d, and sewer, 2½d, total, 11½d; occupiers, water, 7½d, health, 1½d, sewer, 2½d, and general, 10d, total, 1/9½.

11-12-99: During a three day failure in gas supply, a concert was held in the Town Hall when three lamps were used; James Wood, owner of the gas works, was asked to pay 3/- expenses re lamps.

Local contractors, including farmers, put in offers re cleansing of Burgh streets. The Burgh streets were grouped into five different contract areas.

1) Andrew Law offered to clean streets in this area for £45 – from Bathville Row to the Cross including Lower Bathville, Mount Pleasant and Monkey Row.
2) David Sibbald - £60 for The Marches, East Main Street, North Street, Mount Pleasant and Thomson's Land; also Etna Cottages, Bathville Row, cottages in Station Road down to railway crossing in South Street, £35.
3) John and George Sinclair - Hamilton's property, east of Blair's property, Mill Road, Academy Street, £21.11/-. If Commissioners provide a man and pay him to wheel out, offer reduced to £18.11/-.

4) James Drake, of Middlerigg, - Marches, East Main Street, North Street, South Street, Mount Pleasant and Thomson's Land, £110.
5) Alex Smith - £30; all ash-pits south of level crossing, (all ash-pits standing full of water to be drained, also a coup provided for rubbish).

A plan was approved for a new hall for Armadale Free Church submitted by the Deacons Court of the Church.

22-12-99: Appeals heard - nine exempt, including five widows, one spinster, one blind person and one woman whose husband was at 'seat of war' in South Africa. Four to pay half assessment; during 1899, there were 170 births, 36 marriages and 54 deaths, mortality rate 14.6 per annum per 1000 population; 21 deaths were under one year, one case of rickets and one of diphtheria.

Gathering in East Main Street at The Cross
Star Inn Vaults on left of photo prior to second storey being built

20th Century

Barbauchlaw Colliery was in production from 1900 to 1973. c.1900, James Wood sold Bathville Estate to the United Collieries Co.. On 9th June 1900, Armadale celebrated the capture of Pretoria in South Africa, Armadale Brass and Jubilee Bands played in the Volunteer Field; possibly the forerunner to the Annual Children's Gala Day.

Armadale Silver Band (1937)

1900

From Bathgate Parish Council Minutes - four Parish Councillors representing the Burgh of Armadale all resigned, they were Robert Cameron, William Marshall, John Simpson and John Shearer. Adam Wilson was paid for hires of horse and carriage and three new Councillors were nominated to represent Armadale Burgh - Adam

Wilson of the Crown Hotel, George Grey of the Star Inn and George Boyd, tailor, West Main Street.

Robert Muir of Bathgate represented Armadale Burgh on the Parish council, James Thomson was Registrar. At a meeting in Armadale Town Hall, Armadale ratepayers elected these four persons to represent them on Bathgate Parish Council - John Shearer, John Simpson, Robert Smith (Organising Agent) and Andrew Wylie, butcher.

Ellen McIntosh or Anderson lived in Armadale, Janet Westwood or Hill lived in Armadale. William Gillies, engineman, lived in Bathville. Two Armadale parents refused to have their children vaccinated so legal proceedings were threatened by the Council. Two Armadale men refused to allow Dr. Kirk to vaccinate their children on a Sunday. The Burgh Analyst found 3% water in a sample of milk from a town dairyman, there was no prosecution. The Burgh met the cost of an Armadalian who was a patient in Drumshoreland Hospital (£5.12/6). The Medical Officer ordered the destruction of a bed.

Joseph Paul, scavenger, resigned; the Burgh to advertise for a replacement scavenger at 27/- weekly (1 weeks warning to be given). The Burgh's street pillar gas lamps now taken down and stored during summer months. Residents of Armadale to be invited to subscribe towards a bed in a Cape Town Hospital to be named 'The Linlithgowshire Bed'. Robert Muir and Co., brick-makers, to erect an office in South Street. William Somerville to have a stance at the slaughterhouse where he will operate as an offal dealer. Plan approved re a proposed two storey house for Andrew Wylie. David Sibbald, cleansing contractor, complained that there was neither barrow nor cart road to one ash-pit in East Main Street.

Following on from complaints from the owner of Barbauchlaw Estate on behalf of tenants, £12 to be paid out, in compensation for Burgh sewage discharging into fields and Colinburn. Burgh to provide Birkenshaw with water supply for cattle. A reference was made to £10 in the 'Common Good Fund'. A cattle drinking trough to be provided in a field near the slaughterhouse. Water has now been led inside a number of houses in the Burgh. John Frew, Burgh Sanitary Inspector, delivered a very detailed report on water supply, drainage, nuisances, common lodging-houses and dairies. Nuisance complaints included full ash-pits, privies, dirty premises, filthy pigsties and overcrowded and damp houses.

During the first six months of 1900, there were 15 cases of scarlet fever and one of typhoid fever. A request was received for the use of the Town Hall for two or three Sabbaths. There was being planned a fairly complex drainage scheme for part of Barbauchlaw Estate involving way-leave. An objection to ice-cream shops etc. being open on the Sabbath was considered by the Commissioners. The Christian Brethren were granted the use of the Town Hall for three Sunday Services, for £7. The lamplighters for the season 1900-1901 were Higgins and Kerr (for £12 for season). John Forsyth, joiner, submitted plans for Oriel windows, attics and scullery. The Gospel Hall in South Street was built c.1900, it replaced an earlier wooden building.

An Annual General Meeting of Ratepayers to be called by the Burgh bell man. Rates fixed for 1900-1901 – owners - water, 9d, public health, 1d, and sewer, 2d, total, 1/-; occupiers - water, 9d, public health, 1d, sewer, 2d, and Burgh general, 9d, total, 1/9. The Town Hall was let to Bathgate Saturday Evening Concert Association for 22 Saturdays at 30/- a night. After the annual elections, Adam Wilson was Provost and James Gillon was Senior Baillie, John Shearer was Junior-Baillie; new Commissioners elected were Andrew Wylie, James Gillon and Adam Wilson.

The Burgh borrowed £800 for construction of sewers. The Commissioners were given a petition signed by ratepayers in favour of Armadale Public House Ltd.. As a result of an outbreak of fever in the Burgh, the Medical Officer to be assisted by a nurse. The Burgh to establish its own cleansing department in 1901. A harness was bought for a Burgh horse, for £3. The Appeal Court decided to exempt eight people, five others to pay half assessment; two residents in Drumshoreland Hospital from Armadale cost the Burgh £12.6/6; James Main of Eastertoun was employed as Burgh carter, on a 5½ day week.

Some of the inhabitants of Armadale (from the 1900 valuation Roll) –
In East Main Street lived the following families - Greig, Gillon, Wilson, Mathieson, Wilson, Pearson, Nimmo, Dodds, Murray, McNab, Arnott, Brown, Brodie, Thomson, Tweedie, Imrie, Higgins, Russell, Simpson, Johnston, McGregor, Leckie, McKay, Craig, Lambie, Hamilton, Kerr,

O'Donnell, McDonald, Walker, Wardrop, Johnston, Hamilton, Black, Strang, Baird, Cameron, Forrester, Inglis, Holt, Reilly, Russell, Crane, Robertson, McKechnie, Watson, Stafford, Green, Wardlaw, McLay, Greenwell, Anderson, Lees, Calder, Wright, McGowan, Drake, Hempstead, Ross, Gray, Buchanan, Burnett, Craig, Scott, Ronald, Bishop, Friell, Park, Hunter, Douglas, Potter, Edwards, Fowler, Cameron, Bennet, Kay, Wallace, Boyle, Sproule, Fraser, McNeil, Bowden, McConnell, Louden, Somerville, Smart, Galloway, Dickson, McDougal, Robertson, Wardlaw, Spiers, McLurg, Riddell, Benson Darragh, McIntyre, Mathieson, Anthony, Dobbie and Stirling.

West Main Street

In West Main Street lived - Wilson, Gibb, Duthie, Wall, Graham, Hutton, Fraser, Scott, Kirk, Shearer, Forsyth, Pearson, Gibson, McCorrie, Marshall, Dougan, Bryden, Snedden, Ballantyne, Gillon, Wilson, Easton, Wark, Drysdale, Syson, Wardlaw, Nimmo, Smith, Brown, Walker, Harrison, Donaldson, Ramsay, Steel, Waddell, Baxter, Pearson, McNab, Whyte, Easton, Watson, Waddell, Poe, Love, Baxter, Morrison, Bowie, Hunter, Ellis, Ross, Wilson, Marshall, Maxwell, Smith, Stewart, Leckie, Storrie, Easton, Knox, Waugh, Thomson, Bulloch, McNair, Morrison, Anderson, Brown, Love, Dowie, McAdam, Brown, Harrower, Mungall, Bishop, Forrester, Morrison, Boyd, Brown, Pow, O'Donnell, Stafford, Rodger, Ross, Wilkinson, Williamson, Knox, Strang, McCulloch, Gorman, Loudon, Kennedy,

Dowell, Roberts, Stewart, Bisset, Fraser, McDonald, Drysdale, Clemenson, Innes, Boyce, Henderson, Morris, McNab, McIntyre, Russell, Boyd, Drummond, White, McAlpine, Peden, Geddes, Prentice, Anderson, Fraser, Drysdale, Ferguson, Babbington, Anderson, Smith, Cunningham, Hamilton, Jeffrey, Thomson, Weir, Purdie, Hutton, Cunningham, White, Pow, Rowans, Campbell, Duncan, Marsella, Anderson, Brownlee, Brown, Marshall, Clark. Cook, Laird, Russell, Stewart, Birrell, Thomson, Condie, Johnston, Reid, McKinlay, Marshall, Sands, Murray, Archer, Bower and Maxwell.

In Mill Road Street lived - Prentice, Kirk, Boyle, Boyd, Russell, Given, Bonnar, Baxter, Bell, Muir, Brown, Bennie, Hutton and Whitfield.

Mill Road

In North Street lived - Kerr, Scott, Verrier, McCorrie, Williamson, Lind, Anthony, Clarkson, Kerr, Harkins, Bennet, Smith, McLeish, Cunningham, Knox, Bennet, Purdie, Watson, Lochhead, Drysdale, Sheriff, Brown, Russell, Gillespie, Fraser, Ross, Smith, Pearson, Noble, Smart, Chalmers, Ramsay, Miller, Gillespie, Sprott, Baxter, Boyd, Donaldson, Smith, Hailstones, Snedden, Cook, Purdie, Campbell, Gordon, Nesbit, Balloch, Galloway, Baxter, Spratt, Smith,

Higgins, Kerr, Gillespie, Pow, Blades, Wilson, Baird, Hunter, Haldane, Brodie, Eyre, Brown, Williamson, McKenzie and Aitken.

These people lived in South Street - Kerr, Ezzi, Brown, Jones, Forsyth, Rodgers, McDonald, Easton, Walker, Douglas, Spiers, Tweedie, Bulloch, Kerr, Hailstones, Green, Ritchie, Smart, Williamson, Alexander, Rankin, Duncan, Brown, Ramsay, Swan, Wilson, McMillan, Wardlaw, Birley, Fraser, Sanderson, Smith, Baird, Ellis, McGowan, Wardrop, Pane, Kerr, Boyd, McKay, Purvis, Prentice, Edwards, Morris, McGarrity, Flemington, Brown, Muirhead, Knox, Smith, Rankine, Mungall, Hodge, Clerk, Pollock, Law, Russell, Love, Russell, Sprott, McGarrity, Marshall, Anderson, McKinnon, Marshall, Sneddon, Wilson, Brodie, Craig, McQue, McKinnon, Ramsay, Clark, Wylie, McKay, Thomson, Muir, Prentice, Hogg, Purves, Howatt, Neil, Alexander, Wilson, McLean, Middleton, Thomson, Smith, Thorn, Smart, Marr, Henderson, McKenzie, Sharp, Paterson, Bisset, McLaren, Findlay, Strang, Black, Edwards, Kerr, McDonald and Pow.

There lived at Mount Pleasant - McKeown, McDonald, Brown, Wilson, Simpson, Smith, Forsyth, Hill, Bishop, Stirling, McAlpine, Owens, Ronald, Tweedie, Gillies, Watson, Smith, McDowell, McCabe, McKechnie, Young, Sheridan, Kerr and Duff.

They lived in Thomson's Land - Thomson, Maxwell, Nelson, Mowbray, Hutton, Gallagher, Aikman, Bennie, Loudon, Smith, Fisher, Brand, Gibson, Sinclair, Alexander, Hill, Burnett, Rooney and Lynn.

South Street residents - Chalmers, Baird, Sharp, Brown, Wilson, McAlpine, Currie, Selkirk, Dunlop, Torrie, Christison, McIntosh, Brown, Wood, Lawson, Russell, Pennycook, May, Simpson, Nelson, Garvie, Stones, Reid, Oliver, Gardner, Brett, Baillie, Muir, McAra, Friell, Johnstone, Mark, Polland, Stafford, Casey, Brand, McGill, McNamee, Hickey, Townsley, Baxter, Logan, Douglas, McIndoe, Marshall, Duff, Eadie, Fisher, Easton, Polland, Hartley. Walls, Cowie, Murphy, Wilson, McLaren, McInulty, McClory, Wilson, Ellis, Logan, Craig, Gallagher, Duffy, McInulty, Hart, Falconer, Boggins, Crossan, McPhillips, Neilson, Young, O'Neil, Torrie, Currie, Shaw, Morrison, McAlpine, Shaw, Middleton, Russell, Banks, Pollock and Love.

1901

The Gothenburg public house was built in 1901 and it opened in October. It was built as a meeting place for miners. Called 'The Goth', it was owned by Armadale Public House Society Ltd.. It was at first refused a licence. The original Goth apparently incorporated part of Marshall's bakery, which was altered to suit the change of use of the property. The Goth donated part of its profits to local charities and causes such as Armadale Football Club, old folk, widows, the blind; the Goth also built Armadale Bowling Club premises.

Two football teams in Armadale were Armadale United and Armadale Rising Star. Armadale United played in part of what was to become the Public Park. Earlier football teams in the district were Woodend Jubileeans F.C., which was founded 1887, it became Woodend Athletic; Woodend Excelsior c.1902; and Woodend Thistle and Armadale Athletic F.C. who both played Junior level.

Andrew Wylie and Malcolm Mallace were Parish Councillors for Armadale. By 1901, Armadale school roll exceeded 1000. In 1901, for the first time, meetings were minuted as being meetings of Armadale Town Council and, from now on, the members were described as Councillors and not Commissioners. During 1900, 24 children died under one year old. The condition of Burgh footpaths "beggars description" (probably resulting from the laying of gas pipes).

Burgh representatives to take part in a "memorial service for the late lamented Queen Victoria"; local public works to close on the day of her funeral. The Burgh to ask local organisations to attend a local service, including the Brass Band, the Volunteers and the Friendly Societies. The Burgh sent a letter to the new King and Queen Alexandra, in which reference was made to the prosperity of the British Empire under Queen Victoria.

There was an epidemic of smallpox. The Volunteer Field to be cleaned up, a recent circus had left a "decayed matter" nuisance. The new Burgh Carter to be paid a salary and not by commission; the Burgh horse cost £64 and the cart £16. There was a dispute over the bing at No.2 Pit, Hardhill, in Mayfield Park.

A stable, cart-shed and loft to be erected at the slaughterhouse for the Burgh horse. The Independent Order of the Good Templars urged the Council to support a Parliament Bill prohibiting the sale of alcohol to children under 16. Accounts passed included nurse's fee, also feeding stuff for a horse. Alterations to be carried out to property of Mr. Marshall, baker, West Main Street, on behalf of Armadale Public House Society Ltd.. Armadale Brass Band to hold a three-day bazaar.

John Torrance was co-opted on to the Council "in room of" John Shearer, blacksmith, who resigned. Council to co-operate with other committees in arranging the Annual Children's Day. A 'Welcome Home' to be given to the Volunteers on their arrival. On learning of a case of smallpox at Craig Inn, Blackridge, free vaccination was offered to the inhabitants of Armadale over five years old. The Burgh was alerted to the possibility of plague being imported from the Cape, a disease spread by rats. During the painting of the Town Hall, the Christian Brethren to get the use of the Volunteer Hall. Large parts of the town's streets, or footpaths, have been laid with concrete recently.

The Lodging House is now to be designated a private boarding house. The Urinal at the foot of Academy Street has to be repaired. The Scotch Education Department offered grants for Technical Education. The Co-operative was given permission to build a tenement of houses in South Street. Burgh rates were payable at the Collector's house. The Town Clerk, James Thomson, gave notice of resignation on the grounds of ill health. He had been Burgh Clerk for 37 years. Mr. Simpson became the new Town Clerk. Tippethill Hospital now open chiefly for cases of scarlet fever and enteric fever. The Burgh purchased a safe.

1902

Armadale's first Gala Day was held. This year the Model Lodging House was built. The owner of Barbauchlaw Estate planned to lay out two new roads on their land, the streets were named George Street and James Street. Woodend Excelsior F.C. played in 1902. Some Burgh footpaths now being described as pavements. The private road through Thomson's Land was described as sufficiently levelled, causewayed and flagged. The Council is considering setting up a Burgh Court. The Burgh is to pay a share of the cost of the mortuary at Bathgate Cemetery. Armadalians are to get a holiday on the day of Bathgate Procession. Councillors expressed their appreciation of the value of James Thomson's work as Town Clerk for 37 years.

Bandstand, James Wood Public Park, Armadale.

High Academy Street was by now in existence. Dr. Anderson got 19/6 for vaccinations. James Wood offered a field at Bathville as a Public Park, he also offered swings and a bandstand.

Volunteer Hall in South Street to get a porch. Armadale to join the Convention of Scottish Burghs. Bathgate (Landward) School Board submitted plans for a new school, a janitor's house and offices. Luigi Brattesani now lived in West Main Street. Mrs. Thomson of Thomson's Land, died.

Armadale Model Lodging House Association submitted plans for a Model Lodging House in South

Street. Armadale's 1902 Children's Gala Day celebrations were to be held on the same day as the Coronation of King Edward VII. Armadale Co-op to extend their bake-house. The Boys Brigade to hold a concert in the Town Hall.

The owner of Barbauchlaw Estate sought compensation re way-leave through his land of the Burgh sewer. The James Wood Public Park to be opened on 26th June, so the Councillors formed a Park Committee. A water trough has been placed on Whitockbrae as the natural watercourse had been polluted by the Town sewage. The town lamplighters got a £1 extra for carrying a ladder and using matches to light the lamps for a fortnight.

A stretch of Colinburn to be piped through 50 two feet diameter pipes. £750 to be borrowed for the new sewer track. Robert Drysdale was appointed Park Ranger of the new Public Park. Water supply to Robertson's Iron Foundry being negotiated with Armadale Iron Co. Ltd. Some private properties in the burgh by now have a scullery, wash house and water closet. John Forsyth applied to build a hall off South Street.

The Provost received a Coronation medal from the Secretary for Scotland. The Established Church to get the use of the Town Hall for a two-day bazaar. The Burgh to have a Dean of Guild Court. Full water rates to be paid on licensed premises, barber's shops, chemists, fishmongers and ice-cream shops. James Brodie recently erected a brickwork at Colinburn. Persons in receipt of parish relief were exempt from paying rates.

1903

Photographs of old Armadale survive from this year of West Main Street, Wood Park bandstand and decorated lorries on the Gala Day. The two 1903 holidays to be on Bathgate Procession Day and the third Wednesday of September. John Shearer, blacksmith, was given permission to erect a smithy on North Street. The Burgh is to buy a humane cattle killer at £1.16/- for the slaughterhouse.

Station Road, Armadale.

Station Road (now South Street) behind the lorry is the level crossing and, on the left, the Model Lodging House

From 1903 to 1946, the Model Lodging House in South Street had accommodation for over 100. The level crossing in South Street to get a wicket gate and a fence. Baillie Smith reported on distribution of profits made by Armadale Public House Society. Unpaid rates due from about a dozen people to be written off - c.20 to be sued for non-payment. A swing or swings now in position in the Public Park. A cottage, byre and milk-house to be built in High Academy Street. An application was considered from Andrew Graham who planned to add a bathroom, water closet and stair to his house in West Main Street.

The new Model Lodging House is to be controlled by the Town Council. The Burgh paid £136.0/4 to Tippethill Hospital, being the cost of Armadale patients.

The United Collieries offered to pay the Burgh 25/- for each feuar who lived outside the Burgh Boundary to have their drains connected to the Burgh sewer. Provision of water to the whole Burgh cost

£516.12/- for the year. Trustees of the late Maurice Thomson applied to build a tenement of shops and houses fronting South Street. Mr. Baird of Airdrie (Burgh Surveyor and Master of Works) pointed out that Thomson's plans failed to comply with the more stringent rules that were now applied to new building work sanitation and drainage. The proposed plans brought objections that the tenement blocked off servitude rights of way. The Co-op applied to provide water closets at the back of Gladstone Terrace. The County Sanitary Inspector and Colonel Hope of Bridgecastle complained about Burgh sewage polluting Barbauchlaw Water. The Council insisted on a higher standard of drainage in the Burgh, properties outside the Burgh were connected to the town sewers.

The Burgh borrowed £150 to pay off Tippethill Hospital costs and £200 to pay off Town Hall deficit. The Burgh was considering buying the gas works, which was expected to come on the market - the Council later voted by five to four not to buy it. By August, the new sewage filters at Colinburn were nearing completion (the new sewage work cost £917). Two new lamplighters to work to the following rules - lamps to be lit at dusk from 1st September to middle of April 1904, extinguished on Sundays at 9 pm and Saturdays at 11 pm, other nights at 10 pm, except 31st December and 1st January when lamps lit all night. Mount Pleasant and Thomson's Land to get gas street lighting.

Two Burgh slaughterhouse users to be sued for refusing to pay dues of 4/2 and 5/-. With the completion of the Burgh sewers, the Council decided not to pay anything towards cleaning the ditch at Whitockbrae in future.

William Caesar became Depute Town Clerk. Elected in November were - new Provost Adam Wilson of the Crown Hotel and James Gillon, grocer, the new Senior Baillie. Committees appointed were sanitary, lighting, slaughterhouse, hall, park and finance; also Dean of Guild Court. United Collieries, owners of Mount Pleasant, were asked if they would put gas fittings into their houses.

The Burgh borrowed £360 from two local Friendly Society Lodges (the Olive Lodge and the Shepherds Lodge). The Armadale Dramatic Club got free use of the Town Hall for a charity performance. The Burgh streets were divided into three groups and three local farmers put in offers to cart away the manure. Thirty people were exempt from paying rates.

1904

Preparations were made at Tippethill Hospital for an influx of smallpox patients, temporary accommodation to be provided. There was a case of smallpox from Birkenshaw Mill. The Post Office Telegraph Department wanted the telegraph poles in West and East Main Streets moved from backs of houses to front. The Council considered a request for a contribution towards the provision of secondary education in the County. The Town Hall keeper was allocated a bigger council-owned house and the Clerk was instructed to 'peacewarn' the present occupant to look for other accommodation. Armadale Burns Club to get the use of the Town Hall for a children's evening and the Boys Brigade for a concert, at reduced charges.

The Town Clerk's salary was increased to £50 per annum and the Collector's to £45. Thomas Dalling was appointed Burgh Veterinary Inspector. The Postmaster General sent a written request for permission to erect a line of telegraph poles along the commodious main street of Armadale. A sink is to be installed in the hall-keeper's house. Mr. Readman, owner of Barbauchlaw Estate suggested that the two new streets in Academy Park be named George Street and James Street.

Gas street lamps to be erected in Thomson's Land, High Academy Street, James Street and George Street. Complaints to the council included the pollution of Barbauchlaw Burn and somebody's hens at Lower Bathville. The Burgh share of cost of the new Smallpox Hospital recently provided at Tippethill is £88.13/11. The Burgh to pay £31.4/-, being the cost of smallpox patients from Armadale. The Burgh was asked to pay towards provision of technical classes throughout the County.

The Sanitary Committee to meet at the Burgh coup to look into the burning of rubbish. The Council agreed to purchase two patent fire extinguishers after Baillie Gillon saw them at an exhibition in Volunteer Park. Three Councillors elected to serve 1904-1905 were

Robert Smith of Gladstone Terrace, Charles Gillon of West Main Street and John Brown of Unity Terrace.

There was an outbreak of typhoid fever in Thomson's Land. Two Burgh private middens were described as unsanitary. Armadale Draughts Club was allowed use of room at the Town Hall. Water rates were fixed at 7d in £1. The Town Hall to be insured for £1000 value. A press to be provided in the Town Hall to store the town brass bands' instruments. A local farmer agreed not to charge the Burgh for damages if the Council laid 300 carts of ashes on his field. About 50 people appealed against their annual rates assessment, most were sustained, several were refused and a number were shown to be in receipt of parochial relief.

1905

The Scottish Motor Traction Co. ran a bus service between Bathgate and Armadale - the bus was a steam-propelled charabanc. In 1905, James Wood sold Woodlands to Alex McAra. Armadale Burgh employees carted street manure to Burgh depots situated outside the Burgh and local farmers bought it. Each farmer uplifted manure from the depot at so much a cart (usually 3d or 4d). (Sibbald took manure from Hopetoun depot, and Hardhill crossing, Robb took it from Colinshiel and Muirhall depot)

It was reported that the recently completed road at Thomson's Land was very irregular and blinded with mud. When laying a new sewer in the field to the west of Academy Street, many large boulders were encountered.

A large number of houses in the Burgh now have water closets, all new buildings must now have water closets. Cost of overnight accommodation in the Burgh lodging houses to be increased to 6d. The Co-op Society hired the Town Hall for a performance. The Committee told the police that some unknown persons were lighting the Burgh street lamps on moonlight nights. A new sewage works was being planned. The Temperance Dancing Club were not given the Town Hall at a reduced rate for their annual social and dance. The Councillors met High Academy Street property-owners re road and footpath improvements, the owners were Messrs. McKenzie, Burnett, Hunter, Cunningham and Morris.

General Booth of the Salvation Army visits in August 1905

The main block of housing known as the Shoogly Building is where the library now stands

The merchants of Armadale wanted fire plugs fitted in case of outbreak of fire. The Co-op claimed compensation for loss of part of their carcase eaten by vermin in the slaughterhouse. The new sewage works to cost £2,178, if built in concrete, and £2,243 if built in brick; the Council decided to call a public meeting by bell, to seek public approval of these proposals. The farm tenants of Barbauchlaw Mill and Whitockbrae complained about the fences next to Colinburn. William Thomson was engaged as green-keeper of Public Park at 6/- a week during season. Two separate accounts were paid re both hospitals at Tippethill (the Fever Hospital and the Smallpox Hospital). Ten contractors submitted estimates re the building of the new sewage works; only one (McGregor) was from Armadale, others being from as far afield as Edinburgh & Baillieston. The Burgh to arrange a loan of £2,250 on security of sewer assessment.

Provost Wilson died. The Town Hall revised charges to be 30/-, where professionals on stage, 15/-, where local performers and 4/- for dances. There was an outbreak of enteric fever in Bathgate. Piquila Borza was an ice-cream vendor in the West End. The Town Brass Band got the use of the Town Hall at 1/- a night for practice. Cement arrived for sewage works in unsealed bags in violation of the specification. The four Councillors elected for the year 1905-1906 were Allison Howatt, James Currie, George Greig and William Forrester. Baillie Smith was elected Provost, Cllr. Gillon was Senior Baillie and Junior Baillie was George Greig. Six Committees were appointed for sanitary, lighting, slaughterhouse, Town Hall, Public Park and finance. Land was acquired next to the new sewage works for a settling pond. Cllr. Brown became Dean of Guild, nineteen people were given rates relief.

The Council Agenda was described as a Billet. A new water meter at Bathville became a pedestrian hazard and danger as it was in the middle of a footpath, sticking two feet above the footpath level (later removed).

1906

James Wood gifted Wood Park to Armadale. William Marshall was in Barbauchlaw Farm. The Railway Tavern became the Masonic Arms. Lodge Hope Bridgecastle is dated 1906. Hugh Clarkson was co-opted in place of Baillie Gillon who resigned. The new sewage works had a siphon, regulating tank and grit chamber, sluices, settling tank, detritus tank and sludge pump. Improvements to the Public Park included a railing round the bandstand, provision of seats, planting of shrubs and re-siting of urinal. The Burgh had a holiday on Victoria Day (23rd May).

The account re wages of workmen who cleaned out the sewage works detritus tank was signed by the Convener of the Sanitary Committee as the workmen were unable to write. John Fraser was appointed a 'Burgh Servant' (i.e. Burgh Official); his duties included seeing to the filters and the Public Park. His wage was 28/- a week, with one months notice to be given; he got a free house, his duties also included work given to him by the sanitary, lighting and Town

Hall Committees. The Burgh Scavenger's wages increased to 25/- a week. A pair of watertight boots was bought for the attendant at the sewage works.

Ten Burgh property-owners were instructed to deal with nuisances on their properties concerning ash-pits, privies, drainage, rhones and water closets. Mr. Robb of Colinshiel Farm supplied hay for the Burgh Horse. The Burgh claimed from the District Council for scavenging (cleaning) the town's main streets (a District Council responsibility). Tippethill Smallpox Hospital was being considered for treatment of patients with consumption. Owners of the ice-cream and aerated water shops in the Burgh were informed that they should close earlier (11.00 pm on Wednesdays and Sundays and 11.30 pm on Saturdays).

Baillie Grey and Cllr. Gillon resigned and Provost Smith had been ill for several months. Five new Councillors elected for 1906-1907 were - John Bishop, James Brown of Unity Terrace, Hugh Clarkson, Andrew Graham and Andrew Wylie. Town Officials were all reappointed – A.P. Simpson, Town Clerk; John Simpson, Town Chamberlain and Collector; William Baird, Burgh Surveyor; Dr. Anderson, Medical Officer; Stevenson MacAdam, Analyst; John Frew, Sanitary Inspector and Thomas Dalling, Veterinary Inspector.

Mr. Somerville to remove the offal shed at the slaughterhouse. New instructions re slaughterhouse - the shallow midden stead has to be kept full before the deep one is used.

At least seven townspeople who appealed against rates assessment were in receipt of parochial relief. As usual, about ¾ of those granted rates relief were widows. 35 people applied for the position of Burgh Officer, with free house and 28/- per week - John McIndoe was the successful applicant.

Six local farmers who submitted offers for the Burgh manure were - Robert Law of Netherhouses, John Robb of Colinshiel, David Brownlee of Stanerig, Alex Smith of Tarrareoch, William Marshall of Barbauchlaw and David Sibbald of Hardhill.

1907

Street lamps were not to be lit on moonlight nights, except during cloudy weather. Reference made to Dougan's Land. Gas mantles to be stored in a press in the Town Hall. Station Road was mentioned. Property-owners of Bathville and Station Road who had to pay for kerbing and channelling were - W. Muirhead, Mathew Balloch, J. Alexander, J. Edwards and the United Collieries. An account for £4.5/6 was paid to Armadale Iron Co.. A tripery to be erected at the slaughterhouse and a boiler to be purchased. The Town Hall was made available for bazaars at 30/- a day.

The Burgh Medical Officer was authorised to report cases of spotted fever (cerebra-spinal). During the first three months of 1907, the Sanitary Inspector served 135 interdicts of nuisances on property-owners involving drainage, privies, ash-pits, etc. and the emptying of slop water on to footpaths and road gutters. Several property-owners were threatened with closure of their properties because of choked drains, privies with no keys, filth, slops, plaster, dampness and no washhouse. Children's Day to be on 29th June.

Tables to be bought for social gatherings in the Town Hall, cooking facilities to be looked into. (A gas cooker was bought for 5/-) The Burgh paid £1.7/- being payment of William Lightbody's funeral expenses. Victoria Day to be on 22nd May. (Licensed premises to be closed all day) The Council paid £20 to the Jessie o the Dell Lodge of the Royal Order of Ancient Shepherds Friendly Society, in respect of loan, and £30 to the Olive Lodge of the Free Gardeners (also re loan).

Four Burgh Officers were now insured - the Burgh Officer, Slaughterhouse Superintendent, Scavenger and Carter. An account was paid in respect of a sick child in Strang's Land, nurse's keep for three weeks, £1.10/-, three gills of brandy, 3/-, and two bottles medicine, 1/-, total, £1.14/-. The Burgh borrowed £200 from Mr. Frederick Green of East Main Street at 4%. Farmers to be paid 1/3 per head for cattle offal and 2/- per score for sheep offal. Offal selling prices to be - cattle tripe, 2/-; cattle blood per gallon, 2d, cattle guts per bundle, 6d, sheep tripe, 2d, sheep guts per bundle, 1/6.

Armadale Labour Party to be allowed use of Public Park for meetings on weekdays only. The County Education Committee have organised a series of fifteen evening lectures on horticulture in Armadale Evening School. Armadale's first Roman Catholic School was built. Owners of restaurants and billiard rooms in the Burgh to be asked to close at 11.30 pm on Saturdays and 11 pm on week nights. Armadale Cricket Club applied to turf a suitable pitch in the Public Park. (John McNicol wrote the letter)

Three Councillors elected for 1907-1908 were James Currie, blacksmith; John Wilson, grocer and Farquhar, draper. The Co-op to be told to burn their paper, pasteboard, boxes and keep their tins, etc. in a separate part of the midden-stead so that no rubbish mixed with manure. The Council considered taking over all roads in the Burgh and extending the Burgh boundary. About 50 people appealed against rates assessment, several people (probably those in receipt of parochial relief) were described as Poor Margaret, Poor James, etc.

1908

The Burgh received a letter re access to the slaughterhouse. The well in Academy Street wasn't operating. Nineteen applications came in for the position of Burgh Carter. Slaughterhouse windows had been broken. There was a sewage defect between Episcopal Church and Armadale Iron Co.'s Foundry. The charge for a wedding reception in the Town Hall was £1. The Co-operative had property in Station Road. A property-owner's dry closet was considered satisfactory for the time being. A dispute arose between the tenant of the tripery and butchers over the removal of their offal. The Council made a very thorough comparison between Armadale and the Burghs of Bathgate, Linlithgow and Tranent to help them decide whether to take over the responsibility for maintaining the Burgh Roads from the County Council. Nuisances reported by the Sanitary Inspector included the emptying of slop water into the street channels, dilapidated and dirty privies and ash-pits; also dilapidated and uninhabitable house property. Proprietors to be compelled to replace their old dry privies with flush water closets. Bills to that effect that were circulated through the town had an effect.

Of eight applicants for position of Town Clerk, Mr. William Caesar, solicitor, was chosen. The Council view was invited re proposal to extend Tippethill Hospital for treatment of all consumptive patients. Printed regulations to be displayed in the Model Lodging House. Several organisations met the Council re alterations to the Town Hall platform for public theatrical productions - there were representatives of the Co-op Education Committee, the Catholic Dramatic Club, Choral Union and Amateur Dramatic Club. A number of un-letable houses in the Burgh had doors locked and windows barricaded. The Councillors were invited to the Public Park on Children's Day. After seeing the model of a cart, the Council decided to buy one for the Burgh for £16. (all wood and not lined with iron)

July issues included slaughterhouse way-leave deed, the new Burgh cart, pipe track deed, claim for damages, Lodging House Byelaws, the painting of the bandstand, Town Hall fire appliance, accident to Burgh Scavenger, faulty drain, auditing of accounts, transfer of roads and Colinburn Road right-of-way.

Tops of street lamps to be painted as they were rusting. Several property-owners were taken to court over outstanding debts re rates, footpaths, kerbs, etc.. The Council, in response to an Act of Government, formed themselves into an Old Age Pensioners Committee. The Temperance Party, or Council, applied for use of the Public Park and Town Hall. They were granted permission to hold meetings in the park provided no political questions are discussed. The United Collieries asked permission to lead their sewer into the Burgh sewer, also to erect dry closets instead of flush closets. A portrait of ex-Councillor George Greig to be hung in the Council Chambers. Burgh Scavenger's wages to be increased to 28/- per week. Paid to James Waugh for feeding stuff, £7.18/10. One Burgh property-owner was instructed to lay his footpath with clean, well-burnt, engine ashes. The Temperance Party accepted offer of Public Park with conditions on restrictions on speaking on political matters. The local Independent Labour Party successfully appealed for reduced hall charges re two meetings held for charitable purpose. Rates fixed - general charge, 10d, general improvement, 3d, sewers, 9d, water, 1/3 and public health, 5d.

Clinkers to be cleared and manure sold. Council considering street lights being lit all night, including moonlight ones. Clerk to write asking the North British Rail Co. to restore 1 o'clock train because of great demand. All three newly-elected Councillors' addresses were given as Armadale Station although they lived in Gladstone Terrace, Hardhill Terrace and Bathville Road. Their names were Smith, Bishop and Leckie. Sergeant Fullerton of Fauldhouse was appointed Slaughterhouse Superintendent at 15/- per week. Sewage work's sludge tanks were cleaned out.

Sanitary arrangements in several Burgh properties to be compulsorily improved. The Council agreed to take over the Burgh roads from the County Council, with conditions. The Council to consider provision of hose and fire plugs. Most of the 60 people who appealed against rates assessment were successful.

1909

Forsyth's Hall was in South Street. The date 1909 is on a chimney in West Main Street. There was a further reduction in the train service to Glasgow. Reference was made to dilapidated WC accommodation in the Burgh and to a midden-stead. Councillors considered a motion "That the Burgh lamps be lighted the whole period of the lighting season irrespective of the moon's convenience". A small stove to be installed in the slaughterhouse. The minutes of meeting on 2nd February included a very thorough appraisal of the financial state of the Burgh giving records of loans, cost of public works (sewers, hospital, etc) and expenditure during previous years. The Burgh to meet the expense of two funerals.

A Pipe Band Concert held in the Town Hall was a failure. Mr. James Wood now lives at Wallhouse, Torphichen; as feu superior of a property in South Street, his approval was needed before Colin Christison could erect a gate at his property. Mr. Wood was still owner of the gas works. The Dean of Guild Court approved plans from Mrs. Mary MacDonald for buildings in East Main Street (possibly MacDonald's Square), but two flush water closets had to be erected for the property. At another Burgh property alteration, a coom ceiling had to be incorporated to give the statutory 9'6" floor to ceiling height.

The Council borrowed £660 at 4% over 30 years for these purposes - to repay a small loan, to provide stable accommodation, new sewers and Burgh share of Tippethill Hospital. Gas street lighting costs had gone up 20% on previous year.

Two slaughtered cows were found to have tuberculosis. A child, who was buried at the Burgh's expense, was found to be privately insured. Councillors representing the Burgh at future meetings involving personal expenditure to be fully recompensed. The Medical Officer reported on the Factory and Workshop Act. Rev. Robert Cameron of the Parish Kirk died. Government Acts to be considered involved children, offenders and poisons. Difficulty was experienced in finding a 'suitable' person to fill a vacancy on the Council. A person who died in the Model Lodging House to be buried at Council's expense. A water hydrant was fitted in the Burgh water mains.

Police were told of vandalism to the water fountain in the Public Park. (The damaged part was later replaced and two new cups attached) Footballers in the Public Park had to cease using the swings as goal posts. Mr. Findlay and the Armadale Distress Committee each to be allowed the use of the Town Hall for Distress Relief. The Temperance Council to be allowed to use the bandstand in the Public Park for a demonstration. It was learned that neither Messrs. Button nor the Co-op Society sold any poisons or drugs mentioned in the Pharmacy Act. The Town Hall to be painted by Hastie. The Hall Committee to consider how to prevent boys sitting on the window sills and damaging the paint. Councillors learned that the park fountain was in order, the seats painted and fencing done in time for the Children's Day. Problems included slops being thrown out on to streets and cesspool filth. Russell's property to get W.C.s.

The Clerk to communicate with the Post Office with the view to having the telephone introduced into Armadale. The Council considered the introduction of electric lighting into Armadale. Burgh streets to be renumbered. Armadale to get a telephone exchange if enough subscribers to warrant one. The slaughterhouse to be altered to accommodate sheep as well as cattle. The Temperance Society objected to the setting up of a whippet race course in Armadale. The Provost and Town Clerk signed an agreement to the effect that the Council would take over responsibility for the burgh roads. The council considered buying the implements needed for road maintenance and decided to find out terms for hire of Bathgate's Road Roller.

To deal with sewage effluent fouling Barbauchlaw Burn, a deputation to visit Penicuik to learn their method of purification. Police cells to be altered and a Burgh Surveyor's Certificate granted before occupation. Armadale Post Office to be open from 8.00 am to 8.00 pm. Letters and circulars were received re a new disease, milk supply, King's Police Medal and explosive substances. A series of public lectures were being considered on milk supply and other subjects. Mr. Brown, whose horse had been injured resulting from the state of the Burgh road, sued the council. Some issues - widespread disinfecting, weighing machine to be oiled and Burgh manure to be advertised.

1909-1910, total expenditure estimated at almost £2,000. Interest on Burgh loans was paid on Whitsunday and Martinmas of each year. Burgh to buy a road scraper.

Three Councillors elected for 1909-1910 were - Andrew Graham, James Grey and Andrew Wylie. Committees elected for the next 12 months - O.A.P., sanitary, lighting, slaughterhouse, Town Hall, Public Park, finance and roads. Officials re-elected were - William Caesar (Town Clerk), Kenneth MacLellan (Depute Town Clerk), John Simpson (Town Chamberlain and Collector), John Frew (Sanitary Inspector), William Baird (architect), Dr. Anderson (Medical Officer), Thomas Dalling (Veterinary Inspector), Stevenson MacAdam (Analyst) and Reginald Collie (Auditor).

Some footpaths in the Burgh to be re-laid with Dander ashes. Most of the 55 people who appealed against rates assessment were successful. Hawkers of butcher-meat from outwith the Burgh to be stopped as the Burgh derives no dues from them. The Burgh experimented with the use of slag riddlings in footpath repair.

1910

Armadale Thistle Juniors were established by 1910 and Armadale Rangers (Juveniles), also Armadale Northern and Armadale United. On 15th March 1910, about 100 attended a special meeting in

Forsyth's Hall to found Armadale Thistle Juniors. The Thistle joined the Scottish Union. Armadale Thistle was admitted to the S.F.A., they were once beaten 2-0 by the Rangers at Volunteer Park.

A photo taken on Armadale Gala Day at Toll Brae / South Street survives. Cinders and offensive matter had been thrown on to the Public Park. The school closets had been greatly improved. Armadale Rangers Football Club had occasion to write the council. Armadale's first public lecture was on "our milk supply". The Council received a letter from the Scotch Office re cinematograph exhibition. There was insufficient water-pressure to reach the second storey of the school. The pavement, kerb and channel of High Academy Street were to be repaired by the occupiers, thereafter the Burgh was to take over the street.

Mr. Readman's agents agreed to pay £3 towards the cost of cleansing James and George Streets, which were in a bad state. Gusta Vogel, of Cupar, Fife, was the new tenant of the slaughterhouse tripery. Lodge of Freemasons, Hope Bridgecastle, was granted a renewal of certificate. An account for £4.4/11 was paid to Lothian Quarry Co, which was apparently owned by James Wood. Council to remove a burgh sewer pipe that interfered with the foundation of the new gas holder at the gas works.

Armadale Public House Society donated £500 towards erection of a replacement Town Hall and recreation rooms. Four additional water hydrants were connected to the water mains. Armadale to get a telephone exchange if five subscribers join, five eventually did. Council received a circular on public health, re foreign meat. Council received a letter from the Territorial Force Association re a summer camp. King Edward VII died, the proclamation of the new King George to be read out at Armadale Cross and a public service to be held.

Three more pillar boxes to be erected in East Main Street, the Cross and Mrs. Marr's premises in South Street. Treasurer to send the County Council 15/6 for 31 carts of water at 6d per cart, used for road purposes. Account passed to Craigpark Quarry Co, £45. Streets of Armadale were being renumbered at 2d per door. Ashes at Bucks Head to be removed every Monday. Slaughterhouse walls had been lime-washed inside.

After discussion, it was decided to continue the name of South Street, from the town Cross to Bathville Cross. Armadale had two Post Offices including one called Armadale Station Post Office. It was reported that Mr. Vogel (the tripery tenant) was preparing offal from outside quarters, he was obliged to take gut only from the district. New gate erected at slaughterhouse, power was given to slaughterhouse committee to sell the old gate. Circulars before Council included ones on Aliens Act, aviation meeting and the housing of potato diggers. The Council supported the retention of the wall postal box at Mill Road. The Co-op requested that all refuse from Gladstone Terrace and Unity Terrace be removed. James Scott was given a certificate to allow a cinematograph exhibition in the Town Hall. Accounts passed for payment to Robertson Love and Coy. and Shotts Iron Coy.. Three years accumulation of unpaid rates was written off. One of the Burgh carts to be sold. The Town Hall to be available free of charge for public lectures. Burgh weighing machine now repaired.

Three Councillors elected were James Currie, George Farquhar and John Wilson. The town's inhabitants were notified by bell that anyone throwing refuse on to streets or gutters would be prosecuted. The new scullery in the Town Hall was now being used. Armadale Public House Society extension plans were approved. Council considered alterations at Burns' Hall in George Street. Burns also applied for erection of an engine house for generating electricity for the production of the cinematograph shows; the alterations were approved but the Burgh Engineer to examine engine house plans.

1911

Armadalians witnessed a pageant held to celebrate the Coronation of George V and Queen Mary. In 1911, a licence was granted to Mr. Burns to hold cinematograph exhibition in his George Street Hall. The Burgh purchased 100 tons of road setts. Permission was given to Falkirk Labour Exchange to fix up a notice plate on the Town Hall railings. The Convener and Baillie Wylie had purchased a new Burgh horse for £58.10/-. The council considered insuring the new Burgh horse. A new harness was bought and a new cart to be bought.

Mr. McIndoe was now installed as foreman over the Burgh workmen, carter, scavenger, roadmen, etc.. One of the Burgh's 1911 holidays to be 21st April, Bathgate Procession Day. The floor to ceiling height in the attics of a new house in Armadale to be 8 feet. The old Burgh horse, cart and harness to be sold. A proposal "that the horse be not sold meantime" was defeated by four votes to three. The Burgh Medical Officer was supplied with anti-toxin. Hugh Harper of Whitburn bought the old cart, horse and harness for £20.10/-, after a vote was taken. The side exit of George Street Hall was to be made safe. The Burgh had now 67 street lamps.

A deputation met Mr. Readman, owner of Barbauchlaw Estate, with a view to obtaining a grant of a field to be used as a Public Park for the north part of the town, they left disappointed. Councillor Greig drew attention to motor speed within the Burgh, four signs to be erected to make the streets safer. Plans submitted from the Territorial Force Association of the County for a new Drill Hall in High Academy Street, plans were passed subject to thickness of walls and various scantlings shown and armoury and quartermaster's store to be lit by windows facing High Academy Street. Buckets to be removed from streets immediately after being emptied. A new cart was bought for £21.10/-. The Burgh to buy a hand barrow (covered) for removing dust and papers, also a water cart or horse. Mill Road wall post-box to be moved to East Main Street. Rates paid amounted to £1,961, £37 was written off and arrears amounted to £61.

The Scottish Automobile Club offered the Burgh danger post signals at £1 each. Councillors were invited to the combined Children's Day / Coronation celebrations and to meet Mr. and Mrs. Wood. A bonfire to be erected on No.3 bing and Armadale Branch of the British Women's Temperance Society asked permission to sell temperance refreshments from a tent in the Public Park on the Gala Day. (Their sales to be restricted to tea and coffee so as not to unduly interfere with the widows' monopoly of the sales of lemonade, etc.)

West Main Street

A dust cart was bought and a coup to be found. A Horticulture Show to be held in the Town Hall. J. Smiths whippet field was assessed at £25. Instead of insuring the Burgh horse, the council opened a horse replacement account. Mr. Readman declined to give a donation to the new Town Hall Fund, James Wood donated £1,000 to the fund. The Town Hall needs work done to walls, floor, joists and exit. A fire-hose was bought for £36.19/-. A letter came from Armadale Football Club re fencing.

A proposed new Town Hall is to accommodate 1,000 people. The very ambitious scheme, which was being considered for a New Town Hall, was to be two storeys, with Council Chambers, Burgh Foreman's Room, Caretakers House, etc.. Adverts to go in the Scotsman and Glasgow Herald inviting architects to submit plans of Town Hall complex, costing no more than £2,500. Two prizes, £15 and £10, were offered for the two best plans.
The United Collieries to be told that their property at Mount Pleasant requires at least eight flush closets. Buckets in East Main Street to be lifted every second day. October correspondence covered subjects as diverse as cholera, fair wages, ice-cream shop legislation and also Masonic Bazaar.

Three Councillors elected 1911-1912 were - William Gibson, Neil Hailstones and Robert Smith. Additional committees appointed were fire and Old Age Pensioners committees. James and Thomas Smith, spirit merchants, applied to erect a new cinematograph hall in Armadale. Most of the 55 who appealed against rates assessment were relieved of payment. Two wire baskets to be put on lamp posts at Armadale for the collection of papers. Burgh to pay workmen full pay for one fortnight in the event of illness. A committee was appointed to look into lighting West Main Street from the Cross to Academy Street with electric lighting.

1912

Armadale played Aberdeen at Pittodrie. Armadale Rangers Juniors played at Marjorybanks Park at the Marches. In May 1912, the Atlas Steel Foundry and Engineering Co. Ltd. took over the premises of the defunct Armadale Iron Co.. George Balfour, electrical engineer, applied to the Board of Trade, with the Council's approval, to supply Armadale with electricity. The new cinematograph hall in South Street was certified. A demonstration of the Burgh's fire apparatus proved satisfactory. Dr. John Anderson, the town's Medical Officer, died, he was described as a friend and family physician of the whole community.

The Clerk was instructed to issue to Mr. J Bowden a six-day cinema licence, two houses per night and Saturday matinee. The Council considered variety licences. Robert Boyd of Armadale Picturedrome Company Ltd. applied successfully for a variety licence. Two Armadale policemen, who acted as his sureties, were T. Smith and James McGowan. The Burgh supplied overalls to Council Workmen for work on roads, sewage works, etc.. The Council considered the Government House Letting Act, also the Rag Flock Act, also a circular from the National Suffrage League and the Shop Act (concerning a weekly ½ holiday on Wednesday, etc). The Council was advised to take out insurance with an approved society. The Rechabite's Friendly Society arranged for a lecture on the National Insurance Act.

The Council organised a competition, in respect of a new Town Hall, which is to cost no more than £2,500. About twenty architects submitted plans, some of which were exhibited for public appraisal. Fred Smith, measurer, of Motherwell, submitted the winning set of plans. All plans submitted in competition for the new Town Hall failed to fill conditions laid down and were returned to the architects.

Dr. William Anderson became the new Medical Officer. A photo survives of Dr. William Anderson and his father Dr. John Anderson, in a horse drawn carriage. In the interest of public health, all cesspools to be connected to sewers and lavatories provided at whippet and football grounds. On considering the town's water closet provision, it was intimated that the bucket system was now in operation at Mount Pleasant. Waste paper baskets had now been fixed to lamp posts. Property-owners to be asked to lay a pavement in front of their properties. Council got a communication from the Lord's Day Association. A closure order was placed on Marches property. United Collieries applied to alter Bathville Cottage. D. Sibbald claimed £5 compensation for accident to horse through its foot being caught on a water toby. An application was received from William Drummond to build a tenement of dwelling houses in West Main Street.

The new Picturedrome to be assessed for rates. The Burgh's share of Tippethill Hospital's caretaker's house to be £38.13/5. Hope Bridgecastle Masonic Lodge to be registered as a club. Armadale Picturedrome in South Street to be licensed in the name of John Smith, Mill Road, manager. The Burgh's Fire hose was tested and found satisfactory. The Co-op ashes to be lifted once a week. The Burgh Foreman was given power to instantly dismiss any Burgh employee for insubordination. The Convener of the Roads Committee was criticised for issuing instructions without the consent of the Committee. The Burgh is to be covered by seven additional fire hydrants. The slaughterhouse has been re-whitewashed.

Waste paper and litter now being collected on Sundays (at 1/- extra cost) described as a great improvement. New Public Park fence to be completed for the Children's Gala Day. James Wood refused to give a 10% reduction on Town Hall gas bill, on principle. A claim was received from Captain W.D. Allan of Linlithgow for an accident to his bicycle arising from road defects at the gas Works level crossing, the claim was dismissed as the level crossing is outside the Burgh. The

Atlas Steel Foundry and Engineering Co. submitted plans for adding to their steelworks.

Golf was being played in the public park to the danger of the public. 350 tons of road metal to be laid from the Cross to the Public Park entrance and two tons of tar chips laid at Lower Bathville. The Pall House in North Street to be leased for three years. Rates were still being handed over to the Burgh Collector at his house. Patrick Burke, whose daughter Ellen was accidentally drowned in the Public Park, submitted a claim for £200. Council considered a communication from local government board re housing of the working classes. An intimation came from Paisley Burgh re foot and mouth disease. When considering laying pavement at South Street level crossing, the Councillors expressed concern in case horses get their hoofs entangled. Councillor Farquhar died. The Burgh decided not to make a collection for King Edward Memorial Fund. Most of the 39 who appealed against rates assessment were relieved of paying (some received poor relief). Police to be asked to prohibit football playing in the streets. Councillors met at the site of the drowning accident in the Public Park to consider the claim for compensation.

1913

From a 1913 map of Bathville, there are miner's rows at Mount Pleasant, brickworks and tramways, quarry and reservoir, Pit No.5, Stanerig filter beds and pumping station, Cappers Rows, golf course, Northrigg Colliery Pits No.1 and 2, smiddy, Atlas brickworks. Boghead brick and fireclay works, Bathville House, Woodlands, Atlas Steel Works, Wester Hardhill and Baptist Church.

From 1913 to 1918, John Shearer was Headmaster of Armadale Public School. In 1913, there was a Gala Day arch at top of the Toll Brae.

The Council decided to defend the action by Patrick Burke against the Council in respect of the death of his child Ellen Burke by drowning in the Public Park. Three wagons of road patching material to be bought. Councillors decided Burgh workmen to be paid for seven days off in year through ill health, thereafter workmen to come under

National Health Insurance. Council learned that the new crane and bucket at the sewage works emptied the detritus tanks satisfactorily. Police to be instructed to stop slides on the streets during the winter. The Established Church unsuccessfully applied for a reduction on charge for use of the Town Hall by their Sabbath School. Places of refreshment in the Burgh to be registered in accordance with new byelaws. Mr. Frew, Sanitary Inspector, resigned. Council received a circular on sanatoria. The Council threatened to cut off a sewer connection made without authorisation by a property-owner, unless payment made. The footpaths in West Main Street were "being cut up by rivulets". The several houses owned by the Council to be let at 16/- and 14/6 per month (inclusive of rates). It was not known whether Dr. William Anderson had the necessary qualifications to be the town's Medical Officer. Two licences were renewed by the Council - Armadale Picturedrome and Burns' Variety Cinema.

Mr. Simpson, Town Chamberlain and Collector, died. His son Thomas was appointed interim Town Chamberlain / Collector. The Council decided to combine the two vacant positions and placed an advert in the Scotsman and Herald for a Burgh Surveyor / Sanitary Inspector / Town Chamberlain / Burgh Collector at a salary of £120 per annum. As a result of advertising and an attractive salary, 27 applications were received. The five short-leeted came from as far afield as Glasgow and Dunbar. Robert Bamburgh of Bathgate was the successful applicant. The new official's £120 salary was charged against the various Burgh accounts thus - Burgh Surveyor, £20; Master of Works, £10; Sanitary Inspector, £50; and Town Chamberlain / Collector, £40.

The Co-op Society had a branch at Bathville. The Town Hall floor had to be extensively repaired (probably through lack of underflow ventilation). In preparation for Parish Council elections, the Parish to be divided into wards and the number of Councillors increased. The Burgh stock, horse, cart and harness to be insured for £150.

The Council challenged the account of a local carter as to why he charged a full man's rate for a lad attending the watering cart. Dickson & Mann to put rhones on their property, also drop pipes to drains. An Armadale Publican successfully requested the 21st May (Victoria Day) as the annual holiday for the trade. Daniel McConnell lived at McNab's Square, John Smith in Hutton's Land, Alex Black in Dougan's Square, and William White in Thomson's Land.

The new owner of the Pall House was Mr. Murphy. A request for the use of the Public Park from Armadale District Loyal Orange Lodge was refused. The Burgh Foreman resigned and was replaced by Alex Brodie at 30/- a week. An additional scavenger to be employed at 25/- a week and two lamplighters were engaged for the season at £15. Armadale Steel Foundry Co. requested permission to connect drains from their eight new houses into Burgh sewer.

The Council contested Mr. Burke's claim re drowning of his daughter Ellen in the Public Park The case, held in Edinburgh in June, went against the Council, who paid out the total expenditure of £411.2/2 which included £75 damages and interest to Mr. Burke. Soon after, the Council decided to take out third party insurance with the Employers' Liability Insurance Co. (the Council was anxious to know if the policy covered accidents as in Burke's case, children falling over low parapet wall and persons or property injured in the street through misplaced toby).

The annual rates grant from the government (£135.16/11) was divided three ways - to general account, 5/12th; to general improvement account, 5/12th, and to public health, 2/12th. The annual income from Burgh rates is now over £2,000 per annum. Part of the 1913 rates was allocated thus - general, £773.2/-; sewers, £313.2/6; roads, £276.16/-; and public health, £185.

The Town Hall committee was to see to the urn, which seemed to be needing repaired. Armadale Dancing Association was a user of the Town Hall. The Ancient Order of the Hibernians got the use of the Town Hall for charitable purposes, at a reduced rate. Local Authorities were apparently paying Income Tax. A public committee, including all Councillors, was formed to consider ways of raising the balance needed for a new Town Hall. Proprietors responsible for lighting back courts. Street lighting of Burgh by electricity to begin soon.

The Council was concerned that Dr. Anderson, Medical Officer, had not yet taken his Diploma in Science. The Local Government Board instructed the Council to appoint a qualified Medical Officer as Dr. Anderson hadn't the necessary qualifications.

1914

About 100 Armadalians were killed during the 1st World War (1914-1918 - see the town's War Memorial for names).

Empire Palace Theatre, George Street

c.1914, The Empire Palace Theatre was in George Street. A circular was received, on tuberculosis. The Burgh Surveyor has an office in the Town Hall. 2,900 cubic feet of gas was consumed each year by the 70 or so street lamps. A circular was received re fire danger from cellulose articles. The Burgh to celebrate its 50th year with a Jubilee Social. A Sanatorium was being planned to serve West Lothian / Linlithgowshire and other counties. The Town bellman to intimate a public meeting to discuss the proposed new Town Hall. The Medical Officer and Sanitary Inspector to carry out an experimental treatment of scarlet fever. Hydrant indicators to be erected. The Burgh received a grant of £335 from the Roads Board. The United Collieries requested that the Burgh cease using the refuse coup near their properties.

Dr. Anderson, Medical Officer, was given six months to acquire his diploma. H. Brown, Burgh Servant, became Town Hall caretaker at £6.10/- a week, with free house; he was to give two weeks notice. Council agreed to light private streets but the proprietors to light their own back courts. Council were asked by the moulders of Bathville and Atlas Steel Foundries to press for a Labour Exchange in Armadale. The Council decided they could not interfere, but they would support any move to save unemployed moulders walking to Bathgate to get their insurance cards stamped.

Five Burgh tenants to be prosecuted for failing to take their turn of cleaning the common WC. Armadale Cricket Club was refused the use of the Public Park (they later offered to provide an insurance policy). Plans for Armadale's first council housing scheme were being prepared. Mr. Waddell's offer of £5 for slaughterhouse manure and 9d per cubic yard of Burgh sewage was accepted. Armadale Burgh opposed the City of Glasgow being given the power to divert water from Loch Goil. An application received from William Drummond for a proposed new street from Manse Avenue to North Street. An application from Mr. Murphy for erection of a projecting signboard at the corner of the Cross for his garage.

Council to meet the superiors (Messrs. Wood and Drummond) to consider new streets for council housing scheme. The Council took steps to purchase Russell's Row property. Metal from Westcraig Quarry to be used for road maintenance purposes. The Dean of Guild Court started holding meetings on a different night from Council meetings. The Convener of the Public Health Committee reported that a new cistern was to be placed inside his building in South Street, the cistern and its connections to remain "during the pleasure of Mr. Greig". The inhabitants of the town were requested to burn all refuse paper and other combustible rubbish. The Public Park swings were being abused by youths.

Armadale Co-op applied to build a hall, offices and boardroom, subject to the WC being against outside wall and having a window. Armadale Horticultural Society to get the Town Hall at ½ normal charge (later given free, as proceeds went to Prince of Wales Relief

Fund). The proprietor of one of Armadale's last dry privies was given 21 days to replace it with a W.C.. The Registrar General wanted to know the number of inhabited houses in the Burgh. The Burgh Boundary to be extended to take in the proposed housing scheme. The proposed new council houses to be one and two storey and to have one or two rooms as well as a kitchen, scullery and bathroom. Mr. Drew got permission to hold open air services in the Public Park on Sunday evenings.

At the 7th September meeting, the proposed new housing scheme was shelved until some improvement takes place in the present European situation. The Council approved the formation of a Civic Guard. A very detailed estimate of Burgh expenditure and payments for the year 1914-1915 was prepared in September. Ratepayers now paid rates to Mr. Bamburgh at his office in South Street. Three Councillors elected were William Gibson, Neil Hailstones and Robert Smith. The new Provost was John Wilson. The Council were asked to support Glasgow Corporation who wanted the Government to give war widows and dependent mothers of soldiers killed £1 each per week, also to every front line soldier's wife, £l weekly and £1 weekly to every soldier, sailor etc. permanently maimed.

The Sanitary Inspector reported eight nuisances involving choked drains and choked and dirty closets. One case each of scarlet and enteric fever, also about 40 cases of infectious diseases (mainly diphtheria and scarlet fever). A storm in November 1914 damaged many street lanterns.

1915

c.1915, Robert Muir bought Boghead Fireclay Works, Bathville, from Gillies Brothers, who owned the works from 1889. Bathville Cross street lamppost to be moved from Dougan's shop to Dowell's Buildings. No rent charged for the use of the Town Hall in connection with the Belgian Fund meeting. Applications for cinema and variety licences came from Mr. C.B. Wood for licence of Pavilion, Armadale (George Paddle, Manager). Mr. Burns applied for a licence for the Star Theatre, an operating box was erected within the hall.

The Burgh Carter resigned. The Burgh horse died, another horse to be hired from Mr. Roberts at 4/- a day, with keep. Soon after, a new Burgh horse was bought for £87. The Council homologated the action of the committee and authorised a blank cheque to be signed. The Sanitary Inspector to keep a record of cows slaughtered. Robert Bamburgh (Chamberlain / Surveyor) also acted as Treasurer to the local section of the National Relief Fund. The slaughterhouse sleeper fence to be tarred and 50 decayed sleepers to be replaced.

The Provost was asked to authorise flag days for the following - Edinburgh Infirmary, Lowland Forces Association and Belgian, Russian and Serbian Distress. As an experiment, the town's gas lampposts to remain in position during summer months. No charge to be made for the use of the Town Hall for a concert in aid of Red Cross Funds. Permission was given for Bathgate Band to play sacred music in the Public Park in aid of the Royal Infirmary. The Council requested that there should be no bands playing on the Gala Day because of the war situation. Mr. Baird, of Airdrie, former Burgh Surveyor, gifted a large photograph of the town's purification works.

Burgh minutes recorded the railway accident involving a troop train at Gretna, about 500 soldiers killed. £500 of Burgh funds was invested under the Government War Loan Scheme, a further £1,000, held by the Gothenburg Public House Society for a new Town Hall, was also invested. Miss Cuthbert to get the use of the Town Hall, free, to hold a Red Cross Day. Mr. Bamburgh (Town Chamberlain / Collector, also Burgh Surveyor) applied to be relieved of his duties in order to enlist. John Frew was appointed Sanitary Inspector and temporary Burgh Surveyor. A. Reid became permanent Burgh Surveyor and Master of Works. Kenneth MacLellan became Chamberlain and Collector. A signpost at the Cross had been broken by a local motor. The Burgh paid burial costs of a woman.

Officials and enumerators who helped with National Registration duties were thanked. £10.18/- was collected in Armadale during the Poland and Galicia Flag Day. A very detailed estimate for the current year was recorded with recommended rates to be levied in respect of Burgh General Account also the sewers, roads and public health accounts. There was an overflow from sewage water at Buttries Row. Street light gas mantles were bought from Messrs. Hutton. Extensive improvements to West Main Street to cost about £620.

The factory holidays in 1915 were on 19th April and 20th September. The Town Hall was made freely available for - soldiers' and sailors' work parties, evening classes for continuation work and Armadale V.A.D. for Saturday Red Cross Day. Saturday Dancing Club to pay full rate for the Town Hall. Muirhead's water closet was nearing completion. A tribunal committee was appointed to help to recruit more men to armed forces. A communication came from Glasgow Corporation about acquiring land for smallholdings. Persons relieved wholly or partly from paying full rates were - soldiers who were head of family (½ relief), those in receipt of permanent Parish Relief and old age pensioners. Nearly all of 90 who appealed were successful. Dickson & Mann applied to erect latrines at their foundry. Circular re measles. Communication from the Ministry of War and from the Board of Trade re tar. Complaint re South Street coup.

1916

There was a road problem at the top of Mill Road, next to Livingstone's property. Slops are still being thrown out on to the street and some buckets were left out on the street all day. Carter to inform the townsfolk of times for collecting refuse. The Provost was authorised to buy from Brownlee of Bathgate a stable rug and girth for the Burgh horse. Several local factors agreed to collect rates from their tenants on 2½% commission. Burgh to buy a road sweeper. Petrol licences were now necessary. The Local Government Board dispensed with the need for Dr. Anderson sitting for diploma till after the war. Council received a communication re Midwifes (Scotland) Act of 1915.

The Pavilion got its cinema and variety licence for a further year. Licence for Star Inn held up until Mr Michael Burns submits two names of sureties. Mrs. Burns later applied giving two cautioners, application again refused. She applied again, naming Mr. Darby of Blackridge Cinema and Mr. MacAndrew of Electric Cinema in Lanark as cautioners, application again refused. Her next application was successful.

Statement on Burgh rates arrears to be intimated by bell. South Street coup still in use. Part of income from Town Hall concert to go to War Funds. Reference was made to the slaughterhouse tripery man. Communication re Defence of the Realm (Liquor Control). Annual Burgh rates now draws in c.£2,300 per annum. It was agreed to adopt the Burgh Coat of Arms as represented by the Marquis of Bute's book. The Surveyor reported to the Council that the horse brush machine had arrived. The Episcopal Church got permission to erect a sign in East Main Street so long as the Council was "relieved of all blame". Councillors learned that something was wrong with the Burgh horse, the stable was repaired to keep out rats, and a horse collar was bought. Later, the Burgh Veterinary Surgeon reported that the Burgh horse had a cold and should be kept in the stall for 10 days or so, afterwards the stable was disinfected and whitewashed.

The Red Cross got the free use of the Town Hall for a concert. The direction post at the Cross was damaged. Street lighting restrictions imposed by the Government resulted in a reduced gas bill for the Burgh. County Councillor Sibbald was to speak for the Burgh when discussing the Naval and Military War Pensions Act of 1915. East Main Street and West Main Street to be re-sprayed with tar and covered with chips. The band to get the use of the Town Hall for practice. Council to co-operate in War Savings Scheme. Public Park fountain to be put in order and fence repaired before the Gala Day.

The Council met a deputation from the British Women's Temperance Association who pressed for total prohibition of liquor traffic for the duration of the war and during the post-war demobilisation period. The Council discussed the question of treatment of enemy aliens and persons of hostile origin in the country. (The Burgh minutes contain a typed copy of three resolutions passed by the Council on the subject) Warning posts, to curb the speed of motorists, were erected in the Burgh. Seven barrels of asphalt and tar were stored in the Hall Depot. A France Flag day to be held in Armadale. Burgh to use buildings at the Crown Hotel for storage purposes at yearly rent of £3. The Public Park urinal damage was repaired for 10/6. Paper was creating a nuisance in the streets. The Burgh was asked to send the Registrar General the pink forms of young men aged 15 and 16. A detailed typed report on an application for a dwelling house (from Robert Easton of South Street) is recorded in the minute book.

A detailed annual Burgh estimate included these items - weights and measures, property and income tax, fire hydrants, urinals, sale of manure, cleansing private streets, feu duties, sludge (income), hay, cartage, implements, government grant, analyst and hospital charge. Public Health Committee concerned with treatment of tuberculosis. Lord Strathclyde to address public meeting on war savings. Burgh public health was considered very satisfactory. Armadale Parish Church-woman's Guild to get free use of Town Hall for whist drive in aid of war funds.

The Council agreed to support the appeal from Mr. R Johnston, Burgh Contractor, claiming exemption from military conscription. A heavy traction engine recently caused damage to Burgh roads, a haulage contractor was reminded of regulation vehicle weight. The Town Hall was free to the Eastern Star for a whist drive and dance in aid of Red Cross. In future a small charge (7/6) to be imposed for use of hall for charity purposes and 2.30 a.m. break-up time. In cases where the full charge paid, 4 a.m. to be break-up time. The V.A.D. was granted the use of anteroom for collections for soldier's ward No.24 at Bangour. The Burgh accepted W.B. McNair's offer of horse and man for Burgh work. Wage of Burgh Foreman increased to £2 a week. Burgh Foreman authorised to engage a casual man at 32/- a week maximum.

Early in 1916, the Council decided against organising war savings in the Burgh. After Lord Strathclyde's visit, a war savings committee was formed and a fair sum of money paid in. Fred Finlay ran regular dances in Town Hall. The local relief committee held a concert. Town Hall seats to be repaired and a coal cellar provided. Francis Mullen, who died in the Model, was buried at the Burgh's expense. Communication received on Summer Time Act. Miss Kerr and Miss Polly Brown got permission to take contributions to be used to entertain 40 convalescing soldiers at Bangour. A circular arrived from the Scottish Office re the substitution of female labour for male labour. Two women to become employees of the Burgh at 18/- a week (as scavengers).

Council received a copy of the Motor Car (Scotland) Order, 1916, also a circular on venereal disease. Robert Easton, manager of the Pavilion, was granted a cinema and variety licence. An application for a licence for the Star Theatre was refused (later, in 1917, granted after improvements made). A special meeting of the Council was called, to consider future housing, town planning, maternity schemes and child welfare. After several cases of scarlet fever were traced to the Public School, the school was disinfected. The Council were considering employing a District Nurse. A whist drive was held in the Public School. A Red Cross flag day was fixed for 20th January, 1917. Bangour soldiers were entertained in Armadale.

1917

A Committee was appointed to plan future Burgh council-owned housing. The Council considered a resident nurse and a lady health visitor. Atlas Foundry workers hired the Town Hall for a social evening in aid of the Red Cross. Slippery footpaths to be given a coating of ashes. In future, Public Hall dances to end at 11 p.m.. Council to take out a second War Loan (£200). Burgh to purchase £1,000 of War Loan for resale to Burgh people in lots of £50. Allotments to be advertised for cultivation of garden produce. Restrictions on keeping pigs were relaxed. James Wood offered ground near the gasworks for allotments.

Burgh female employees requested an increase in wages. Council refused saying that they had not been properly tested. M. Burns got a cinema licence, but not a variety licence, for Star Theatre. James Wood offered £1,000 War Stock, interest to go towards upkeep of a District Nurse. Waterproof clothes were purchased for the two female Burgh workers, one woman left, wages of two Burgh female employees was increased to 22/- a week. A flag day for limbless sailors' and soldiers' hospital was requested. Allotments offer was taken up, at 5/- each - 28 in Public Park, 12 at gas works and 9 at sewage works. An attempt was made to get supplies of seed potatoes, the Clerk was to write the Board of Agriculture pointing out that seed potatoes were scarce yet they were being sold for table consumption.

16 dozen mantles were bought for street lights. The Town Hall basin had been repaired. Female scavengers to get dust overalls and a smaller size of brush. A communication was received re waste of food and waste paper. United Collieries, Atlas Foundry and Co-op donated £47 to Nursing Association. Council took out five-year insurance with a 10% premium reduction. Street waste paper

collections began. Armadale and District Nursing Association had two Council representatives on it. £9.4/- was sent to the County Volunteers Fund. Red Cross Flag Day approved. Flag Day approved in aid of Veterans Garden City Association. Flag Days requested for Mesopotamia Comfort Fund, also Lord Roberts' Memorial Fund. Burgh circulated 3,000 handbills as part of nationwide food economy campaign. The cleeks on the Public Park swings to be renewed. The Council considered appealing on behalf of carter for exemption of military conscription on grounds of indispensability.

Pythius was a patient from Armadale at Linlithgow Poorhouse. There was a complaint that a farmer's hens were trespassing on allotment ground, the farmer to be told by formal letter to keep his hens on his own ground. Bandstand to be cemented, white-washed and painted. First batch of waste paper now in Burgh shed and a baling hog installed. A dry closet in Mill Road is still in use (condemned). Defence of the Realm food economy and food waste communication. Women employee's wages raised to 25/- a week. Circulars before the Council - on locomotives on highway and use of studs in traction engines and child welfare milk supply. Dr. William Anderson is now a Lieutenant with the Royal Army Medical Corps.

The Burgh horse was suffering from a suppurating foot caused by a nail. Joe Waddell, farmer, offered 1/2 per cubic yard of sewage sludge. A sacred concert to be held in Armadale Pavilion in aid of the Red Cross. Pink National Registration Forms were prepared for males aged 40 to 49. The Burgh sought government aid to build 100 2-room and 100 3-room houses to satisfy the Burgh's housing needs. A nurse was appointed to serve Armadale and District. The Burgh to buy another horse. The Burgh to be represented on the committee set up to deal with cases where a resident of Linlithgow Poorhouse develops T.B.. A football team was criticised for playing in the Public Park too near the bowling green. A cricket match to take place in the Public Park for Red Cross Funds, provided the public were protected. Thomas Milne successfully applied for a cinema and variety licence for the Star Theatre. Dr. Gilchrist now has an assistant. There was to be no more Saturday dancing in the Town Hall. Sheep had ravaged allotments in the Sewer Field. Local Friendly Societies told the Council that there was an inadequate medical service in the Burgh; Council to ask for another doctor; failing that, the recall of Dr. Anderson. Armadale Burgh to purchase a burgh seal without armorial bearings. After an accident in the Public Park caused by a cyclist, bills to be exhibited prohibiting cycling in the Park. Brass Band to get use of the Town Hall and financial help from the council. Mr. Wood asked the Council to meet with the directors of United Collieries re future housing schemes, etc.

Burgh rates were fixed for 1917-1918 - occupiers to pay towards general purposes, road maintenance, public health and sewers; cost to be split equally between owners and occupiers. After a boy sustained an injury playing cricket in the park, Council decided that boys playing cricket in the park must take the risks. Ordinary brown paper to be used for blinds for Town Hall during winter, to obscure lights under lighting restrictions. A meeting took place between Council and retail coal-sellers to attempt to standardise prices. Local sellers present were Sibbald, Brodie, Boyd and Roberts. Coal prices varied from 16/6 to 30/- a ton, coal types were South Blair, Cultrigg, Beaton Best, Hillhouserigg and United Collieries. The water barrel blamed for causing flooding at Forsyth's property was removed. The Council accepted an offer from Mr. Wood for a burgh seal with armorial and heraldic devices engraved thereon, a device to perpetuate Mr. Wood's generosity to the Burgh to be incorporated in the design. An Armadale Allotment Holder's Society to be formed. Councillor Greig replaced Provost Wilson, who resigned through ill-health.

Council decided to relieve from paying rates in full, soldier's dependents who were not in receipt of rent, or coals, or civil liability grants. An offensive smell came from the burning bing at Muir's Works. Mr. Hugh McNeil of the Co-op Defence League put forward the name of Henry Traynor to fill Council vacancy. Ebenezer Calder filled the vacancy. A W.C. and two coal cellars to be erected at Council property. Council considered request from the Episcopal Church Minister to have lamp at Marches lit. A woman employee of the Council resigned over low wage rate paid to female employees. Thomas Milne and Robert Easton applied for renewal of cinema and variety licence for the Star Inn and the Pavilion.

1918

Armadale got a Burgh Seal. The seal was to retain the third bear's head and the tree, representing Mr. Wood's connection with the Burgh. Armadale had a Gillon's Land in 1918. The Superintendent of the County Police authorised lighting of eight additional streets lights in the Burgh. The Burgh's first consignment of waste paper was sold for £18.3/-. A deputation was appointed to petition the Central Medical Emergency Committee for the return of Dr. Anderson to civil employment. Mr. Ezzi submitted an application to open his ice-cream shop on Sundays between 2 p.m. and 8 p.m..

Two delegates to represent the Burgh at the congress called by the Scottish National Housing and Town Planning Association. The Burgh Fire Brigade extinguished a fire at the Co-op before much damage was done (the Brigade's first fire). February correspondence covered a phthisis patient, public health visitor, waste paper, T.B. regulations, housing and Midwives Board. Miss Cuthbert was allowed to take a collection on behalf the Red Cross for Bangour War Hospital. The Ancient Order of Hibernians got permission to hold an Irish Flag Day for charity. Sympathy cards to be sent to dependents of fallen soldiers.

A new hose to be bought for the slaughterhouse. 1,500 handbills to go out calling for recruits to join an Armadale Platoon of Volunteer Corps. Sir J. Balfour Paul suggested 'Ferveant Opera' go on Armadale's Burgh seal. Many more allotments to be provided at the Public Park, etc. including 34 for Russell Row tenants. The Dramatic Club was allowed to raise money for Edinburgh Royal Infirmary and Edenhall Hostel. A fund was inaugurated for Armadale and District Prisoners of War. Harry Chalmers was co-opted on to Council. W. Dougan submitted an application for a piggery at Bathville Cross. Bathville Football Club objected to losing part of their playing pitch for additional allotments. An office to deal with food control matters to be opened in Armadale.

The Council considered erecting a Burgh piggery next to slaughterhouse with 15 double pens. The Council received the Burgh seal die and lever press, also an account for £57.2/-, which they sent to James Wood as he had previously offered to gift the arms and seal. Mr. Wood to be presented with a replica of the coat of arms, another replica to be framed and exhibited. Council to apply for exemption from military conscription for Burgh Foreman, J. Brown. The injured Burgh horse was declared fit to resume work. There was a burst pipe in the billiard room, South Street. Measles prevalent among young Armadalians, several children died. Burgh to organise a child welfare scheme.

The rules and regulations governing the use of the Burgh seal were recorded in the Burgh minutes. Fire hydrant indicators to be provided. Two women started work with the Burgh at 35/- a week. It was reported that parties were in the habit of playing cards on the vacant ground in George Street and on the whippet ground behind the Pavilion and using foul language. A concert was organised for Belgian Relief. A piggery attendant to be paid 10/- a week. A coal committee was appointed - coal overseer, ex-Provost Smith, Provost Greig, owner of the Crown Hotel, Baillie William Gibson, publican, Councillor Ebenezer Calder, engineer, Alex Torrance, Co-op manager and John Sprott, miner. Permission was granted to Post Office Telegraphs to lay wires along West Main Street. The Horticultural and Industrial Society got permission to hold a whist drive and dance in the Town Hall on behalf of P.O.W. Fund.

A letter was read from Soldiers' Christmas Parcel Fund. A letter came from Glasgow Corporation re separation allowances and pensions. At the Council meeting of 8th November 1918, Armistice was referred to and reference made to local soldiers, including some who have won honours in the field. Armadale Picture House to be disinfected daily. Council to advertise for a lady health visitor. A hose to be bought for the Burgh, for £35. Street lights obscuration (a wartime measure) to be removed. There was an epidemic of influenza. During a flu epidemic, public schools closed and children excluded from cinemas. William. B. McNair and James Easton applied for licences for the Star Inn and Pavilion. Dr. Anderson attended December Council meeting when four applicants were interviewed for position of lady health visitor.

1919

Act of bravery - inscribed on an ornamental, decorated, steel or cast iron lamppost, on plinth, with steps, near the Cross in West Main Street – "In memory of Mrs. Elizabeth Kerr, Dunolly Cottage, who near this spot, on 26th November 1919 was fatally injured while saving a child from being run over by a passing motor car. Erected by the public of Armadale". The child was May Easton, who later became Mrs. Forbes and seems to have emigrated to South Africa. Mrs. Kerr was a popular midwife in Armadale.

The Memorial to Mrs Kerr at the Cross
Note the original globe light

In 1919, the Burgh bought land to the east of Armadale Cross from the owner of Barbauchlaw Estate as a site for about 150 council houses. (Greig Crescent, Barbauchlaw Avenue and Wood Terrace) The whole site was bought for £750, the entry was on 1st March 1920, and total acreage was 11.8 acres.

Barbauchlaw Mill, which had a wooden 28 feet diameter wheel ceased production c.1919.

The Mill, Woodend, around 1908

The Council bought a brush to test the sewer drains, for 9/6. Father Rattray requested a lamppost. Sister Stevenson was appointed as lady health visitor at £120 per annum, with uniform. The Burgh Fire Brigade did a good job controlling a chip shop fire in the Burgh. A letter sent to Council re voters roll. The Burgh Foreman and Burgh Carter both resigned, the Burgh got the use of a carter from Bathgate, when needed. Council meetings had, for several years, been held in the Town Clerk's office in East Main Street. Sewage purification works overhauled. Burgh Foreman's wages now £3 and carter's wages £2.15/- per week.

Council considering sharing, with neighbouring local authorities, an up-to-date fire extinguishing apparatus. Councillors were shown an excerpt from Edinburgh Gazette on Education (Scotland) Act. A circular received from the Y.M.C.A.. A card was received from Falkirk Labour Exchange re Mr. Bamburgh's demobilisation. Council to meet with the Armadale Branch of the Discharged Soldiers' and Sailors' Federation to discuss "a war memorial to our fallen heroes". (Mr. Mack and Mr. McKerron represented the Federation) Hugh Brown, now demobilised, to resume duties as Burgh Foreman. Some North Street tenants still threw rubbish out on to footpaths and channels. The Council decided to end the tripery tenancy, if the tenant was discovered to be an alien. (After police report was considered,

Gustav Vogel was allowed to continue as tripery tenant) Public Park allotments to continue for at least one more year. The Council was offered custody of polling booths and boxes but declined for lack of storage accommodation. £25 interest from James Wood Bequest was given to the Nursing Association. Rates arrears dating back to 1909 were written off as irrecoverable.

The provision of council housing became the main issue before the Council. A special housing meeting on 29th April was held. Mr. Roberts, architect, was to prepare plans of one room house, with kitchen and large scullery, in blocks of four flats, also two room houses, again in blocks of four flats.

A power line to go through Armadale, overhead, except underground at Muir and Co.'s works in South Street. Wartime Sanitary Inspector Mr. Frew resigned and Mr. Bamburgh, now demobbed, to resume duties. Councillors saw Mr. Roberts' housing plans and requested fireplace to be moved from the kitchen to the scullery. Armadale's first council housing scheme to be built at Russell's Row site.

Mr. Mighton became the new Burgh Carter. Communications re Parish Council elections and the treatment of T.B.. The Temperance Vigilants were allowed to hold a demonstration in the Public Park with the use of the bandstand. A Council meeting on the 20th May was attended by Mr. Roberts, architect, and a representative from the Local Government Board. Sites considered for Armadale's first council housing were at Mill Road, Mount Pleasant, Mayfield and Russell's Row. Fifty houses to be built within two years, the final choice of site between Mayfield and Russell's Row depending on cost. Mr. Reid was the temporary Sanitary Inspector.

Ex-Provost Smith resigned after 25 years service. A small pig reared at the Burgh piggery was sold to the Co-op for £4. Football playing in the streets was a nuisance. Council was considering whether to re-lay Burgh footpaths with tar-macadam or granolithic concrete. The Burgh was gifted a brass plate from the Red Cross inscribed 'The Armadale West Lothian Bed'. Pig sales earned £82.19/4 for the Burgh. The Burgh co-operated with the county scheme re venereal disease. The Council were anxious to learn whether Mr. Bamburgh wished to return to his former position with the Burgh. Request for use of Town Hall came from a new association, Comrades of the

Great War. A Burgh horse took ill and was later put down. Nurse Stevenson was complimented on her work. The vet reported that two pigs died at Burgh piggery died of a swine disease, sometimes called 'purples' or 'measles'.

Peace celebrations, subsidised from the rates, were being planned. Muir and Co. to provide W.C.s at their property. The Co-operative, Russell and Marshall got permission to make vehicle entrances off West Main Street. The Local Government Board told the Council that the new council houses must be no smaller than three apartment. A mining engineer was engaged to check out mineral workings under the proposed future housing sites. Malarial fever and pneumonia were now notifiable diseases. The slaughterhouse boiler was valued at £750 for insurance purposes. To save paying £1.15/- for private maintenance of weigh machine, the Burgh Foreman to inspect and keep well oiled.

The 23rd August was Peace Celebration Day. The Temperance Vigilance Society and two Armadale churches requested that licensed premises close on Peace Celebration Day. The Council learned that they could buy Russell's Row property for £2,800, land at the Russell's Row site could be bought from Barbauchlaw Estate for £6 per acre, land at Mayfield could be bought from Mr. Wood at £8 to

£10 per acre, inclusive of minerals. A woman was appointed pig attendant and feeder at 12/6 weekly.

A new Town Hall was being considered as a War Memorial. Nurse Stevenson reported no infantile mortality and a high birth rate. Where inpatient treatment was needed, Burgh cases to be sent to Glasgow Maternity Hospital and the Royal Hospital for Sick Children, Edinburgh; suitable cases of sick children to be sent to a convalescent home. Food and milk to be provided, where instructed by the Medical Officer of Health. Burgh Foreman to get six days holidays in the year, Burgh workmen three days and, if they prefer to work throughout holidays, to be paid extra for these days. Provost Greig was appointed to the school management committee.

The Town Hall

The Council was looking into raising money for the Town Hall / War Memorial by weekly contributions from wage-earners. The new revised Town Hall rates were - weekly dancing, 9/-; social and dance, all night, £1.10/-; concert, £1.10/-; lectures, 3/6 for first hour, 2/- per hour thereafter; and ante-room, 1/6 per first hour, 1/- thereafter. Coal was being conserved because of rail strike. A local motor damaged the Town Hall property. In response to a Board of Trade circular, the

Council suggested that representatives from these bodies sit on a Profiteering Tribunal - the Council, women members, Food Control Committee and the working classes. The Co-op and Mr. McNaughton were invited to submit offers re waterproof suits for Burgh employees. A van broke three panes of glass on a North Street lamp. Smallpox outbreak feared. It was reported that the street lamps would be available after change of moon. The United Collieries was alerted to the unsanitary conditions of the W.C.s at St. Helen's Place.

Six new Councillors elected were - Robert Hynd-Brown, Henry Chalmers, William Forrester, John McNicol, John Williams and Martin Prentice. Committees formed included cleansing and sewer, Public Park and Fire Brigade. Representatives were chosen to represent the Burgh on these bodies - Hospital Board, Venereal Diseases Committee. Nursing Association, Fuel and Lighting Committee and School Management Committee.

Interim Chamberlain retired. Mr. Caesar, Town Clerk, resigned through ill-health, Kenneth MacDonald succeeded him. Mr. Bamburgh to be asked if he approved of the Council applying for his demobilisation. The Horse Purchase Committee failed to purchase a horse at Lanark Fair because of high prices. Issues before the November meeting of the Council were - van entrance for the Co-operative, two street lamps broken by vehicles, waterproof suits, stable fodder, slaughter-house rats and condemned carcase, defective gully and Burgh share of painting of cemetery mortuary. Water supply was blamed for prevalence of goitre. Robert Easton applied to make alterations to the Picture House. Three cases of diphtheria dealt with. Mr. Bamburgh's telegraphic acceptance was read out to the Councillors. Council to hire Mr. McNair's horse for 15/- a week, Council to feed and shoe the horse. Council expressed sympathy to the husband and family of the late Mrs. Kerr, who was killed by a motor-car while trying to save a child.

1920

Armadale Football Club played in Senior League along with Hibs, Clyde, Dundee, etc. Armadale had Girl Guides. Mr. Bamburgh, following his return from military service, resumed duties as Town Chamberlain, etc. An office was provided in the Town Hall for the new Town Clerk, Kenneth MacDonald. The railway gates at South Street crossing were smashed by runaway wagons. The public were not making proper use of slops drainage. £4.7/6, being proceeds taken at a ceremony held at the Pavilion Theatre, was given to the War Memorial Fund. At the ceremony, medals were presented to returning soldiers. A further donation came from Peace Celebrations Fund.

Armadale residents were experiencing difficulty in obtaining coal. The Public were endangered by subsidence in south-east corner of the Public Park. A circular came from the Board of Health on lousiness and itch. A special meeting was held on 19th January on the proposed council housing scheme. The Council heard a very detailed report on the state of the Burgh footpaths and recommended action. They were told of the advantages of granolithic pavements and kerbs. An estimate of the cost of laying grano pavements throughout Armadale came to £2,400 based on 6 feet wide footpaths, 13,109 square yards at 3/9 a square yard, and tradesman's rate 1/10 and labourer's rate of 1/6 per hour. Part of the Burgh's reserve stock of coal to be released.

The Soldiers' and Sailors' Parcel Fund was closed. Because the Burgh Model Lodging House had increased their charges beyond those recommended, the Model was now outwith the Burgh supervision and control. The Co-op bought three Burgh pigs for £58.5/-. Armadale's first housing scheme was delayed as the purchase of the site was still being negotiated. During January, 61 cattle, 43 sheep and 25 pigs were slaughtered at the Burgh Slaughterhouse. On 23rd February, for the first time, the business agenda was recorded.

Mr. Drummond attended a housing meeting as Mr. Readman's law agent for Barbauchlaw Estate. The site for Armadale's housing was acquired from Barbauchlaw Estate for £750, giving entry on 1st March

1920. The Council bought Russell's Row (about 60 houses) for £2,100 (entry 28th May 1920). The Council wanted the new council houses to have this ratio, 70% three apartment, 25% four apartment and 5% five apartment. Councillors saw plans of new houses. The Council campaigned for establishing of a National Bank to provide housing loans free of interest.

Council passed a resolution calling for the adopting of an improved system of meat inspection. The Public Park allotments to discontinue at the end of the year. About £75 was collected for a memorial to Mrs. Kerr. Free vaccination against the spread of smallpox was recommended. Armadale to benefit from a Joint Sanatorium Board's decision to build a large hospital at East Fortune. During March, four cases of infectious diseases reported in the Burgh. All Councillors visited the town's sewerage purification works, which were in a dilapidated state. Atlas Steel Foundry Co. Ltd. criticised the Council's housing policy. Burgh property-owners were to construct granolithic pavements, at their expense, then the Council to take them over.

West Lothian Foundry with Atlas Foundry in background 1920

Council Employees' salaries and wages reviewed thus - Town Clerk, £150 per annum; Town Chamberlain, £300; Lady Health Visitor, £150; Road Foreman, £3.15/- per week and £12 annually for lighting street lamps; Carters, £3.5/- and 2/6 for weekend stable duty for one carter; Scavenger, £3 and 2/6 for Sunday work for one scavenger.

Burgh to borrow £130,000 for housing. Local butchers objected to 50% increase in slaughterhouse charges. The Atlas Foundry Co. asked what help they could expect from the Council with their plans to erect houses for their workers. The Burgh's free vaccination service to be given publicity because of an outbreak of smallpox in Glasgow. Armadale's lady health visitor started to provide a weekly child welfare service for the Burgh. Armadale's first council housing scheme to have 158 houses comprising 88 3-room, 58 4-room and 12 5-room houses. Mr. Marshall claimed for damage to his wheat crop from the Burgh sewer's overflow, Council paid £2.10/- without admitting liability.

Permission was sought from Armadale Temperance Vigilants Society to hold open air meetings in the Town Hall forecourt. West Lothian Housing Association applied to erect a wooden dwelling house in Armadale. The Council disapproved of such houses and insisted on ceiling height being raised to 8'6". Armadale's council housing to be a mixture of south and north aspect housing types. 1919-1920 was probably the first year in the Burgh's history when there were no rates arrears. Allotments no longer in the Public Park and fences removed.

A cow with T.B. was destroyed, chicken pox now a notifiable disease, free vaccination within the Burgh. A Burgh diphtheria patient died. Armadale to share the administration of Tippethill Hospital for the first time. New road contract - East Main Street to be scarified and excavated, re-laid with consolidated ashes, clean metal layer and surfaced with tarred aggregate. South Street and West Main Street to follow on. Specification and alignment of replacement Burgh footpaths detailed by Burgh Surveyor.

Mr. Marshall, farmer, to buy the slaughterhouse manure and sewage sludge for a further year. The council homologated the purchase by the Piggery Convener of 18 young pigs at £4.10/- each to restock the Burgh Piggery. There were no cases of infectious diseases in the Burgh during May. To protect schoolchildren, signals warning motorists to be erected at the foot of Academy Street. The North British Railway Co. refused to provide a footbridge at South Street level crossing. Loans borrowed for council housing to be repaid thus - 80 years for land, 60 years for housing and 20 years for streets. Council decided to get permission from the Secretary of State for Scotland to erect 10 miles per hour speed restriction signposts. The Burgh's emergency reserve of coal to be disposed of and Control Committee wound up. Council to organise a poll under the Temperance (Scotland) Act of 1913.

Councillor Forrester died in August. Council to advertise for offers of work on the building of the new houses, in July. The Council, who became owners of Russell's Row in May, considered increasing rents in terms of the 1920 Act. During July, three cases of scarlet fever and three of diphtheria in Burgh. The Atlas Foundry planned three blocks at the Marches, outside Burgh. 73 cattle, 162 sheep, 50 pigs and two calves were slaughtered at the slaughterhouse. John Wardrop was co-opted on to the Council. Street lighting to start when daylight hour was changed. Smoke and noxious vapours abatement circular. The Council asked for £20 per annum to clean two private Burgh streets owned by Barbauchlaw Estate - James and George Streets. A Burgh delegate to attend conference on electricity supply.

East Main Street with the new Council houses on Wood Terrace

On 6th September, Councillors learned what was to be the cost of 158 Council houses (Wood Terrace, Barbauchlaw Avenue and Greig Crescent). The total cost was over £150,000. William B. McNair of Armadale submitted the lowest offer for brickwork and plasterwork, and won both contracts. Local carpenter Forsyth won the carpenter contract, although his offer was second lowest, David Marr of Armadale won the plumbing contract and Robert Easton of Armadale won the slater and rough-caster contract.

Because of industrial uncertainty, the Council decided to retain coal stocks (they could have sold them off). Armadale to pursue with the Secretary of State for Scotland the urgent necessity of introducing a speed limit on roads. In August, there were two cases of diphtheria, one of scarlet fever, one of pneumonia and one of chicken pox within the Burgh. 46 Russell's Row tenants protested against the increase in rent. Mr. Wyper engaged as Master of Works for housing schemes in Armadale and Bathgate, for £8 per week (£4 from each Burgh).

1921 census day to be 24th April 1921. Atlas Foundry planned to build 100 houses. A Poll was taken on 2nd November 1920 in terms of the Temperance Act of 1913 - for no change, 755; for no licence, 435. Council now had standing orders to help them conduct their business. A Ceremony was arranged for 6th October 1920 to mark the beginning of Armadale's first council housing scheme. Provost Greig to cut the first sod. A street lamp, in memory of Mrs. Elizabeth Kerr, to be erected at the Crown Hotel corner. William McNair offered to cart bricks from Etna Works for 3/- a 1,000.

Because the road surface at East Main Street was now, after relaying, much higher than the rail line, the line had to be also raised. Five street lamps to be lit throughout the night were at the Cross, Mill Road Street, two level crossings and Bathville Cross. 11.8 acres were bought from Mr. Readman of Barbauchlaw Estate for council housing. Whitburn and Armadale Burghs urged the rail company to improve the intercity service by arranging for more trains to stop at Armadale. Mr. Somerville, Headmaster of the Public School, successfully requested the use of part of the Public Park for hockey. Mr. Muir, brick manufacturer, bought 17 tons or so of coal from the Burgh reserve stock for pumping purposes to prevent flooding at his mine.

Four Councillors elected were James Greig (840 votes), William Gibson (690), Neil Hailstones (730) and John Wardrop (676). Armadale's first speed warning sign posts were erected at Academy Street / West Main Street junction and near the Crown Hotel. There was a shortage of coal and cement. Academy Street was judged to be too steep for the road roller. Lighting Convener recommended that a bracket lamp be fixed in the wall at Mrs. Webster's shop to help improve lighting at the Cross. By November 1920, the road from the Cross to the Marches had been entirely re-laid and resurfaced. The Council asked Armadale Public House Society for a loan of £1,200 to pay for sewers to service new housing. The Council asked the Board of Health to advise them on a fair level of rents for Russell's Row, they recommended no increase. The Council received £18 from supplier of road materials used in East Main Street to compensate for inferior materials.

The new boiler for the tripery cost £75. The Council learned that 50% of income from the sale of National Savings Certificate to be reinvested in loans to local authorities. Circulars sent to Council at end of 1920 concerned pollution, National Savings, local authority loans, cleansing and salvage, sanitary conditions of theatres, Public Works Loan Board, etc.

1920's

R.C. Chapel School

1922: A third school building was in use on Academy Street, it was multi-denominational. A new R.C. School was also built.

1923: The former Miners Welfare Institute in East Main Street has the inscription 'Ferveant Opera 1923'.

1924: Inscription on Goth Tower – 'AD 1924. Erected in memory of Malcolm Mallace President A.P.H.S Ltd 1901 to 1922'.

1925: Saw the start of the annual pageant.

1926: The 28th West Lothian Scout Troop was founded.

1928: Buttries Pit on Barbauchlaw Estate ceased production. Robert Muir and Co. owned Boghead Fireclay Works, Bathville, from c.1915 till 1928.

Old place names up till the 1920's

Taken from the Valuation Roll, Linlithgowshire, 1912-1913, Parish of Bathgate (Armadale Burgh) and based on information from Jim Somerville with the map based on Ordnance Survey 1922 edition.

PROPERTY	STREET	No.
Aitken, John (carriages)	South Street	23
Alexander's Place	West Main Street	30
Boyd	West Main Street	3
Bucks Loan	West Main Street	28
Buttries Rows	North Street	8
Castle Poorie	North Street	9
'Curly' John Wilson	East Main Street	13
Dandy Row	South Street	21
Dougan's Square (was Russell)	West Main Street	24
Drummond's Building	West Main Street	29
Gillon's Loan (Charles)	West Main Street	26
Gillon's Loan (James)	East Main Street	11
Holmes Place	North Street	10
Linton's Loan	East Main Street	15
Lonie	East Main Street	17
McDonald's Square	East Main Street	16
McNab's Square (was Edward's)	North Street	6
McNab's Building	East Main Street	14
Model Lodging House	South Street	20
Monkey Row	High Academy Street	22
Pavilion Picture Theatre	South Street	19
Penny Geggie / Empire Theatre	George Street	25
Russell's Row	East Main Street	18
Shoogly Building	West Main Street	4
Shotts Rows	North Street	7
Star Theatre	North Street	12
Syson's Loan	West Main Street	27
The Beeches	West Main Street	2
The Place	West Main Street	1
Verrier's Property	West Main Street	5

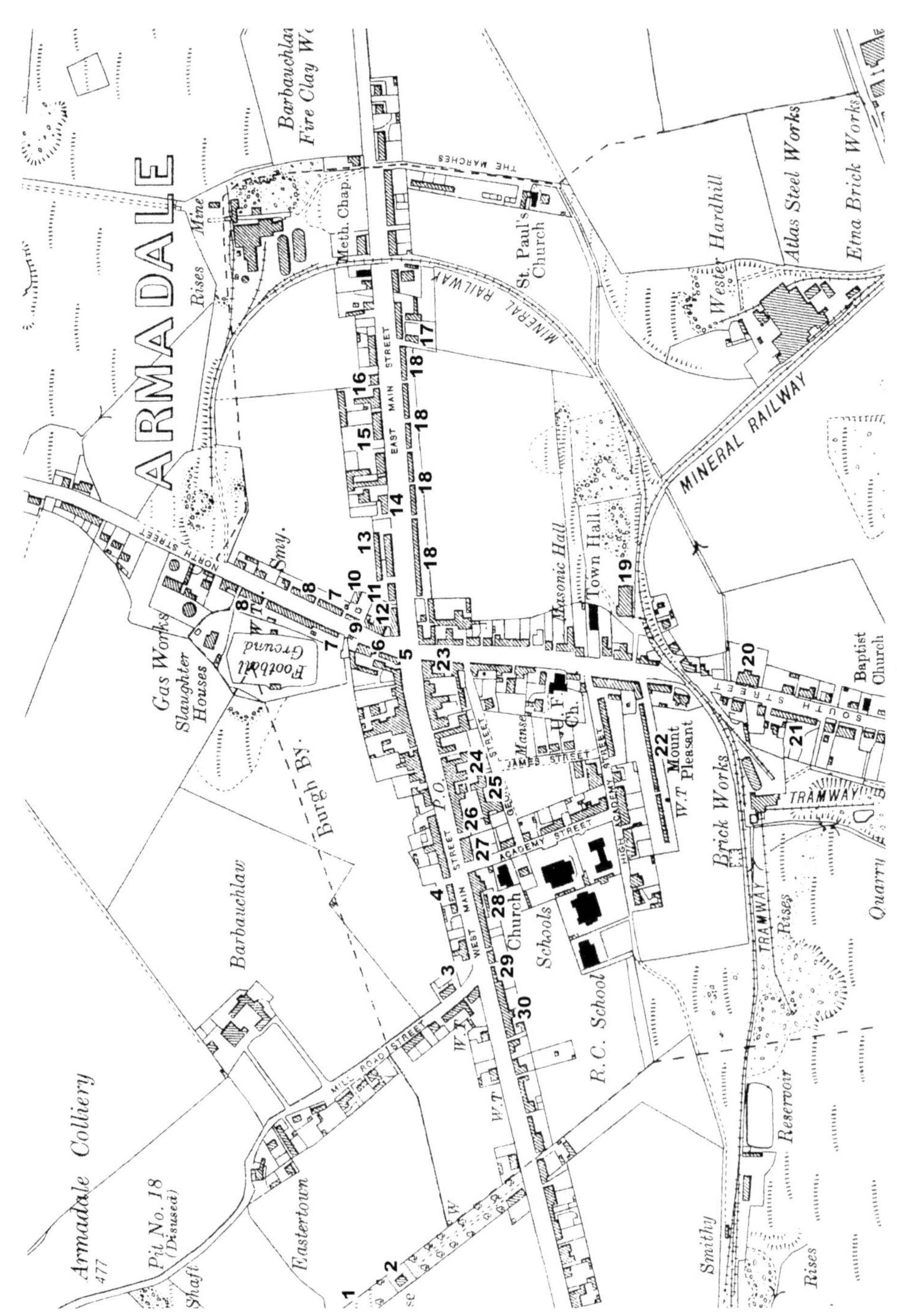

Armadale 1922 O.S. map with old place names

1930's

During the few years before 1931, Armadale Thistle played in the Scottish Senior League.

1931: Armadale Free Kirk in South Street became Armadale East Kirk and, in the same year, Armadale Parish Kirk in Academy Street became known as Armadale West Kirk. Because of the depression of 1931, there was not the usual Gala Day that year, only a fancy dress competition and sports.

1934: The directors of Armadale gas works were William, Thomas and Mary Wilson. There was a Scout Gathering in Volunteer Park. There were Jungle Dances, Highland Gathering and music by Airdrie Scout Pipe Band. Among the participants - Assistant Scoutmasters J. McCracken and Alex Smith, P.L. Jim Christie, Rover Leader R. Morton and Scout Master Joe Hall. Armadale Greyhound Stadium was established in 1934 or 1935 (in the old Volunteer Park).

1935: Atlas shareholders had £37,000 in shares. Armadale had two Friendly Societies - Good Templars and Free Gardeners. Woodend children had an outing to Ayr instead of a Gala Day. Armadale Cricket Club beat Avonmills of Linlithgow. Jean Barnard of the Dell married John Brown of Millhaugh, Bathgate. Barney Rice (who emigrated to USA in 1889) visited Armadale.

1936: Armadale Cricket Club formed. (Photo by J. Lockhart survives from 1937) Armadale Thistle Juniors founded. Armadale's new sewage works and house open. Presentation to Cub Sixer, Anderson Russell and Cub-mistress, Miss Jean McHattie. There was a Jessie O the Dale Burns' Club in Detroit. Armadale had a Cycling Club and a Harmonica Band (W. Sanderson and R. Ure). A Social was held in Woodend Welfare Hall. Mr. Hailstones ran Armadale Good Templars Juvenile Lodge.

1937: James Aitken died, he ran a horse bus to and from the station. Thomas Sanderson won £3,337 on football pools. Regal Theatre was opened to replace the Star Theatre, the Regal seated 1,250 people, Harry Lauder and Harry Gordon performed. (The Regal closed in

1972) On 12th June, was held the inauguration of Armadale Sewage and Purification Works.

At last ! The new Sewage and Purification Works

1938: Woodend held a Gala Day. Armadalian Dr. Alex Shearer died, he was son of blacksmith and Cllr. John Shearer and was Medical Officer of Health for the Highlands and Islands. Poem written on Gowanbank.

1939: Barbauchlaw Fireclay Works, owner Robert Muir and Co., from the 1890's to 1939-45, makers of building bricks. Participants in a Rover Scout Burns' Supper - Baillie Hall, Joe Hall, Alex Smith, Alex Bisset, D. Kerr, J. Kelly, James Marshall, N. Hailstones, Roy Taylor, T. Johnston and G. Halliday. Four generations of Robert McKay's family were photographed together in Armadale. Ronald McNicol was appointed to the Gold Coast. Rovers Hudson, Marshall, and MacDonald attended a Rover Moot at Crieff.

Mrs. Dougan, of Detroit and Armadale, sister of Mrs. Philip Kerr, Barbauchlaw Avenue, was saved when the Athenia was sunk. 21

year old James Ramsay of Armadale was saved when Glasgow steamer Clan Chisholm sunk. Harvie Watt, son of Mr. and Mrs. Watt of Woodlands, was in command of an anti aircraft battalion. The names of around 40 Armadalians killed in the 2nd World War (1939-1945) can be seen on the Town War Memorial, South Street.

Armadale Co-operative Society on West Main Street

1940's

1940: Poems by John Craig – 'Sweet Armadale' and 'Doon the Auld Whitockbrae'. Armadale Scout premises were enlarged. Airman James Boyd of Mill Road went missing, George Coyle of Armadale was killed in France, Gabriel Hunter was wounded and three Armadale men missing - Walter Brown, Andrew McKay and Private Currie.

1941: There was a social and presentation in Woodend Miners' Welfare Hall. Tom Morrow lost both hands in an accident involving hand grenades.

1942: D. Baxter and Thomas Craig were missing. Walter Marshall of Armadale was killed. Mrs. and Mr. Philip Kerr, who were married in 1892, and lived then in Russell's Row, celebrated 50 years of marriage.

1943: Mr. Watt, manager of the Atlas Steel Foundry, died. Armadale Atlas had a Tam O Shanter Burns' Club. Jimmy Nish was killed by enemy action. Walter Russell (son of the Provost) got an award for bravery in the Gold Coast. Thomas Morrison got a Military Medal for Bravery.

1944: Armadale Scout Pipe Band entertained patients at Wallhouse Hospital. Thomas Hanlin of Mayfield Drive won £500 for his 35,000 words novel, 'Once in Every Lifetime'. Two Armadale soldiers (Hanlin? and Evans) were killed.

1945: John MacDonald won the D.F.C.. As part of the War Victory Celebrations, Armadale Boy Scout Pipe Band led a march to bonfire at Trees Farm.

1946: William Jeffrey, poet, died in Glasgow; he was son of Woodend manager and spent his youth in Armadale. 86 year old Andrew Barnard of the Dell, died, he was a poet and wrote 'The Sparrows that Bide in the Lum' etc..

1947: 43 Europeans were housed in Bevan Hostel, Armadale. They volunteered to work in the Scottish shale mines. They came from

Latvia, Estonia, Lithuania, Poland and Ukraine. Dr. Anderson wrote 'The Sport of Pigeon Racing'.

1949: John McNicol retired.

Scene at Railway Cottages, Station Road

1950's

The Cross in the 1950's

1950: Sergeant J. Hutton of Armadale was in China. Mrs. Murgatroyd wrote the poem 'Armadale Glen'. W.B. McNair died. There was a two-way broadcast between Armadale, Scotland and Armadale, Australia.

1951: c.12,500 saw Armadale play Broxburn at Volunteer Park.

1952: Edward Blades of Armadale, Director of Education, died. Barbauchlaw Farm was demolished to make way for council housing. Rev. John Drummond of the West Kirk died.

1953: Rev. Emmanuel Robertson was minister of Armadale West / Parish Kirk until c.1994. Dr. Anderson died; also Helen Cunningham.

1954: Ex-Provost John Wardrop died.

1955: Mrs. Murgatroyd wrote poem 'Auld Russell's Raw'.

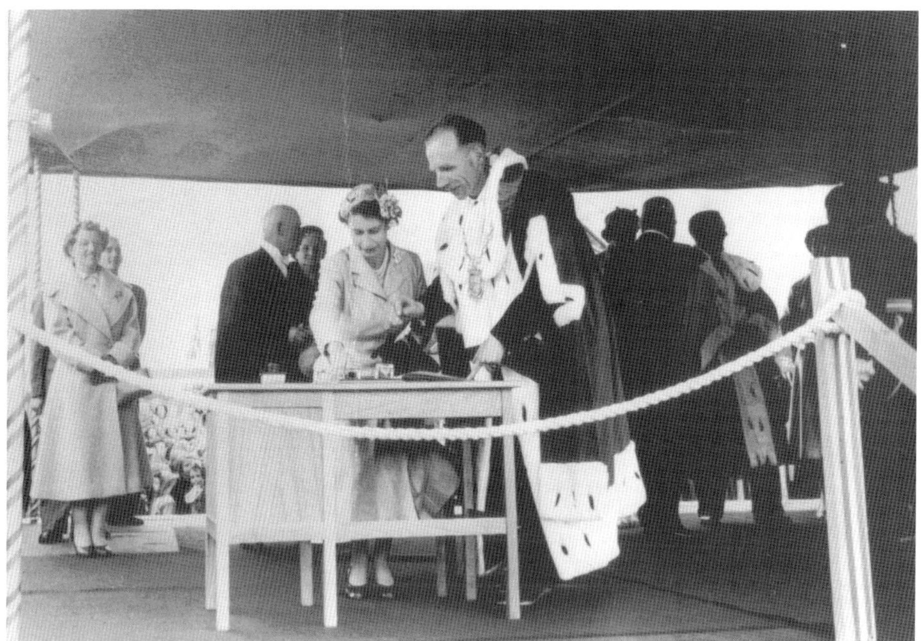

H.M. Queen meets Provost Willie Ferrier 2nd July 1955

1956: Provost Ferrier sent greetings to Armadale in Victoria, also Armadale in Western Australia and Armadale in Ontario. Armadale featured on the wireless program 'Matters Arising'; there were questions from Mrs. McKeown, Esau Edwards, Martin Prentice, J.F. Miller, Hugh Wotherspoon, Peter King and Mrs. Sharp.

1957: Woodall & Duckham bought the United Fireclay Products.

1958: Miss Dean retired after 42 years as a teacher at Armadale Public School. 170 were paid off at Atlas Steel Foundry.

1959: Tom Fleming died.

1960's

1960: West Works brickworks built; it had a 400 foot long tunnel kiln. Dickson & Mann's premises were extended in 1960.

An aerial view of Bathville showing Atlas Steel Foundry, West Lothian Steelworks, Etna Brickworks & United Fireclay Products Pipe Works

1961: The Courier carried an article on Maxwell Flood. Alex Notman retired after over 50 years with United Fireclay Products. An Armadale man became the Mayor of Taurango in New Zealand.

1962: Kenneth MacDonald, former Town Clerk, died, he was a native of Brora. Armadale gas works closed.

1967: Armadale Academy was opened.

1970's

1970: Bathville Pipeworks closed. The United Fireclay Products had made fireclay goods (salt glazed pipes, chimney cans, bricks, etc.) Colinshiel Home opened. Swimming pool opened.

1972: Armadale Community Centre opened.

1973: Atlas Steel works closed to become part of the North British Steel Foundry group (ceased trading in 1990). The ships Queen Mary and Queen Elizabeth both used Atlas-made castings.

1976: Armadale Free Kirk, built in South Street c.1860 and later, c.1930, renamed the East Kirk, was demolished. A plaque in South Street says - "On this site stood Armadale U.F. Church, the foundation stone of which was laid by Sir James Young Simpson, discoverer of the anaesthetic properties of chloroform".

The East Church on South Street

1980's

1981: Steetley turned the West Works into a facing-brick brickwork. The Etna was sold to Giscol. Armadale's population was 9,455.

1983: Ochilview Court sheltered housing was open.

1984: The Regal Theatre was demolished.

1985: The annual Gala Day crowning ceremony was held in Watson Memorial Park.

Buck's Head Tavern
Armadale's telephone exchange was housed for a time in the wooden building to the right

Assorted snippets and fragments

Bulletting or Hainching was once a popular competitive sport in the Armadale area; it involved the throwing of stones along the road with the least number of throws over a set winding course winning – as in golf.

Armadale had Lodges of Free Gardeners, Shepherds and Rechabites. The annual summer parade of Friendly Societies was the highlight of the year.

Between 1862 and 1975, Armadale Burgh had 26 different Provosts; all were men, three of them did two stints as Provost - they were Thomas Robertson, Adam Wilson and Willie Ferrier. Many of Armadale's streets were called after Provosts including Greig, Hailstones, Wardrop, Wotherspoon, Calder, Russell, Ferrier, McNeil, King, Watson and Ewart.

A photo survives of Provost Charlie King and fifteen former Gala Day Queens.

1900, telegraph address, Robertson Love, Armadale.

'British' address, c.1900, Armadale Station, West Lothian, N.B. (N.B. = North Britain, which was for a time used instead of Scotland).

Armadale's third Subscription School (later the Town Hall) seems to have been built in 1859, and not 1873 and seems to have been in South Street; Armadale's Last Subscription School Headmaster was Mr. Thomson.

Acknowledgements

When the History of Armadale Association asked me to edit Robert Kerr's "History of Armadale (West Lothian)" with a view to publishing this book, I received a great deal of help from many people.

History of Armadale Association members

Robert had already done all of the research work and my task was to lay out the text and add the photos and maps. I was greatly helped in tracing photos by Betty Hunter of Armadale Library and Sybil Cavanagh of West Lothian Library HQ. Our thanks are extended to the owners of the photos for permission to use them. Iain Davidson researched the maps and I only had to tidy them up. Davie Kerr, Robert's brother, was my sub-editor and his comments, as always, made my task so much easier in completing this volume.

Jim McGregor
Editor

Photo Credits

The photographs used in this book have been used with the permission of the following people and organisations. The description refers to the West Lothian Library code.

Page	Title	Reference
008	Lord Armadale from Kay's Edinburgh Portraits 1790's	© Edinburgh Central Library WL A2 596
009	William Honyman of Graemsay, Lord Armadale caricature by John Kay	© Edinburgh Central Library WL A2 088
010	Jessie o the Dell - Victorian illustration with the words of 'Sweet Jessie o the Dell'	Armadale Library A2 585
011	Shepherd's Stanes	© Jim McGregor
012	Shepherd's Stanes	© Jim McGregor
016	Whitockbrae at the end of the 19th Century	© Mr Jim Ferguson
018	Public School	Armadale Library
020	Butress Pit miners 1912 – note the oil lamps in their bunnets	Armadale Library
023	United Fireclay Brickworks at Bathville No date, perhaps 1960's	Armadale Library A2 411
026	Gowanbank	© DMT Davidson Associates
028	Bridgecastle Avenue	Armadale Library
031	Railway Station around the 1950's	© Mr Jim Somerville A2 140
033	South Street looking south	Armadale Library
035	South Street or the Toll Brae from Townson's Grand Photgraphic View Album	EF 1997:176:043 A2 012
038	Parish Church from a coloured postcard by Archer, Stationer, Armadale 1925	© Mr Douglas McIndoe A2 513
041	East Main Street	Armadale Library
046	The Bowling Green c.1910	© Mr Jim Somerville A2 149
055	Woodend Village. No date possibly 1920's EF 1997:176:047 A2 313A	© Mr Charles Colquhoun A2 313
057	Bathville House from a coloured postcard by Mrs A. Marr, Stationer, Armadale 1908	© Mr Douglas McIndoe A2 512

058	Station Road looking north Girls with shawls	Armadale Library
062	Public School & Parish Church	Armadale Library
067	North Street pre First World War	Armadale Library A2 129
068	Armadale Thistle Lodge of the Ancient Order of Free Gardeners No date	A2 010 WLDCM 1995:001:9 P
094	West Main Street looking east from Townson's Grand Photgraphic View Album	A2 014 from Townson Album
099	West Main Street by Archer, Stationer 1904 No Goth knock	EF 1997:176:042 A2 294
100	Kerr Family in 1900	© Mr Davie Kerr
101	Volunteer Park football ground. No date, probably 1920's EF 1997:176:040 A2 311	Armadale Library A2 311
127	Tippethill Fever Hospital	Armadale Library
130	Star Inn possibly on a Gala Day	Armadale Library
131	Armadale Silver Band 1937	A2 001 WLDCM 1995:001:1 P
134	West Main Street looking east No Goth knock	Armadale Library
135	Mill Road Armadale from the top No date, possibly 1920's/30's EF 1997:176:032 A2 310A	© Scottish Ethnological Archive C.24217
137	The Goth in the 1960's	Armadale Library
139	Bandstand, Wood Public Park from a coloured postcard by Archer Stationer 1923	© Mr Douglas McIndoe A2 514
141	Station Road - on the left, is the Model Lodging House c.1920's / 30's	Armadale Library A2 312
145	Visit of General Booth of the Salvation Army 1905	© Scottish Ethnological Archive C.24202
157	West Main Street showing the Goth knock from a coloured postcard	Armadale Library
163	Empire Palace Theatre, George Street No date, possibly c. 1914	© Scottish Ethnological Archive C.24200
175	West Main Street with Kerr Memorial	EF 1997:176:030 A2 142
176	The Mill, Woodend from a postcard by Mrs A. Marr, Stationer, Armadale c.1908	© Mr Jim Somerville A2 102
178	Pipe Band in Gala Day on West Main Street	EF 1997:176:049 A2 163
179	Armadale Public Hall with brass band playing outside - from a postcard	© Mr David Hedges A2 599

182	West Lothian Steel Foundry in foreground and Atlas Foundry in background c. 1920	A2 008 WLDCM 1995:001:7 P
184	East Main Street looking east from Cross Motor bus on the left No date c. mid-1920's	© Scottish Ethnological Archive C.24208
186	East Main Street with billboards	EF 1997:176:036 A2 301
187	Roman Catholic Church School, High Academy Street Postcard Mrs A. Marr EF 1997:176:024 A2 52A	© Scottish Ethnological Archive C.24223
191	Sewage purification plant No date	A2 022 WLDCM 1995:001:13 P
192	Armadale Co-operative Society, West Main Street No date	© Mr William Evans A2 303
194	Railway Cottages: Suzanna Martin, Mary Mulcahy & Lizzie Higgins	Armadale Library
195	The Cross looking down North Street 1950's	Armadale Library A2 302
196	H.R.H. The Queen with Provost William Ferrier of Armadale on the 2nd July 1955	A2 015 WLDCM 1995:036:92 P
197	An aerial view of Bathville showing Atlas Steel Foundry, West Lothian Steelworks	© Aerofilms Library Negative no. C17763
198	East Church	Armadale Library EF 1997:176:055
199	Buck's Head Tavern c.1960	A2072A WLDCM 1995:001:100 P

Map Credits

The maps used in this book have been researched by Iain Davidson and Jim Somerville and adapted by Jim McGregor.

Page	**Title**	**Original work**
003	Some of the earliest estates and farmsteads around Armadale	© Mr. Iain Davidson
022	Industry in Armadale	© Mr. Iain Davidson
189	Old place names in Armadale before the 1920's	© Mr. Jim Somerville

Bibliography

Here are some of the manuscripts, study papers, etc. that Robert Kerr has researched and produced over the years including "A History of Armadale (West Lothian)" upon which this production of "Armadale in Minutes" is based.

Title	Notes	Publ.
A history of Armadale, West Lothian	86 pages	1996
A history of Barbauchlaw	2 pages	
A history of Bathville	5 pages	1996
A history of Bathville II	6 pages	1996
A history of the ancient Barony of Ogilface in the parish of Torphichen		1993
A revised history of the ancient Barony of Ogilface : Giving owners or lessees of lands of barony		1994
A history of the land occupied by the ancient Barony of Ogilface in the parish of Torphichen	Manuscript	1994
A history of the estate and lands of Cathlaw	2 pages	1996
A history of the West Lothian town of Armadale and surrounding area	Manuscript	1992
A history of the West Lothian town of Armadale and surrounding area	Manuscript	1994
A history of Westfield and district near Armadale	3 pages	1994
A history of Woodend, near Armadale, West Lothian	Single sheet	1995
Bridgecastle and Bridgehouse	2 pages	1998
Gowanbank : Notes on Gowanbank, north of Blackridge	½ page	1998
Plan of lands of Hardhill and lands of Harestanes in the ancient parish of Bathgate : Showing boundaries of the two estates, and the farms and other notable sites they included		1990
Sketch map showing the boundaries of Coustoun, Bridgecastle, Barbauchlaw, Hardhill and Polkemmet estates	Sketch map	1990

Title	Notes	Publ.
Sketch maps of Armadale c.1850 and of surroundings c.1773 and 1820	Sketch map	1990
A history of Blackridge, Woodend and the lands of Ogilface		1995
Bedlormie House, West Lothian	2 pages	1998
A history of Balbardie, Ballencrieff, Barbauchlaw, Bathgate, Boghall and Boghead estates		1995
A history of Bathgate	Manuscript	1993
A history of Bathgate	Typescript	1994
A history of Bathgate	Typescript	1996
A history of Bathgate	78 pages	1997
A history of Bathgate (Edited Robert Harkness)		2006
A history of Lochcote estate and lands	6 pages	1996
Historic map of Bathgate	Sketch map	1990
Sketch map of Bathgate : farms and estates, with dates	Sketch map	1990
Sketch map of Bathgate : industrial : Mainly industrial places of employment (pits, quarries, etc.) c. 1850	Sketch map	1990
Sketch map of Bathgate c.1898 : Historic places in and near Bathgate town, overlaid on road and rail system of c.1898 (with dates)	Sketch map	1990
Sketch map of the farms and estates of Bathgate district - with dates : Historic maps, map 1	Sketch map	
Sketches of Bathgate buildings : S3		
A history of places within and near Beecraigs Country Park in West Lothian, to be read with the historic map of the park		1997
Lochcote - miscellaneous information and map of Lochcote estate		
Historic map of Beecraigs Country Park, West Lothian : Scale c. 6 inches : 1 mile		1997
Sketch map of Beecraigs Country Park, West Lothian : Showing boundaries of earlier farms of Whitebaulks, Hillhouse, Balvormie lands and many of the old field names.	Sketch map A3 size	1997

Title	Notes	Publ.
A history of Blackburn, Stoneyburn, Seafield and district		1994
A history of Bo'ness and district	Manuscript	1994
A history of South Queensferry, Kirkliston and district		1995
A history of South Queensferry, Kirkliston, Winchburgh and the parishes of Dalmeny and Abercorn		1994
A history of Broxburn, Uphall and Ecclesmachan		1995
A history of the parishes of Strathbrock, Uphall and Ecclesmachan (including Broxburn)		1994
A history of Fauldhouse, Longridge and district		1994
A history of Fauldhouse, Longridge and district	3 pages	1995
A history of Whitburn, East Whitburn and district		1994
A history of Linlithgow	29 pages	1994
A history of Linlithgow	44 pages	1995
A history of Livingston parish		1994
A history of the Livingston New Town area		1994
A history of the Livingston New Town area		1995
A history of the three Calders and Kirknewton parish		1994
A history of Torphichen, West Lothian : the first 4 thousand years	Manuscript photocopied	1991
A history of Torphichen, West Lothian : Book 2, pages 13-20, brothers, knights and preceptors. How James Sandilands became Lord Torphichen. Also the first tenants and farms of Torphichen parish.		1992
Assorted information on Torphichen 's history	10 pages	
Persons buried in Torphichen Kirk graveyard	Handwritten	
The estate and lands of Wallhouse	5 pages	1996
The well, the square, Torphichen	2 pages	1998
Torphichen's first council housing scheme at Greenside	2 pages	1996
A history of West Lothian (county and district)	Manuscript	1995
Glimpses of West Lothian past	8 pages	1998

Title	Notes	Publ.
Glimpses of West Lothian past		2006
Notes on West Lothian place names	Manuscript	
Robert Kerr's histories of West Lothian towns and villages : Vol. 1	Typescript	
Robert Kerr's histories of West Lothian towns and villages : Vol. 2	Typescript	
Robert Kerr's histories of West Lothian towns and villages : Vol. 3	Handwritten	

All of these, plus other drawings and maps of the West Lothian area, can be seen by contacting West Lothian Library HQ, Connolly House, Hopefield Road, Blackburn, West Lothian, EH47 7HZ. Information courtesy of Sybil Cavanagh.

Index